SPORTS BUDGET

FAMOUS FOR LONG COMPLETE STORIES

2ᴰ

No Holding the Old'Uns!

FOOTBALL'S COMIC BOOK HEROES

FOOTBALL'S COMIC BOOK HEROES

The Ultimate Fantasy Footballers

Adam Riches

with Tim Parker and Robert Frankland

MAINSTREAM
PUBLISHING

EDINBURGH AND LONDON

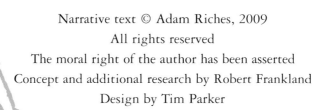

Narrative text © Adam Riches, 2009
All rights reserved
The moral right of the author has been asserted
Concept and additional research by Robert Frankland
Design by Tim Parker

Associate Publisher: Iain MacGregor
Production: Neil Graham & Gill McColl
Jacket design: Emily Bland & Kate McLelland

First published in Great Britain in 2009 by
MAINSTREAM PUBLISHING COMPANY
(EDINBURGH) LTD
7 Albany Street
Edinburgh EH1 3UG
ISBN 9781845964085

The Hotspur, Wizard, Rover, Scoop, Buddy, Victor, Adventure, Spike, Hornet,
Champ, Skipper © D.C. Thomson & Co. Ltd.
All associated characters © D.C. Thomson & Co. Ltd.

With some exceptions all other titles published before 1969 are © IPC Media.
Titles published after 1969, including Roy of the Rovers, are © Egmont UK Limited.
For clarification please contact Egmont UK Ltd or IPC Media Ltd.

No part of this book may be reproduced or transmitted in any form
or by any other means without permission in writing from the publisher,
except by a reviewer who wishes to quote brief passages in connection
with a review written for insertion in a magazine, newspaper or broadcast
A catalogue record for this book is available from the British Library

Printed in Great Britain by
D.C. Thomson & Co. Ltd., Dundee

REFERENCES

Back Page Football, Stephen Kelly (Aurum, 1988)

Boots, Balls & Haircuts, Hunter Davies (Cassell Illustrated, September 2003)

British Comics: An Appraisal, The Comics Campaign Council (1955)

The British at Play – A Social History of British Sport from 1600 to the Present,
  Nigel Townson (Cavallioti, 1997)

Charles Buchan's Football Monthly (various)

Football is My Business, Tommy Lawton (Sporting Handbooks, 1946)

The Football Man, Arthur Hopcraft (Penguin, 1968)

Gas Masks for Goal Posts, Anton Rippon (Sutton Publishing, 2005)

Manliness and the Boys' Story Paper in Britain: A Cultural History, 1855-1940,
  Kelly Boyd (Palgrave Macmillan, 2003)

The Mavericks, Rob Steen (Mainstream, 1994)

Old Boys' Books: A Complete Catalogue, Bill Lofts and Derek Adley (private publication)

Penny Dreadfuls and Comics, Kevin Carpenter (V&A, 1983)

Soccer at War, Jack Rollin (Headline, 2005)

Take a Cold Tub, Sir!: The Story of the Boy's Own Paper, Jack Cox (The Lutterworth Press, 1982)

Those Feet: An Intimate History of English Football, David Winner (Bloomsbury, 2005)

The Ultimate Book of British Comics, Graham Kibble-White (Allison & Busby, 2005)

Uppies and Downies: The Extraordinary Football Games of Britain, Hugh Hornby
  (English Heritage, 2008)

The Daily Mail
The Guardian
The Observer

Blakiana, www.sextonblake.co.uk

Bunterzone, http://www.geocities.com/bunterzone/

Donmouth, Patrick Brennan (http://www.donmouth.co.uk)

Dudley D. Watkins' website (www.thatsbraw.co.uk)

National Army Museum (www.national-army-museum.ac.uk)

Sporting Heroes: Footballers and the First World War,
Ian Maxwell (www.soccerhistory.org.uk)

For Harriet and Eleanor

CONTENTS

THE ULTIMATE FANTASY FOOTBALL COMIC
GREAT STORY ACTION FEATURING COMIC BOOK
FOOTY STARS FROM DOWN THE AGES
page 219

"FANTASY IS VERY IMPORTANT IN MODERN FOOTBALL. WITHOUT IT, IT CAN BE IMPOSSIBLE TO SCORE GOALS."

Fabio Capello, England manager (June 2008)

INTRODUCTION

I doubt there is anyone reading these words who did not, in their youth, dream of one day becoming a professional footballer. More than that; fantasised about scoring the winning goal in the cup final, of being the talismanic presence in a triumphant England team (substitute Scotland, Wales or Ireland here). Or of saving a penalty-kick in the last minute, or executing a last-ditch clearance off the line, to become the hero for school, club or country. A very few gifted, determined and lucky boys actually get to achieve this ambition; for the rest of us it is the office, the factory, the farm or the foundry. Eventually, the day dawns when we realise that, actually, we're not going to be the next Bobby Moore, George Best or Jim Baxter. For most young men this realisation comes between the ages of 14 and 18 (although my brother was 27 when he finally conceded that he was not going to be "discovered" by a West Ham scout). But up to the tender age of, say, 15, when reality kicks in, there is always the dream. And there was one place where this dream was played out, every week of the year – and that was in the pages of the comic books. OK, so we worshiped the 11 men who crossed the white line every Saturday afternoon at 3 p.m. (those were the days) sporting the colours of our favourite team, but these gods, it inevitably transpired, had feet of clay. Our real heroes played for Melchester Rovers or Blackport Rovers, wore "Dead Shot" Keen's old football boots; or could kick a ball so hard that an opposing goalkeeper who had the misfortune to get in the way would find themselves hurtling through their own goal net and into the crowd behind. These players frequently scored the winner in the Cup final to become the hero of the hour; and the reason we loved them was because, vicariously, they were us. This was fantasy football in its original sense – Charlie "Iron" Barr, Nipper Lawrence and Andy Steele Playmaker were projections of ourselves, and they never let us down.

Our bond to these heroes goes far deeper than football; for, invariably, the footballer faced bigger hurdles off the park than on it. Frequently the underdog, even the outsider, our comic book hero has to overcome almost insurmountable obstacles including, typically, a rich, prejudiced chairman, bullying and jealous team mates, a sceptical, even abusive, crowd and, even more profoundly, poverty, homelessness and physical disability. But all were overcome, thanks to the protagonist's sheer force of personality; a mix of courage, determination, moral fortitude and, frequently, huge slices of luck.

We also loved the comics for what they were. Who can forget their excitement on hearing the clank of the letter-box and plop of our favourite comic hitting the doormat? It was always so. In a 1955 paper, *British Comics: An Appraisal*, the Comics Campaign Council said that, "All of us, whether children or adults, enjoy some leisure reading. It is a retreat from the serious business of living which can be recreational in the true meaning of the word: the retreat can create us again. Complex situations can be pictorially presented in ways beyond the reach of words. It is not just that the pictures save people the bother of reading; some situations can be grasped in reality or pictorial form which can scarcely be conveyed in words. If the subject is interesting to us, we gaze at the picture while silently relating our own experience to it... Children of all ages enjoy a good story, whether it is inspired, exciting or funny, through the vivid medium of cartoon; what would become boring under any but the most brilliant telling can be seen in a flash through a brilliant picture." Early in 2008, author Philip Pullman described the comic medium as "a wonderful way of telling stories, of imparting narrative". They are, he said, "vigorous, swift and immediate... they combine the immediacy and vigour of cinema with all the advantages of the book".

The Comics Campaign Council estimated that, in the 1950s, 350 million comics were sold annually in Britain. Today, that market has shrunk drastically, and the boys' football paper is all but extinct. But forget about the present; indulge yourself in these pages, and glory in the past triumphs of the comics. I fervently hope the story of your particular favourite comic book character is related here. Sincere and heartfelt apologies if they have been omitted. At the outset I made a conscious decision not to put too much emphasis on the "famous" and iconic comic-book footballers; so Roy of the Rovers, "Hot Shot" Hamish and others, while included here, are not the book's major figures. This is not to denigrate their importance, influence or popularity. But plenty has been written about those characters elsewhere, obviating the need to make further reference to them in these pages. There are a thousand other stories to be told, stretching across over a century of comic publishing. Some characters you will know; others will be new to you. I hope you enjoy reading all their stories.

Adam Riches, March 2009

"GOOD-BYE, DEAD-WIDE DICK!" SEE PAGE 86

THE HOTSPUR

No. 500 · OCTOBER 7TH · 1944 · PRICE 2D

"FOOTBALL, IN ITSELF, IS A GRAND GAME FOR DEVELOPING A LAD PHYSICALLY AND ALSO MORALLY, FOR HE LEARNS TO PLAY WITH GOOD TEMPER AND UNSELFISHNESS, TO PLAY IN HIS PLACE AND 'PLAY THE GAME', AND THESE ARE THE BEST TRAINING FOR ANY GAME OF LIFE."

Scouting for Boys (1908)
Lord Baden-Powell (1857–1941)

CHAPTER ONE

PLAY UP, AND PLAY THE GAME!

AS CERTAIN AS DEATH AND TAXES is that, on the subject of football, your father, or grandfather, will one day have said to you: "Things were better in my day!"

Of course we all know that things are better now than they have ever been. We've got the Premiership – the best league in the world, right? There's wall-to-wall coverage of the "beautiful game" on television, offering instant access to the world's superstars.

The old times are for the old-timers. Jumpers for goalposts, stubbing out a fag on the centre-spot before kick-off; footballs as heavy as bowling balls with laces protruding like battlefield scars. We've all seen the comedy sketches. In football as in life, as L.P. Hartley once wrote: "The past is a foreign country: they do things differently there."

But was it so very different? In many ways the answer is a resounding "yes" – at the birth of the professional game the vast majority had "proper" jobs (particularly in the close season) as well as being paid for playing. True, the major football grounds of old have been developed out of all recognition, particularly in the past 30 years. A regular visitor to Old Trafford in the inter-war years would not recognise the current stadium and would no doubt be shocked to be asked to pay £48 to watch the current crop of Red Devils – in 1930 this represented more than 12 weeks' wages.

Below The boys' story-papers such as *The Boys' Friend* were quick to latch on to the growing interest in sport in the late Victorian era

A GRAND NEW STORY STARTS THIS WEEK.

1D.
½

THE BOYS' FRIEND

1D.
½

No. 24. Vol. I.]   ONE HALFPENNY WEEKLY.   [EVERY WEDNESDAY.

But things were not so different, especially for non-Premiership professional clubs. Brunton Park would be recognisable to our inter-war-years' Carlisle United supporter; the geography of the ground would be utterly familiar and the chances are he (or she) could even stand on the same spot he did all those years ago. And as for having a proper job, speak to Dagenham & Redbridge midfielder Dave Rainford – he combined playing in the Daggers' inaugural season in the Football League (2007–08) with a job as a teacher.

Even the briefest flick through the football history books shows that there is more than a grain of truth in the old expression that "the more things change, the more things stay the same". There's nothing new under the sun. From the outset, professional footballers were heroes – nay, superstars – in the communities in which they lived and worked; but they were also open to offers from the highest bidder. The clubs exerted huge influence and they attracted vast and loyal support – and were commercially-minded, money-making organisations. Owners steeped in the rampant entrepreneurialism of the Victorian age were quick to realise that football, to use the modern vernacular, was "a results business" – and there was money to be made. Comic publishers were quick to recognise this, too. Almost from the birth of the professional game players became a saleable commodity – indeed, the first £1,000 transfer took place in February 1905, when Alf Common left Sunderland for local rivals Middlesbrough. This was just 17 years after the inaugural English league season (1888–89), when Preston North End beat Aston Villa into second place to become the first-ever English champions in the first competition of its type anywhere in the world.

That 1888–89 season does not mark the

Above In 1909, *The Boys' Realm* took the bold step of launching a dedicated football paper

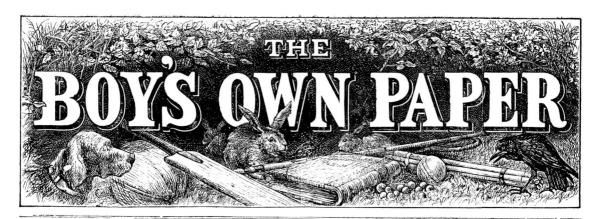

THE BOY'S OWN PAPER

No. 1.—Vol. I.   SATURDAY, JANUARY 18, 1879.   Price One Penny.
[ALL RIGHTS RESERVED.

MY FIRST FOOTBALL MATCH.

BY AN OLD BOY.

IT was a proud moment in my existence when Wright, captain of our football club, came up to me in school one Friday and said, "Adams, your name is down to play in the match against Craven to-morrow."

I could have knighted him on the spot. To be one of the picked "fifteen," whose glory it was to fight the battles of their school in the Great Close, had been the leading ambition of my life—I suppose I ought to be ashamed to confess it—ever since, as a little chap of ten, I entered Parkhurst six years ago. Not a winter Saturday but had seen me either looking on at some big match, or oftener still scrimmaging about with a score or so of other juniors in a scratch game. But for a long time, do what I would, I always seemed as far as ever from the coveted goal, and was half despairing of ever rising to win my "first fifteen cap." Lately, however, I had noticed Wright and a few others of our best players more than once lounging about in the Little Close where we juniors used to play, evidently taking observations with an eye to business. Under the awful gaze of these heroes, need I say I exerted myself as I had never done before? What cared I for hacks or bruises, so only that I could distinguish myself in their eyes? And never was music sweeter

"Down!"

start of our story, however. Football endured a long period of labour before the professional game was born – centuries, in fact. And the period immediately proceeding the 1888–89 season exerted a strong influence on the comics and storybooks that first featured the footballer as the chief protagonist.

A brief history lesson. Football, in its crudest form, was widely played from medieval times. According to Hunter Davies, in his book *Boots, Balls & Haircuts*, whole villages turned out to kick, throw, punch or scrummage a 'ball' to a designated point, or goal. Some of these games survive – in Ashbourne, Derbyshire, Kirkwall in Orkney and Workington, Cumbria. These types of games were played in Europe, too – the game Calcio is still played in Florence, annually. The game in Ashbourne is thought to have started around 217AD, while in the 1870s special trains were laid on to bring thousands of 'fans' to enjoy the spectacle in Workington. But this type of "football" was considered a disreputable pastime for the lowest in society, and was frowned upon – through the ages. Football attracted the ire of Elizabeth I, no less, who is reported to have said: "No foteballe play to be used or suffered within the City of London"; and James II of Scotland, in 1457, banned both football and golf.

It seems incongruous, but the fact is the game we know and love owes more to the playing fields of the public schools of Victorian England than the blood-and-thunder pell mell of the people's street "football".

For it was in this rarified environment that football found strong support; the headmasters of the major public schools – Charterhouse, Rugby and the like – saw football as a way of promoting the Victorian ideal of "a sound mind in a healthy body"; as a wholesome activity for adolescent boys. These head teachers saw the game – although there was no unified structure or set of rules at this juncture – as a means of instilling discipline and courage into their young charges. It would help them become good Christians.

And as these boys grew into young men, so they took football with them to Oxford, Cambridge and the other universities. It is in these famous old institutions that the game developed. Here the "Corinthian" ideal was born – the sense of fair play that the comics and the storybooks of the day reflected each week in their pages. Winning was not important – it was the taking part. Football was a game for the "gentleman amateur" – the Englishman. But by the 1870s, "football" was at a crossroads. While the Corinthian spirit was alive and kicking with the amateur former public schoolboys, football had spread across the country to all strata of society.

The church was a prime mover in this pollination of the game, and the

Far left Sport changed the face of the comic and story papers. In 1879, *The Boy's Own Paper* put a story, "My First Football Match", on the cover. The match in question was more akin to rugby than association football

FOOTBALL.

Above Free for all… "football" as depicted by *The Boys' Herald* in 1876. The game progressed rapidly from this point to the inaugural Football League season 12 years later, in 1888

impact of this religious fervour was to take the game into the industrial Midlands and the north. Celtic is perhaps the most famous of all football clubs founded by a religious organisation for moral and spiritual reasons; it was set up on 6 November 1887 by a committee led by a Marist, Brother Walfrid, who wanted to "alleviate poverty in Glasgow's East End parishes". Other clubs founded by church groups included Aston Villa, Birmingham City, Bolton Wanderers, Everton, Liverpool and Manchester City.

But as these clubs progressed both on and off the field, they became at odds with their established southern, amateur counterparts. They adopted a bolder, winner-takes-all approach – what we might call professionalism. Payment for the best players began creeping in, and a noticeable schism appeared. While the public schoolboys had formed the Football Association in 1863, these professional clubs were to do their own thing, founding the Football League in 1888, three years after the FA voted to "allow" payments to players. It was the brainchild of one William McGregor, a draper from Perthshire and Aston Villa director, who was fed up with constant confusion that surrounded the fixture list. Of the 12 founder Football League members, six were from the north-west and six from the Midlands. Nigel Townson, in his essay *The British at Play – A Social History of British Sport from 1600 to the Present*, sums up this schism nicely: "... the middle-class sportsmen of late Victorian and early Edwardian England seem admirably romantic in their idealism, viewed from today's world of commercialised, win-at-all-costs sport, where kick-off times and the rules of a game are dictated by the television companies, and where footballers are congratulated by team-mates for their skill in winning a penalty, even if this involves the employment of theatrical dives and rolls.

"The Corinthians, the greatest amateur football team of all time, was made up of former public schoolboys who had learned to love the game at school and who wished to carry on playing while pursuing their careers in London. They found, to their chagrin, that they were increasingly obliged to play against professional opposition because so many of their amateur colleagues had defected to rugby in order to avoid contamination from competing against those who played for money. As money became a factor in the game, winning became more important, and the rules were changed to increase the excitement of the game. The introduction of the penalty-kick was greeted with horror by the Corinthians, for they held that no gentleman would ever deliberately commit a foul. This led them to refuse to attempt to score from or save a penalty. Sadly, their opponents had no such qualms, and the slow decline of the amateur teams had begun. The Corinthians also refused to enter any competition for which a cup was awarded, for this contravened the spirit of participation for its own sake. Winning was not the goal, merely a satisfying outcome of having given of one's best."

Below A true British sporting gentleman: P.M. Walters was an Oxford University, Old Carthusians and Corinthians player. The picture was taken in 1896

At around the time football was being propagated in the public schools and universities, the comics and storybooks of the day were being transformed. The Education Act of 1870, which brought about compulsory schooling for all children, led to a boom in literacy and a massive expansion of reading material to cater for this new-found reading class. The so-called "penny dreadfuls" enjoyed a period of massive sales, employing serialisation to create "cliff-hangers" at the end of each story each week, thus ensuring sales the following week.

Photo by Bob Thomas/Popperfoto/Getty Images

The first popular juvenile weekly publication in England was **The Boys' and Girls' Penny Magazine**. This appeared in September 1832, according to Bill Lofts and Derek Adley's *Old Boys' Books: A Complete Catalogue*. Consisting of eight pages, at least 23 issues appeared. According to Lofts and Adley, issue 21 contained the following statement that emphasises the popularity of these publications: "The Christmas sale of this periodical was... a grand total in figures of 835,000 copies being sold in one week."

The first "penny dreadful" appeared in 1866 – Charles Stephens' **Boys of England**. Many competitors followed, with such titles as **Boy's Leisure Hour**, **Boys' Standard**, **Young Men of Great Britain**, and many, many more.

The most important of these was **The Boy's Own Paper** (1879-1967), which was one of a number of story papers launched to counter what was perceived as the corrupting influence of the penny dreadfuls. The idea for **The Boy's Own Paper** was first put forward in 1878 by the Religious Tract Society, which wanted to launch a weekly paper to provide "first-class stories for boys of all backgrounds" and ensure at the same time that they were exposed to an underlying Christian morality during their formative years. In its earliest version **The Boy's Own Paper** was a weekly paper of 16 pages; while it cost one penny, many copies of this first edition were given away in schools to ensure a good circulation.

Below Front cover designs got more daring – and funnier – as publishers began to feel comfortable with the medium

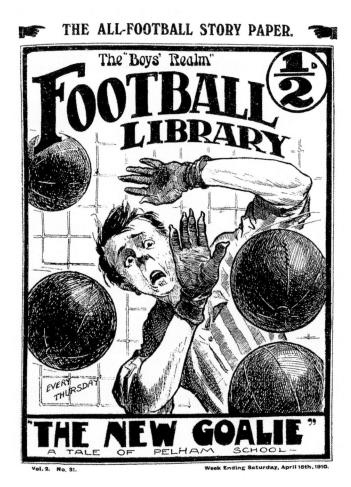

THE ALL-FOOTBALL STORY PAPER.

The "Boys' Realm"

FOOTBALL LIBRARY

½ᴅ

EVERY THURSDAY

"THE NEW GOALIE"
A TALE OF PELHAM SCHOOL —

Vol. 2. No. 31.   Week Ending Saturday, April 16th, 1910.

The Boy's Own Paper was packed with stories and articles on science, natural history and adventure, and competitions were included. Launch editor George Hutchison, who had previously produced a paper for Dr Barnado's, had the foresight to include a story entitled "My First Football Match" by an Old Boy.

The author was Talbot Baines Reed, widely considered to be one of the best-ever writers of public school stories. Although he never attended public school, he was the paper's

THE THIRD ELEVEN.

A Fine Long, Complete Tale of the Football Field.

At the last moment Jack Noble sent the ball whizzing into the far corner of the net. It was first blood to the Juniors!

Above Action from *The Boys' Realm Football Library*, issue 1, dated 18 September 1909

assistant editor and from 1880 to 1893, and his stories were all first serialised in the magazine before becoming best-sellers in book form.

Talbot Baines Reed's success led to other well-known writers exploiting the comic/story-paper format – Jules Verne, R.M. Ballantyne, Algernon Blackwood and Sir Arthur Conan Doyle all had stories serialised in *The Boy's Own Paper*. W.G. Grace wrote articles on cricket; among other regular correspondents was Lord Baden-Powell, the founder of the Scout Movement. He urged boys to do a good deed every day and "to live clean, manly and Christian lives".

A major "comic" of the late Victorian period was *The Boys' Friend*, published by Amalgamated Press, which first appeared in 1895. The first issue, at 16 pages for one halfpenny, represented excellent value. Many prominent writers contributed, often using pseudonyms. Some storybook characters also made the switch from other Amalgamated Press publications; Nelson Lee, the detective, being a notable example.

Around this period the other two major Amalgamated Press papers appeared; *The Boys' Realm*, in 1902, and *The Boys' Herald* a year later. Although both papers began with a similar content to *The Boys' Friend*, the former would later take on sport as its theme while the latter would become a hobby interest paper.

Football was, by now, massively popular – in 1901, 114,815 people turned up for the Tottenham Hotspur v Sheffield United FA Cup final at Crystal

Palace – yet professional league football was only 13 years old. By this time Amalgamated Press had realised that football was here to stay – and continuing to grow in popularity. It launched *The Boys' Realm Football Library* on 18 September 1909. It consisted of two text-led stories – "The Third Eleven", "A Fine Long, Complete Tale of the Football Field" and "The Blue Crusaders", "A Fine Football Yarn. By A.S. Hardy".

The former introduced one of the most enduring characters of the early years of football comics, Jack Noble. He was to grace the pages of the *Football Library* in hundreds of stories and represented all that was seen as good ("noble") about British youth. Noble was honest, brave, loyal and eternally optimistic, characteristics that stood him in good stead to deal with life at "Pelham School". This public school was like those found only in boys' literature; in issue 7 (30 September 1909) Noble foils a plot by the captain of the school's senior side in a grudge match against our hero's Third Form which involved the villain drugging the Third Form's star players (including Jack Noble).

Right The Blue Crusaders' pre-war stories were extremely popular. This issue is dated 28 January 1911 (see page 218)

Below Advertisers were quick to seize the new opportunities the boys' sports papers afforded. This Gamages advert appeared in *The Boy's Own Paper* (1908)

The Blue Crusaders was a more interesting tale. The story follows the fortunes of ex-Brampton College pupils Harry Ewing, Arthur Drew and David Moran. Along with one William Fowkes, who befriends them at the factory that employs them after they leave school, the four form a football team of their own – the Blue Crusaders of the title. Its prose betrayed the grip that football was beginning to exert on the lives of Britain's young men; here they ponder how they can set the ball rolling: "The football fever burned fiercely in the veins of Harry Ewing, Arthur Drew, and David Moran. The love of the game which had been instilled in them by their experience in the Brampton College eleven was not to be easily quenched, and so it came about that on the Saturday afternoon which marked the termination of their first week at Messrs. Keith, Howse & Co.'s works the three met William Fowkes, their new-found friend, and discussed the question, whilst the crowd marched onward to the huge football arena of the Browton Rangers Football Club to witness the League match between that famous side and Newcastle United.

THE "BOYS' REALM" FOOTBALL LIBRARY.

½

"MUDDIED OAFS"
— A TALE OF THE "BLUE CRUSADERS" —

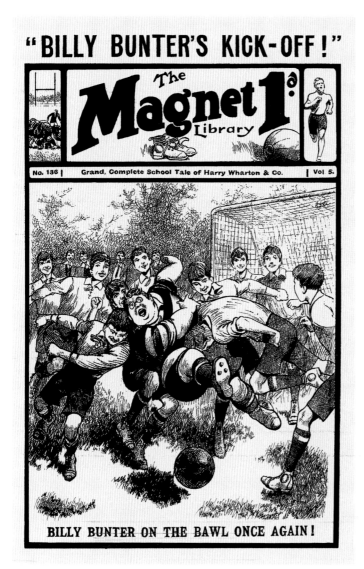

"BILLY BUNTER'S KICK-OFF!"

The Magnet Library 1ᵈ

No. 136 | Grand, Complete School Tale of Harry Wharton & Co. | Vol 5.

BILLY BUNTER ON THE BAWL ONCE AGAIN!

Above Even Billly Bunter was getting in on the action, *Magnet*, issue 136 (1911)

"'Fowkes,' said Harry, addressing the young giant, 'we must form a football club of our own.'" (It was common in the early comics for fictitious football sides to play matches against real clubs.)

The bulk of the Blue Crusaders stories plotted the club's rise from amateur park side to the top division of the football league. They mixed football with adventure and intrigue – the Blue Crusaders visit Africa on tour at one point – but what's interesting is the movement away from the public school amateur game to the professional football league.

"William Fowkes" is an interesting character. William "Fatty" Foulke was a real-life goalkeeper for Sheffield United and Chelsea (among others), who also played cricket for Derbyshire. He also won a single international football cap for England in 1897 against Wales. A larger-than-life character, Foulke, who was 22 stone and, varyingly, 6'2" to 6'7", made his debut for Sheffield United against West Bromwich Albion on 1 September 1894. He led the team to three FA Cup finals (winning two) and a League Championship. He then moved to Chelsea – for a fee of £50. A man with an enormous appetite for life (and food), legend has it that he once scoffed not only his own plateful but also the food put out for his 10 Chelsea team mates, making him the original footballer who ate all the pies. He was made captain of the Stamford Bridge outfit, whose directors felt the big man could put their club on the map. But he stayed for just one season before moving to his final club, Bradford City. Foulke died in 1916, but he lived on, in various manifestations in the comic books; the first, it would seem, was our chum from the Blue Crusaders.

Even the traditional "high jinx" comics that had both feet firmly planted in the English public school were recognising the popularity of football. Launched in 1908, the *Magnet*, within whose pages Greyfriars School first appeared, was clambering aboard the bandwagon, with football introduced into more and more of its stories. Possibly the most famous fictional public school of them all, Greyfriars was home to Billy Bunter, created by the prodigious Charles Hamilton, a.k.a. Frank Richards. Richards was reputed to have written the equivalent of 1,000 full-length novels and could produce a 35,000-word story for the *Magnet* in days. Bunter even appeared on the cover of the *Magnet* playing football, although, true to type, it seems he was a duffer at that, too.

Launched slightly earlier, *Gem* (1907) featured football in its very first issue. "Stormpoint", "A School Tale by Maurice Merriman", featured Rex Allingham, a footballing hero; later, Tom Merry, the footballing maestro of St Jim's, a school that came to rival Greyfriars in the comic books, first appeared in a story called "Playing the Game".

Meanwhile, *The Boys' Realm Football Library* continued to grow, both in terms of readership and the range of stories it carried (it also had various incarnations including *The Boys' Realm Sports Library* and, simply,

Below Sheffield goalkeeper William "Fatty" Foulke in action. He "takes a kick in the Cup Final against Southampton, 1902", according to the illustrator who was there. He was reported to have once said: "I don't mind what you call me as long as you don't call me late for lunch."

FOULKE – THE SHEFFIELD GOAL KEEPER

TAKING A KICK

Photo by Hulton Archive/Getty Images

McCOY COMPETITION. (£25 IN PRIZES.)

The Big Budget. 1d

DID YOU GET "LOVE STORIES," ½d.
YESTERDAY? THE DAINTY LITTLE PAPER.

VOL. II. No. 35.   WEEK ENDING SATURDAY, FEB. 12, 1898.   PRICE 1D.

AIRY ALF AND BOUNCING BILLY INTERVIEW THE ASTON VILLA FOOTBALL TEAM.

1. A. A. and B. B. are commissioned to interview the captain of the Aston Villa Football Team. They had to go by excursion train. "Sit tight," yell the other occupants of the carriage. "We'll get yer aht wiv a sardine-opener, wen we git there."

2. Arrived at the ground, they make straight for the dressing-room. But the bobby outside took them for "dud-pinchers," and ordered them off.

3. As Devey came out they nobbled him. "Wot 'o, Devey!" they cry; "'arf a mo'! We've got to interview you. 'Ow —— ?" But Devey gave them the go-by.

4. "We shall 'ave to wait till 'e's done chivvying that ball," said Alf. But Billy had got the hump, and said nothing.

5. At last the illustrious pair got sick of doing nothing, and ventured on to the field of play to interview Devey while playing. Alf opened his mouth, and one of the players had a pot shot at it. And not such a bad shot either.

6. And then the crowd had their whack. And after they had wiped their boots on A. A. and B. B., and played tunes on them with their walking-sticks, the happy pair remembered an important engagement at home. A— is advertising for a head-ache cure.

Big Budget 35; 12 February 1898 (Tom Browne)

Sports Library ("The Popular Thursday Athletic Paper for Boys and Young Men"). Football continued to dominate right up until the outbreak of war in 1914, at which point all the comics adopted a more militaristic approach.

Characters such as Get-There Gunter, who was "The Disgrace of the School" – although, of course, this was an unfair and undeserved label – were firm favourites; again, the stories combined derring-do and foiled criminals with sporting prowess.

On a similar theme, the story "Shunned by the Team" – "A Powerful Tale of the Football Field", tells of yet another Jack, Jack Strong. He is a "sturdy and clever centre-forward" who "has a hard struggle to keep his invalid mother and sister, and is compelled to scrape together every penny he can get. He is consequently looked down upon by the other members of the team, who regard him as mean and miserly." Jack's traditional virtues – honestly, courage, self-discipline – carry the day. The story was penned by A.S. Hardy, who, with Charles Bartlett, was responsible for much of *The Boys' Realm*'s more popular output.

Left *Big Budget* gets in on the football action with its popular Airy Alf and Bouncing Billy characters (19 February 1898)

Other stories, including "Football Foes", were pot-boilers with a (sometimes tenuous) football link. A tale that appeared in issue 163 (dated 26 October 1912) is typical. Our hero, Jack Carr, "an athletic, manly young Britisher. A champion in the football-field", has been swindled out of his rightful legacy by Seaton Carr, "Jack Carr's rascally uncle, the owner of the mills" in cahoots with George Carr, "the mill-owner's son, as unscrupulous as his father". When Jack is sacked by Seaton Carr from his job at the mill for playing football for the local team (picked ahead of the mill-owner's son) the mill workers strike. Jack signs professional forms, and gradually the full truth emerges – that Seaton forged Jack's late father's will, leaving the business to him. All is found out; Jack is given rightful

Below "Shunned By the Team" first appeared in *The Boys' Herald* on 24 December 1910

SHUNNED BY THE TEAM.

A Powerful New Football Tale.
By ARTHUR S. HARDY.

ARMY LIFE, SPORT, FUN, AND ADVENTURE.

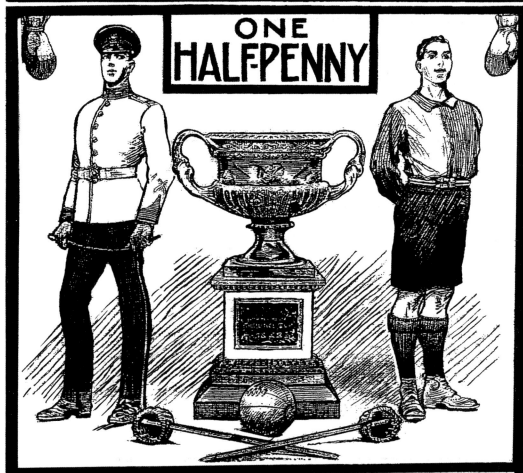

THE SPORTS LIBRARY

ONE HALF-PENNY

The ARMY CHAMPIONS

A MAGNIFICENT TALE OF LIFE AND SPORT IN THE ARMY

"ock banged the ball home, giving the Caleys the lead. But the next instant he was lying upon his face. One of the players had kicked him savagely, and he was down.

ownership of the mill and in disgrace Seaton takes poison rather than face prison. The last line of the story is key: "A minute later Seaton Carr was dead. His sin had found him out – and the wage of sin is death."

The stories became increasingly sophisticated as publishers and their editors became more confident in the genre. "The Army Champions" first featured on 15 February 1913, as the comic picked up a more military tone. It was "Our Glorious New Tale, which will send a thrill through you from beginning to end. Exciting to a degree, it is a veritable masterpiece of Boys' fiction". The Army Champions tracked The Anshires' quest for Army Cup glory, plotting their path round-by-round up to the final. Our heroes, corporals and brothers Ron and Val Brandon, have to deal with the dastardly machinations of a Major Gilbert Marriott as well as their opponents on the field. Full of colourful language and vivid description, the matches are reported in great detail, and full team line-ups are provided (2–3–5 formations, of course). The series culminated in the cup final, against the Irish Fusiliers (26 July 1913), where the Irish team's supporters were "leather-lunged lads, ready to shout at anything". For the home side, "the wide balcony above the gymnasium was crowded with officers and their wives and sweethearts, and among the crowds of the lower ranks fluttered many a gay dress. Mrs Tommy Atkins loves the great national games as well as her husband."

Ron Brandon scores the winner in the last minute to lift the cup for the Anshires and, poignantly, the story ends with the regiment being shipped off to foreign climes as the shadow of war looms ever larger. For the next four years, football was to take a back seat.

Above Football was a man's game, especially if you were playing against the Fighting Caledonians, who featured in the pages of *Sports Budget*

Left The Army Champions were destined to swap the mud of the playing field for the mud of Flanders. The growth in Armed Forces football reflected the massive popularity the game was enjoying

"A TYME THERE IS FOR ALL,
MY MOTHER OFTEN SAYES,
WHEN SHE, WITH SKIRT TUCK'T VERY HIGH,
WITH GIRLS AT FOOTBALL PLAYES."

Sir Philip Sidney, English poet and soldier (1554–1586)

CHAPTER TWO
WAR AND PEACE

BY 1913, **EUROPE WAS IN A FEVERISH STATE**, as tension between the ruling dynasties heightened. Despite the fear and apprehension that was sweeping the continent, little dampened the enthusiasm for football. A significant barrier in the recognition of the sport was broken in 1914 when, for the first time, a reigning monarch, King George V, attended the FA Cup final (Burnley beat Liverpool 1–0 on 25 April in front of 72,778 at Crystal Palace, London.) It was the moment the sport became mainstream, and socially acceptable. As one national newspaper said at the time: "Professional football of the best kind is no longer regarded as a spectacle suitable only for the proletariat. The King's presence at the Cup Final, let us hope, will put an end to the old snobbish notion that true blue sportsmen ought to ignore games played by those who cannot afford to play without being paid for their services." The professionals were here to stay – with the royal seal of approval.

The outbreak of war in August 1914 gave the story-paper publishers a great opportunity to beat the patriotic drum – and increase circulation – and the great conflagration became the backdrop for many of the by-now established "heroes". With the war barely a month old, the *Sports Library* sent one of its main characters to the front line; the "Dandy Champion", a boxer, went to war (14 September 1914).

Others characters were luckier and many of the story-papers' characters were untouched by the conflict. The prolific Charles Bartlett penned the stories of "Redcastle United" in episodes such as 'The Glory of Redcastle' – "A Great Cup Final Yarn of Redcastle United", and "The Trainer's Daughter". This particular tale (published 7 November 1914) concerned one Dolly Larson, a beauty

YOUNG MEN OF BRITAIN !!
THE GERMANS SAID YOU WERE NOT IN EARNEST

Extract from Frankfurter Zeitung :—
"The young Britons prefer to exercise their long limbs on the football ground, rather than to expose them to any sort of risk in the service of their country."

"We knew you'd come—

and GIVE THEM THE LIE !"
PLAY the GREATER GAME on the FIELD of HONOUR

National Army Museum, London

Above By the time the football season started in September 1914, Britain was at war. The authorities put pressure on footballers to forsake sport for 'the greater game on the field of honour', as this army recruitment poster demonstrates only too well. **Left** *Sports Library* (29 August 1914) advertises a sister publication

FOOTBALL
AND
—WAR!—

THE Editor regrets exceedingly that, owing to the serious European disturbances at the time of writing, the Football Double Number has been postponed. These tremendous happenings inevitably cause world-wide ruptures of the ordinary course of things. Therefore, the Editor is certain his readers will perfectly understand the situation and give him their whole-hearted help in other directions.

To save readers as much disappointment as possible, the Editor has arranged a special—

FOOTBALL NUMBER $\left(\frac{1}{2}^{D.}\right)$

for next week. As much as possible that was arranged for the Double Number will be crammed into this issue, and those features unavoidably omitted will appear without fail in subsequent numbers.

who distracted the Redcastle players by turning up to watch training. Once a close-knit bunch, jealousies and rivalries come to the fore, to the point where the players "support each other as much as Labour members support a Tory measure". On the pitch, a series of poor results leads Venner, the coach, to set up a series of boxing bouts among the love rivals – a manly way to settle the matter, during which the players realise how foolish and selfish they had been. As a result, in the next match Aston Villa are beaten 3-0 and harmony is restored (before the "game" the line-ups are named; the Aston Villa team is the full first 11 of the time).

As a reward the players are told by Venner: "Boys, our train doesn't go until five minutes to midnight, so I've booked seats for the whole bunch at the Pyramid Music Hall." And guess who's the star of the show? Dolly, of course, whose football-related turn with her husband (she was doing her research at United) causes much consternation among the pugilistic element at Redcastle.

But the zeitgeist was changing. As the conflict intensified, the Football Association came under more and more pressure to halt play. Critics felt that football was a frivolous pastime in such dire circumstances, a distraction that should be abandoned. Footballers should be encouraging volunteers to sign up by signing up themselves. Sir Arthur Conan Doyle – who himself had volunteered to fight in the Boer War at the age of 40 – said in a recruiting speech on 6 September 1914: "There was a time for all things in the world. There was a time for games, there was a time for business, there was a time for domestic life. There was a time for everything, but there is only time for one thing now, and that thing is war. If the cricketer had a straight eye let him look along the barrel of a rifle. If a footballer had strength of limb let them serve and march in the field of battle."

And heed the call the footballers did. Gradually,

Photo by Topical Press Agency/Getty Images

competitions were wound down; by 1915 both the Football League and FA Cup had been suspended. That same year the footballers of Clapton Orient (now Leyton Orient FC) signed up en masse; they were the first English Football League club to enlist together in a "Pals' battalion". Club captain Fred Parker and some 40 players and staff volunteered. They joined the 17th Battalion of the Middlesex Regiment, which was set up in late 1914 and became known as the "Footballers' Battalion". Leading Orient players Richard McFadden and William Jonas were among those killed during the Battle of the Somme in 1916.

The *Sports Library*'s Redcastle United were quick to follow suit; in issue 285 (27 February 1915) coach Venner addressed a wildly excited crowd who had just seen the team beat Everton in a thrilling match: "As you all know, our Empire is passing through a time of stress just now which is unparalleled in the world's history. As an eminent statesman has said, 'We must put all in.' Every city, every village is doing something in this unprecedented period, and that is as it should be. We of Redcastle United have done something. We

Above Wounded soldiers watch the FA Cup final between Sheffield United and Chelsea at Old Trafford, Manchester, on 24 April 1915. The match has gone down in legend as "the Khaki Cup Final". The Sheffield team won 3-0 in what was the last competitive fixture before football was abandoned for the duration of the war

Left Paper shortages kick in; this announcement appeared in the *Sports Library*, on 29 August 1914

have subscribed to funds for the relief of all affected by this horrible campaign. We have given – and, I hope, given generously – of money, but we can give more. We can give men. Do you hear that? Men! Men! Men! And that is better than money. We can give men, and we are going to. Your boys, your favourites, the men who have amused you and added lustre to the sporting records of Redcastle, are going of their own free will and with light hearts."

Meanwhile, on 15 January 1916, the Footballers' Battalion reached the front line. During a two-week period in the trenches four of its members were killed and 33 wounded.

Below The men of Redcastle United sign up for the Great War

Cheer upon cheer went echoing to the skies as Venner produced the Union Jack and waved it aloft

By 1915, the war provided the raw material for the vast majority of the story-papers' output. The famed Blue Crusaders returned (issue 289) and had their own Pals' battalion, the Browton Footballers' Battalion; subsequent issues carried Blue Crusaders stories called "The Tommies Match" (issue 292); "French Leave" (issue 293); "The German Spy" (issue 295); and "How the Germans came to Browton" (issue 296).

Sports Library readers could also follow the exploits of the "Roughs and Toughs", a story of life in the trenches in which football plays a part. In one yarn (issue 270, 14 November 1914) the lads' football is booted into no-man's land during an impromptu game. Shouting to the Germans, our heroes, Dusty and Jack, agree a truce during which the football is to be retrieved: "'Bravo Bosches! Good on yer!' applauded Dusty, who had always regarded the foe as unmitigated hogs.
'Three cheers for 'em, chummies. They're proper sports, blow me if they ain't! Oooray – 'ooray!'

Above The Blue Crusaders in wartime football action

"The German captain grinned and dropped back into cover again. Jack hurried on and picked up the ball. When he turned back there were his pals lining the trench top, waving their caps and hurrahing. And then – Crash! Bang! Rattle! Zip! A sheet of flame had come from the Bosches' lines. It was a blackhearted ruse, after all, to lure the hated British to destruction."

For a government desperate to recruit, the propaganda this type of story generated was invaluable, and despite the privations of war the story-papers carried on publishing. They continued to espouse the great British virtues that would stand the reader in good stead in the theatre of war as well as in the sporting arena. In March 1916, *The Boys' Friend* celebrated its coming-of-age with a 21st anniversary special issue. Just 12 pages in length, it

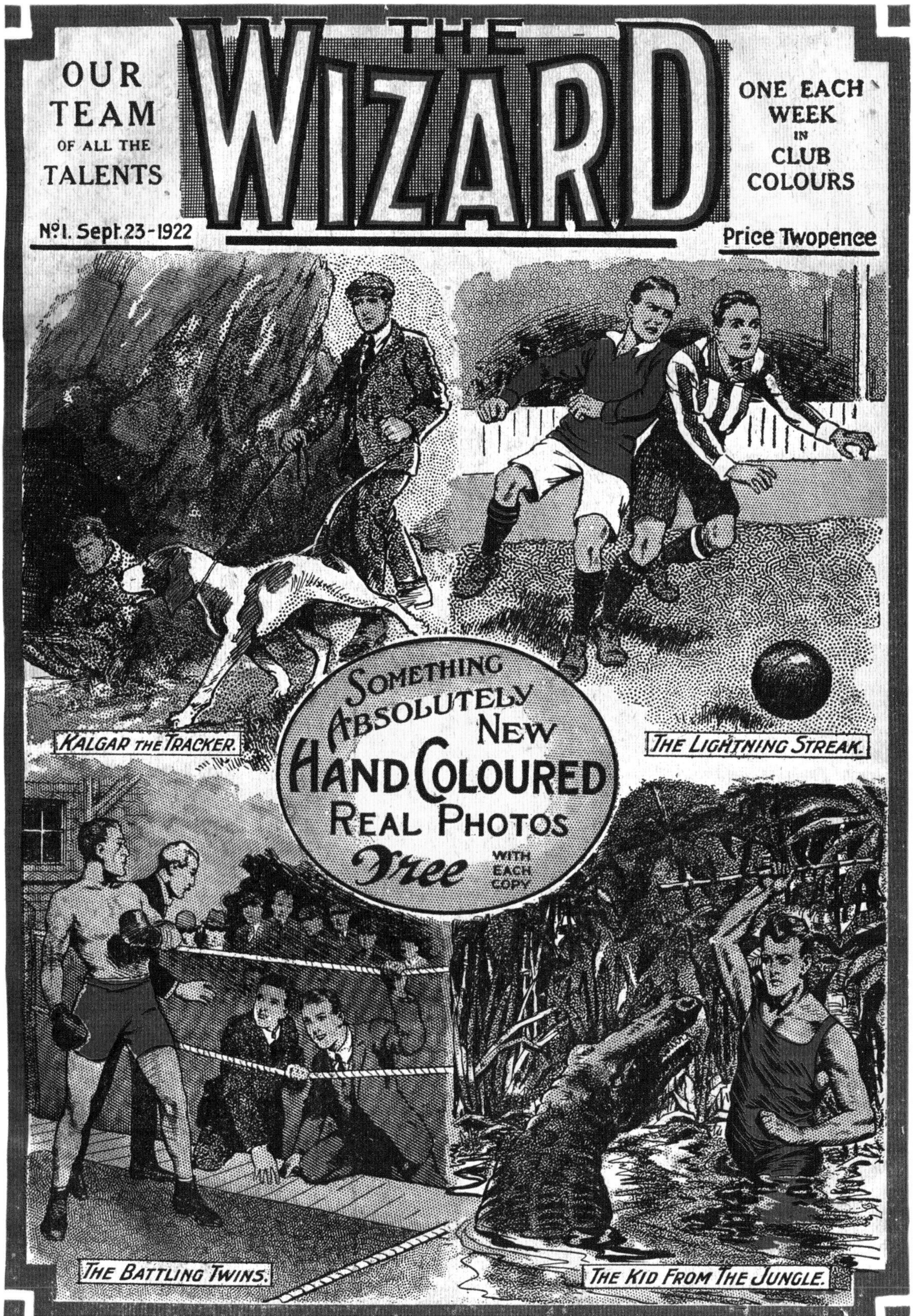
OUR TEAM OF ALL THE TALENTS
THE WIZARD
ONE EACH WEEK IN CLUB COLOURS
No. 1. Sept. 23 - 1922
Price Twopence
KALGAR THE TRACKER.
THE LIGHTNING STREAK.
SOMETHING ABSOLUTELY NEW
HAND COLOURED REAL PHOTOS
Free WITH EACH COPY
THE BATTLING TWINS.
THE KID FROM THE JUNGLE.

carried an article from Hamilton Edwards, a director of Amalgamated Press, publishers of **The Boys' Friend**. In the "In Your Editor's Den" section was "My Message to British Boys". It read: "My Dear Boys – Your Editor has asked me to address you in the great coming-of-age number of TBF, a paper whose interests I have always had dearly at heart.

"One of the first things we were taught at school, and the best and noblest thing which any boy can be taught, is contained in the time-honoured but ever-fresh motto: 'Play the game'.

"What a wealth of wisdom lies in these three words! How infinitely superior is the boy who is a straight, clean sportsman, when compared to the lad who does not scruple to hit below the belt, and who takes defeat badly.

"In any game in which you join, my lads, even in the great and serious game of life after school, you will frequently find yourselves pitted against fellows who don't know the proper rules. They will try to down you by unfair tricks, or try to trip you up when you are off your guard. With the natural spirit of the sportsman these shabby tricks will irritate you, and you may lose your temper.

"A fellow who loses his temper is no earthly use to his side. He cannot shoot straight, and he is a bad bungler. It is annoying to be up against caddish opponents, true, but if you yourselves play the man, the very chaps who act in such an unsportsmanlike way will respect and admire you in their hearts…"

Below New comics sprang up at the end of the war, as interest in football revived. They included *Boy's Pictorial* and *Wizard*, launched in 1921 and 1922 respectively

B ut the Great War changed the world, sweeping away the dynasties that had ruled Europe for centuries, and giving birth to the modern age. The early 1920s were a boom time for the comic publishers; but subtle changes were taking place. In her book, *Manliness and the Boys' Story Paper in Britain: A Cultural History, 1855–1940*, historian Kelly Boyd argues that, by the end of the 19th century, the idea that true manliness emerged only from within the elite classes was under pressure from the ranks of the respectable working class, and Boyd suggests that the period 1890 to 1920 marked a transitional period in which the papers' depiction of manliness was "democratised". Adding to the debate, academic Stephen Heathorn wrote: "The heroes of Edwardian story papers were no longer aristocratic and arrogant; no longer was rugged individualism

A FINE CHANCE FOR AMATEUR DETECTIVES TO WIN PRIZES SEE PAGE ELEVEN.

Boy's Pictorial

THE BOY'S OWN NEWSPAPER   ADVENTURE, PICTURES, SPORT AND COMPETITIONS

No. 17. (New Series)   Week Ending February 4, 1922.   (Every Tuesday.)   Two Pence.

FOUR FOOTBALLERS FACE PHOTOGRAPHER.

" THE BOY WITH THE £1,000 PUNCH "—See Page 5.

Grand English & Scottish Cup-Ties Number

the acme of masculinity. The emphasis switched to sacrifice and communal values within the structured hierarchy of society. In this setting skilled working-class boys could be cast as heroes, becoming so by being team players, albeit for a team on which not everyone was equal. Finally, after the Great War, the shift away from youthful aristocratic arrogance and independence was completed. In the post-war years few of the inter-war heroes were aristocratic; instead, boys from humble social backgrounds were shown what it meant to be manly not so much by the actions of their peers but rather by adult exemplars, most especially teachers. The literature of the inter-war years posited manliness as a process arrived at through education; obedience and respect for adult leadership was thus rewarded in these tales."

Among the launches in the boys' comics sector were **Young Britain** (1919); **Boys' Cinema** (1919); **Football & Sports Favourite** (1920); **Adventure** (1921); **Boys' Pictorial** (1921); **Pals** (1922); **Rover** (1922); **Boys' Magazine** (1922); **Wizard** (1922); **Champion** (1922); **Sports Budget** (1922); and **Triumph** (1924). Proof of the renewed appeal football was enjoying post-war was the entry into the market of Dundee-based publishing giant D.C. Thomson. Along with Amalgamated Press, and its subsequent tie-ups with Fleetway and IPC, D.C. Thomson was to become one of the majors forces in football comic publishing.

After 1918, while the traditional boys' papers varied in content and tone, these new publications stuck to the tried-and-tested pre-war formula of adventure, mystery and action stories. These dramas were regularly played out against the background of the football field, but with the sports action the sub-plot to the melodrama. While the front covers generally had a much more modern look and feel, the papers were still dominated by text-based stories, illustrated with single-frame "action" shots.

Adventure, which marked D.C. Thomson's first foray into the youth market, was typical of the new launches. "Lively, healthy and

Left, Design-wise, *The Football Favourite* led the way with its modern look

Below A notice in the first issue of *Rover*, dated 4 March 1922, advertising issue 2

HI, KID!

D. NICOLL, Dundee.

ADAM M'LEAN, Celtic.

Make sure you get these
TWO DANDY
PHOTOS
given free in special envelope with next week's
ROVER.
First-class photos of first-class players.

D. NICOLL and ADAM M'LEAN
Dundee   Celtic

If you order your ROVER now you'll
be right—if you don't—well, you'll be left.

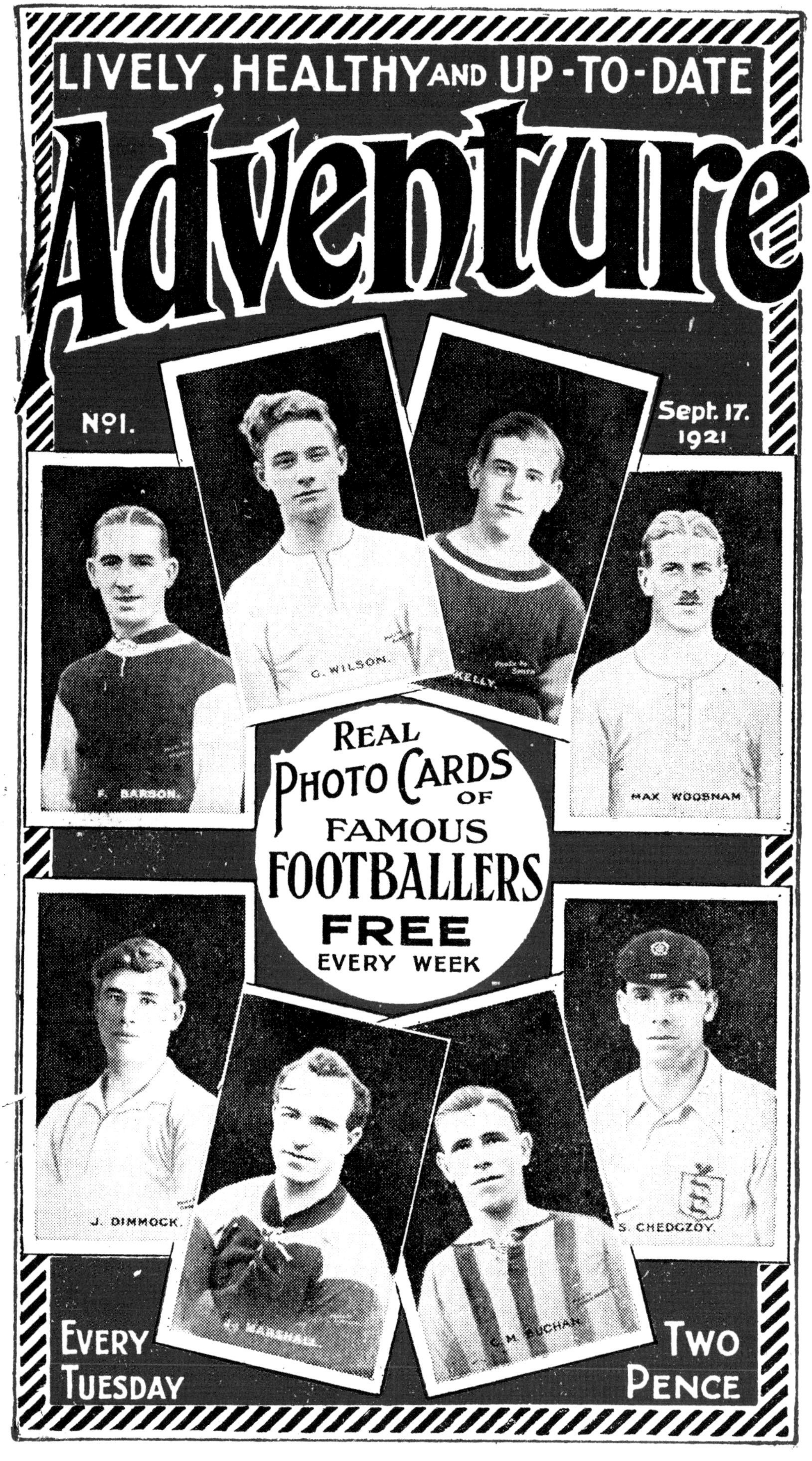
LIVELY, HEALTHY AND UP-TO-DATE
Adventure
Nº1.
Sept. 17. 1921
F. BARSON.
G. WILSON.
MAX WOOSNAM
REAL PHOTO CARDS OF FAMOUS FOOTBALLERS FREE EVERY WEEK
J. DIMMOCK.
S. CHEDGZOY.
EVERY TUESDAY
TWO PENCE

up-to-date", it first appeared on 17 September 1921, offering readers "Real Photo Cards of Famous Footballers Free Every Week". Among the eight illustrious players featured on the first front cover were the legendary Max Woosnam (Manchester City), Jimmy Dimmock (Spurs), Sam Chedgzoy (Everton) and Charles Buchan (Sunderland). The free gift was by now standard practice with new-launch comics; *Adventure* readers were tempted with the offer of one card a week for eight weeks (not eight cards in the first week). The first free card, which was based on the hugely popular cigarette card, was of "Dimmock, the Dazzler", described as "the most famous footballer in London".

Among the mystery and adventure stories ("Dixon Hawke", "the renowned Detective" in "The Smiling Mask"; "Rip", "Our Magnificent New Serial of World-Wide Adventures, featuring the daring Captain Nile and his two boy chums, Rip and Tom"; "Non-Stop Ned", "The Thrilling exploits of Ned Byng, the Dashing Young Motorist") was "The Outcast of the Spurs", featuring Jimmy Power in the "Enthralling Tale of the Boxing Ring and Football Life". Jimmy is found unconcious in the offices of Leversham Spurs by manager-secretary Mr Harder and trainer Bill Sinclair. No one knows how he got there. Fortunately for the Spurs, when their first-choice goalkeeper is injured before a big game, and there's no one to replace him, Jimmy turns out to be a very able

Left *Adventure* hit the streets on 17 September 1921

Below Bold and brash, *Adventure* was D.C. Thomson's first foray into the boys' story-papers market. One of its earliest footballing characters was "The Outcast of the Spurs"

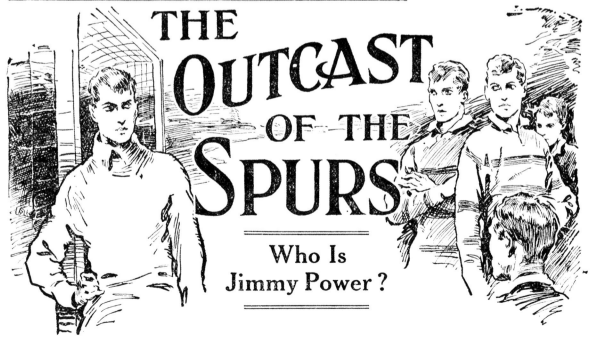

DIMMOCK, The Dazzler,

The Young Hero Who Won The English Cup.

HIS REAL PHOTO PRESENTED FREE THIS WEEK.

The adventurous career of James Dimmock, of Tottenham Hotspur, has been full of romance. Although he has not yet reached his majority he is the most famous footballer in London.

Unlike some boys who flatter only to deceive, Jimmie gets better every day he plays, and, barring unlucky accidents, will be in the limelight for many seasons yet to come.

Dimmock is an Edmonton youth, and was born within a stone's throw of White Hart Lane, the ground where he has won his fame. At school he played good football, and when he left his desk for his father's workshop, chased the leather with a small junior team.

It was while he was with these youngsters, playing in nothing better than a minor grade of football, that Peter M'William, that great wing half who had left Newcastle United to look after Tottenham Hotspur, saw the cheery, red-faced youngster, who played with the zest of a schoolboy and the craft of a veteran.

Mr M'William knew at once that he had found a jewel which required very little polishing in order to dazzle like the genuine thing, and asked the boy to join the 'Spurs' playing staff. Dimmock went.

Within a few weeks the boy had displaced Chipperfield, the 'Spurs' regular outside left.

Last season he played with the 'Spurs' first team in 41 games, and scored nine goals. He won his international cap, playing against Scotland.

Above all, the 'Spurs' played in the final of the English Cup, and Dimmock, unknown to fame but a little while before, scored the only goal which took this most coveted trophy to Tottenham.

The goal is worth describing because it typifies his style of play. Getting the ball on the touch line, Dimmock went away at great speed. He was tackled by the half-back and full back, and for a moment appeared to have been robbed. One of the defenders made a mistake in not getting the ball away, and, like a flash, Dimmock had sprinted upon him, robbed him of the ball, and, showing a wonderful burst of speed, got clear away, and with a great shot defeated the Wolverhampton goalkeeper.

NEXT WEEK : Real Photo of SAM CHEDGZOY, the Everton Outside Right.

Above Adventure featured profiles of real players in each issue, the first being Jimmy Dimmock of Tottenham Hotspur (17 September 1921)

deputy indeed. He also proves to be very handy with his fists when put to the test by club captain Dick "Iron" Butler, a bully and all-round bad egg with connections to the underworld. In fact, he's setting Jimmy up for a fixed boxing match linked to a betting scam.

There were, however, some radical changes, both in society and in the pages of the story-papers. One, perhaps bizarre, consequence of the Great War was to propagate women's football in Britain. As the horror of trench warfare began to take its terrible toll, women were moved into what were previously male occupations, notably in the factories – over 700,000 women worked in munitions factories at the height of the conflict. The growth of this female labour force led to the setting up of many women's work football teams, particularly in the Football League heartlands of the north and the Midlands. The most famous of these was the Dick, Kerr Ladies team. The Dick, Kerr factory in Preston manufactured munitions and other goods to help the war effort; during break times the factory women played football, apeing their male counterparts. Under the guidance of one of the factory's managers, Alfred Frankland, the team played a series of matches to raise money for services' charities. They were an instant hit, and soon Dick, Kerr were the most famous ladies' team in the land. Frankland arranged for the women to play a game on Christmas Day 1917 in aid of the local hospital for wounded soldiers at Moor Park, persuading Preston North End to allow the women to play the game at their ground, Deepdale. It was the first football game to be played there since the Football League programme was cancelled during the course of the war. More than 10,000 people turned up; Dick, Kerr's was able to donate £200 to the hospital (equivalent to £41,000 today).

Dick, Kerr's was one of many hundreds of teams that formed during the latter years of the war. After the Armistice in November 1918, when women began to leave the factories, many of them disbanded. Those who played on drew huge support. Dick, Kerr's Ladies played a game against Newcastle United Ladies at St James's Park, in September 1919, attracting a crowd of 35,000 people and raising £1,200 (£250,000 today) for war charities. Another match featuring the Dick, Kerr's Ladies team, played at Goodison Park, Liverpool, on Boxing Day 1920, attracted a crowd of 53,000 with another 10,000–15,000 reportedly turned away because the ground was full.

This astonishing popularity was reflected in the story-papers, with the appearance of female characters, notably "Meg Foster – Footballer" and "Nell O' Newcastle", both of whom graced the pages of *The Football Favourite*.

By this time the women's game was under attack, from some surprising quarters. According to Patrick Brennan, a women's football historian, "radical feminist writer Sarah Grand (real name Frances Bellenden Clarke) went into some detail in giving her objections; she condemned lacrosse, football, cricket and some forms of gymnastics as positively injurious, stating 'the football-playing girl, the boxing girl, the girl who by gymnastics and physical drill of the too strenuous type, flattens her chest and hardens her muscles will never be the ideal'. This was a remarkable volte-face by the person whose 1893 novel, *The Heavenly Twins*, had launched the concept of the 'New Woman'. Dr Ethel Williams, the first female doctor to practise in Newcastle upon Tyne, who in her

Below Dick, Kerr International Ladies were undefeated British champions in 1920-1921

Photo by Bob Thomas/Popperfoto/Getty Images

MEG FOSTER— FOOTBALLER

If you like this story of the popular mill girl Captain of the Crusaders, be sure you do' not miss the opening instalment of " Captain Meg " next week.

Above Women football characters, such as "Meg Foster – Footballer", were extremely popular in the early 1920s

youth had been a suffragette and had taken part in the famous 'Mud March' of 1907, said that while she was in favour of girls having opportunities to participate in athletics, she had 'always been sorry that they had taken to football instead of taking up some of the more suitable games'."

Perhaps less surprising, given its efforts to re-establish the professional (men's) leagues, was the Football Association's attack on the women's game. It saw the women's game, and the huge crowds it drew, as a threat. Consequently, on 5 December 1921 it adopted the following drastic resolution:

"Complaints having been made as to football being played by women, the council feel impelled to express their strong opinion that the game of football is quite unsuitable for females and ought not to be encouraged.

"Complaints have also been made as to the conditions under which some of these matches have been arranged and played, and the appropriation of receipts to other than charitable objects. The council are further of the opinion that an excessive proportion of the receipts are absorbed in expenses and an inadequate percentage devoted to charitable objects.

"For these reasons the council request clubs belonging to the association to refuse the use of their grounds for such matches."

WHY YOU LITTLE MAGGOT I'LL – – –

The defiant response to this effective banning of the women's game was the setting up of the English Ladies Football Association (astonishingly, the FA finally rescinded its 1921 edict as recently as 1971). "Meg Foster – Footballer" embodied this female empowerment, described as it was as an "Absorbing Tale of a Mill-Girl's Football Club. And Their Plucky Fight for Fame and Fortune". Meg was the popular captain of the Crusaders, a team founded by workers at Blake's Mills.

In an early storyline we see Meg trying to set up the side, imploring her team mates to get involved: "'And why shouldn't girls play football, anyway? Coom to that, why shouldn't they play it as well as t' men? 'Tis all a lot o' rot to say that it's dangerous – 'tis no more dangerous than other sport. There is always a risk aboot everything. Oh, I know we've got plenty o' difficulties to overcome, but we'll manage 'em all reet.'"

Meg, it seems, was inspired by the visit of the real French ladies' team in 1920 to Deepdale, home of Preston North end, to play the Dick, Kerr team. Widely perceived to be the first women's international match, Dick, Kerr's Ladies won 2–0 against the team from Paris.

"Since the visit of the French team of lady footballers to Preston, the idea of playing football herself had taken a very firm hold in Meg's mind. And now, it seemed, was her great chance.

"For the first Girls' Football League had been formed. Some twenty clubs all over Lancashire had been got together. For the first time in Great Britain, football for girls was to come into its own, and it was Meg's great idea that Blake's should form one of the League."

But a suitor, Ted Sefton, tries to deter Meg: "'Look here, Meg,' he said, 'tak' my advice and gi' oop being so silly. Football isn't a girl's game.'

'Why isn't it?'

'Tha know why. It's a man's game.'

'Then why don't tha play it, Ted Sefton, instead o' spending all thy spare time in the public-house and backing horses? It would do thee a lot more good, and make thy owd mother a happier woman.'"

Later, after falling in love with Tony, the nephew of the wicked mill-owner, millionaire John Blake, Meg is kidnapped by agents working for Blake. However, "great crime expert" Martin Trackman uncovers the plot, manages to save Meg from transportation to America, and confronts the mill-owner – with the young

Below Everyone has got an opinion… how one (anonymous) writer saw the debate in *Boy's Pictorial*, 21 January 1921

SHOULD GIRLS PLAY FOOTER?

WHAT THE MERE MAN THINKS ABOUT IT.

PERHAPS many readers will be inclined to dismiss from their minds the question of whether girls should play football, with the thought: "It doesn't matter; they do."

Now that the Football Association has "put its foot down with a firm hand," however, the question has again become one of topical interest.

As a mere man there are just one or two points that strike me in connection with the matter. The first is, are there not enough games quite suitable for women and girls without their wanting to play such a game as football, about which there is a controversial atmosphere?

There are dozens of good girls' games —or perhaps I had better say, good games for girls. It seems to me, however, that the whole business is simply another case of the girls wanting to copy the men.

Girl Training.

Do football girls really get any pleasure out of their play? I very much doubt it. It is the same as with smoking, the majority of them positively detest it—but it looks big, you know!

From the point of view of the spectators, the position is even more ridiculous. The grand old British sport of football then becomes a pantomime. Instead of the spectators watching tactics, they watch antics.

As a music-hall "turn," a girls' football match is in its true company; as a healthy outdoor sport, it is out of its element entirely.

The trainer of one of the best-known girls' football teams has been saying, in a contemporary, that she can see the time coming (in the near future, too) when the best girls' team will be able to play the best professional team in the country.

The comment which comes immediately to the mind is "Don't be silly!" A team of schoolboys would beat Dick Kerr's team, or any other girls' team, with the greatest of ease. Why? For the simple reason that football is essentially a game for the male sex—women are not "built" for it.

A word to the girls who do play— stop it! Whatever you think, you are not admired by the opposite sex.

Right Meg Foster gets a hero's reception in the pages of *The Football Favourite*

lovers Meg and nephew Tony. Facing disgrace and prison, Blake crumples, only to be consoled by our footballing heroine (who now seems to have lost her regional accent):

"'Cheer up, Gaffer!' she said, touched by the old man's misery. 'You aren't going to be hanged, you know. You played foul… I've been having a long talk with Mr Trackman and I agree with him, I don't want any arrests if you play fair now!'" Blake agrees to consent to the marriage – and buy the Crusaders the town's football stadium if they beat rival factory team the Canaries in a forthcoming fixture (the Canaries' boss, Dawson, also has designs on the ground).

"'I've been foolish and wicked!' [Blake] faltered. 'I am most anxious to atone both to you and the girl who shared your terrible experience. It is for you to suggest what sum of money will compensate–'

'I don't want your money!' flashed Meg. 'I'll tell you what will compensate me. Tony loves me and I love him; let us be engaged with your consent, fair and square for all the world to know, and be finished with this stupid sort of on approval business, never knowing where we are. That's the big thing, Gaffer, the other thing is a sporting thing. Two thousands pounds isn't much to you, so will you be a sport? If we beat the Canaries on Saturday will you buy us the Albion Athletic's ground? It's a sporting chance for you, for it's a very open game.'"

The day of the big match dawns, and tension runs high. For there's more than local pride at stake: there's the prize of the ground for the winners, and the game's soul is at stake. "'We don't want men like Dawson in the game!' [Meg] said. 'Well, if we lick them to-day, were not likely to have him in it. Meg, the story is that he has threatened to withdraw his support from the Canaries if we beat them to-day on their own ground.'"

Below Some of the stories bordered on the melodramatic, from the pages of *The Football Favourite*, 1 January 1921

Of course the Crusaders win, but their moment of triumph is met with a portentous and thunderous tirade from the bad-sport Dawson. As the girls went

One of the Best Football Stories Ever Written.

POWERFUL SERIAL OF FOOTBALL, LOVE, AND MYSTERY
By STEVE NELSON

As Meg entered the field a solid mass of Blake's supporters started a great roar of cheering. Then "For she's a jolly good fellow"

NELL O' NEWCASTLE

By *Steve Nelson*

Magnificent Football Adventure Yarn.

Don't Miss a Line of this Topping Story.

up to collect the cup… "a bullying looking man rose, purple in the face, and shook his great fist at them. 'This ends football for girls!' he cried; and there was a fanatical light in his eyes. 'There'll be no more girls' football at my mill, and before long there'll be no girls' teams in this district! I withdraw my offer of the gold cup! Go on cheering, but I'll break the lot of you.'" And the author makes clear the real-world point: "There was a sudden silence in the stand; practically everyone present was a keen supporter of football for girls, and with old Dawson, who had great wealth and influence, and up to now had been a great supporter of the movement, suddenly abandoning them, the outlook was bleak."

Above Nell O' Newcastle – "a very pretty girl and a clever footballer"

T*he Football Favourite* repeated the female footballer as "star" in another major story. "Nell O' Newcastle" featured our eponymous heroine as she battled on and off the field to do what is right. "Don't miss a Line of this Topping story" the comic implored – for this is a "Magnificent Football Adventure Yarn". In truth the 'yarn' is driven by the adventure part of the story; the football is of secondary importance, albeit diverting and interesting. Nell Harmer is "a very pretty girl, and a clever footballer". She is employed at a Tyneside engineering firm owned by her uncle – who is "John Hood, who had defrauded her in her father's will of a great deal of money. For this reason, Hood, aided by his daughter, Cynthia, plots to undermine Nell's team of girl footballers, to get her disgraced and forced to leave Newcastle." Sound familiar? 'Football Foes', *The Boys' Realm* story written 10 years previously, used exactly the same plot, and the similarities do not end there. Nell has to deal with a corrupt professional (a doctor rather than the lawyer in 'Football Foes'), a "scoundrelly foreman at Hood's" who is murdered, and Hood's business rival, Philip Gray, who "is in love with Nell".

Right *Pals*' all-action front cover, Christmas Day 1922, promising a mix of "mystery, sport and adventure"

Many twists and turns ensued in this "Thrilling Story of Girl's Footer Team",

Pals, December 25, 1922.

GREAT NEW FOOTER SERIAL STARTS THIS WEEK

MYSTERY
SPORT
ADVENTURE

Pals

EVERY
2d.
MONDAY

VOL. I.—No. 12.　　[Registered For Transmission By Canadian Magazine Post]　　DECEMBER 25, 1922.

A WONDERFUL EFFORT　::　SEE THRILLING NEW FOOTER SERIAL STARTING ON PAGE 3.

Don't miss this Grand New Footer Story, which is the further adventures of Harold Dark of Milltown City. Start to-day, and ask your friends to do the same.

THE . . .

MILLIONAIRE CENTRE-FORWARD.

The Hero of "The Great Cup Tie Mystery," Harold Dark, has come into a fortune, but this does not stop him following his beloved football. Although now a millionaire he still plays centre forward for Milltown City.

By SIDNEY HORLER.

Harold Dark turned up the sleeve of his pyjama jacket, and on his forearm showed the tiny puncture of a hypodermic syringe.

Above Glamour, footer and mystery, from the pages of *Boys' Pictorial*, 11 February 1922

but, of course, good triumphs over evil, and moral order is restored. It's a sub-text that's repeated time and time again in literally hundreds of stories that were appearing during this post-war publishing boom. Other patterns were familiar; the mystery, crime or adventure story with a football background was a staple for new launches such as *Boys' Cinema* and *Pals*.

Competition was fierce; issues of *Young Britain* in 1924 carried the following legend on the bottom of each page: "Stick to the Four Best Papers Obtainable – 'CHAMPION' (Every Monday) – 'PLUCK' (Every Tuesday); 'ROCKET' (Every Wednesday); and 'YOUNG BRITAIN' (Every Thursday)." Enough reading matter to stretch even the most voracious young reader; and more than enough to stretch the weekly pocket money allowance.

This competition drove the publishers and their editors to more and more outlandish storylines and plot twists, to grab their readers' interest and attention.

Boys' Cinema ran a story called "Winning Goals" about a goalkeeper who was kidnapped before a big game (25 November 1922); *Boy's Pictorial* featured "The Millionaire Centre-Forward" (11 February 1922). The hero Harold Dark – a character who featured in many *Boy's Pictorial* stories – has come into a fortune, but this does not stop him from playing football. Although "now a millionaire he still plays centre-forward for Milltown City". In a story of intrigue, Dark somehow survives an eventual murder attempt; but that was a simple affair compared to "The Mystery Final", from the *Champion Story Supplement* (29 April 1922). In that fanciful yarn, a Sherwood Rovers player is shot on the pitch while celebrating winning the cup, while another protagonist, who was thought murdered by yet another Rovers' player, seemingly comes back from the dead even as the gunman, who

Right *Sports Budget* was another newcomer to the market in the early 1920s

SPORTS BUDGET

EDITED BY "SPORTSMAN"

2d.

HAWTON UNITED
FOOTBALL
CLUB
AN
EXTRAORDINARY
GENERAL
MEETING

Wonderful long complete sports story by Jack Crichton (within)

NO CASH-NO CLUB!

The Champion Story Supplement

A SUPERB 15,000-WORD LONG COMPLETE STORY WITH EVERY ISSUE—that is what I am giving you in THE "CHAMPION" STORY SUPPLEMENT. And here is the first of them—a tip-top football yarn by one who knows his subject from A to Z. There are many other star stories to follow this —stories of mystery, sport, humour, and adventure in all parts of the world. Look out for them, and tell your friends to follow your example and order in advance!

= PAID TO LOSE! =

A Magnificent, Long Complete Story of the Football Field, introducing SEXTON BLAKE, Detective.

By ARTHUR S. HARDY.

Pictures by FRANK R. GREY.

CHAPTER ONE.
A Question of Bribery.

"MR. SEXTON BLAKE!"

It was the trainer of the Benton Rovers Football Club who announced the visitor, and Manager Talbot, who was talking to Richard Creed, the most influential of all the directors, looked up with a cry of glad surprise.

"He has lost no time, Mr. Creed," he commented. "The wire saying he was coming has beaten him by only half an hour."

The door swung open, and Sexton Blake came into the private office.

It was the first time that either of them had set eyes upon the famous detective, and they looked him over with the keenest interest. Sexton Blake was just as distinguished-looking as they had expected, but it was difficult to believe that the fashionable clothes he wore covered a frame whose strength was far beyond the average, or to understand what was passing behind the mask-like expression of his face.

They caught a flash of piercing eyes, and then came the question, short and sharp.

"Mr. Talbot, I believe?"

"Yes, Mr. Blake. This is Mr. Creed, one of our directors. I sent for him the moment I received your wire. You are amazingly prompt. Mr. Creed is the big noise in Benton football, if I may use the expression. Please sit down!"

Sexton Blake put his gloves in his pocket, removed his overcoat and hat, selected a cigar from the box that was offered him, and leant back in his chair.

"I understand you wish me to remain in Benton until I have solved your football mystery for you?" he said.

"Precisely."

Next Week: "SHIPS OF THE DESERT!" A Thrilling Story of Weird Adventure, by REID WHITLEY.

had attempted to bribe Rovers' centre-forward, is apprehended. Phew!

The publishers also turned to another tried-and-trusted publishing device, one that their Victorian forefathers had used to great effect in the era of the "penny dreadfuls": the serialised story with the cliff-hanger ending. Pre-war, many of the story-paper yarns were complete stories – sometimes over 15,000 words long. Serialisation, which led to more and shorter stories being published in each issue, encouraged repeat purchase among readers who no doubt spent the week on tenterhooks in eager expectation of the next instalment.

Editors also sought new, more interesting 'characters' as vehicles for their stories; thus *Pluck* introduced us to Jim Drew, football journalist, in the story "Fighting for Football!" – "An Amazing Account of the Adventures of a Young Journalist Who Set Out to Save Football". This was "Something new in sports yarns!" and "Brimful of gripping incident". *Pluck* boasted that this was "Footer from a new angle!… Really good footer yarns are few and far between, but here you have a stunner! Mr Howard Grant, whose work is well known to all of you, has never written a better yarn than this, and as he has combined footer with the fascinating theme of newspaper production, you have an unusual treat awaiting you. Kick off to-day!" Drew's mission is to dispel the myth that "professional football is not on the square" – in other words, results are rigged.

B y this time *Pluck* already included an eight-page story supplement with each issue, called *The Star* (launched 28 October 1922); a tactic many of its rivals adopted. Others like *Champion* published separate supplements – *The Champion Story Supplement*, which was "A superb 15,000-word long complete story with every issue". It cost 2d and enticed readers by featuring well-known fictional characters from other mediums in its stories. The launch issue, dated

Left The ubiquitous Sexton Blake in a case of football corruption

Below A journalist's mission to save football… Jim Drew is "Fighting for Football"

A YARN WHICH BREATHES THE ATMOSPHERE OF THE FOOTER FIELD!　　　KICK OFF TO-DAY!

FIGHTING for FOOTBALL!
An Amazing Account of the Adventures of a Young Journalist Who Set Out to Save Football. BY HOWARD GRANT.

Below Famous Chelsea player
Jack Cock turns his hand to
writing a football yarn for *Pals,*
1922

Right A typically stylish and
humorous front cover from
The Football Favourite
(12 March 1921)

28 January 1922, contained the story "Paid to Lose" – "A Magnificent, Long Complete Story of the Football Field, introducing Sexton Blake, Detective". Blake was the best-known of all the fictional detectives in Britain at the time. Called the "prince of the penny dreadfuls" and "the office boys' Sherlock Holmes", he first came to life in 1893 in the pages of **The Halfpenny Marvel** shortly after the legendary Baker Street sleuth had toppled into the Reichenbach Falls. "Paid to Lose" was written by story-paper veteran A.S. Hardy. Sexton Blake was also to appear in issue 7 of **Champion Weekly** in a story called "The Golden Wolf". Such was the ubiquity of the character it is estimated that, in different publications, some 400,000 words were written about him in the month of January 1922 alone.

Other publications went for real-life celebrities. The Christmas Day 1922 issue of **Pals** featured a story called "Out for the Cup", by Jack Cock, "The Famous Chelsea Centre-Forward". It was "A Wonderful New Soccer Serial by one of England's Finest Exponents of the Game". In the **Rover**'s launch issue (4 March 1922) the story "The Traitor of the Team" was co-authored by Arthur Grimsdell, the "popular 'national half-back and captain of the 'Spurs".

The huge number of story-papers, with their supplements, meant editors were under immense pressure to generate stories to fill them. This pressure was felt by the writers, too; one of the outcomes was the re-introduction of characters and indeed storylines that had appeared in stories from the previous era. With new editorial teams in place D.C. Thomson was able to inject fresh ideas into the genre – and the competition between the old guard of Amalgamated and the Scottish newcomer was to inspire both to greater and more creative heights in the coming decade.

Commencing in This Number. A Wonderful New Soccer Serial by one of England's Finest Exponents of the Game.
Read how Charlie King answered the Call of the Dreadnoughts and, Despite the Machinations of his Enemies, helped
the Team to Fame and Victory. Don't Miss this Footer Sensation of the Year. Start it Right Now.

OUT FOR THE CUP.
By JACK COCK,
The Famous Chelsea Centre-Forward.

Published All The Year Round!

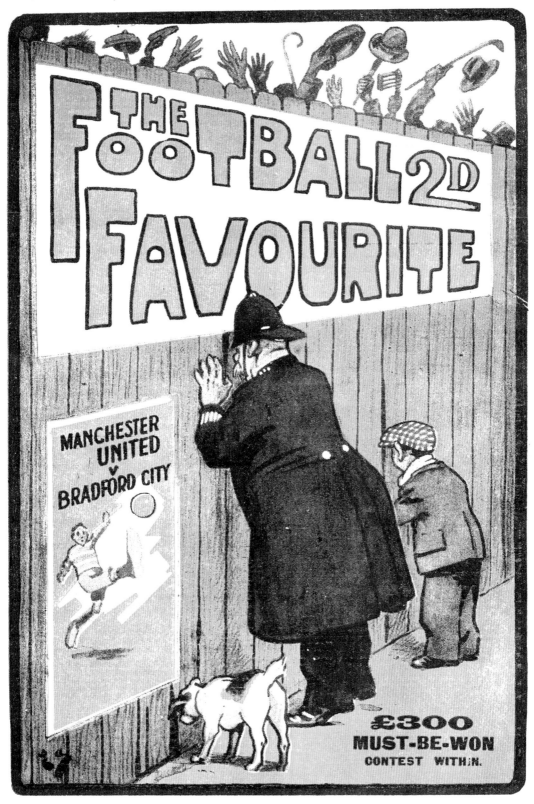

THE FOOTBALL FAVOURITE 2D

MANCHESTER UNITED v BRADFORD CITY

£300 MUST-BE-WON CONTEST WITHIN.

Vol 1. No. 28.

Saturday, March 12, 1921

"TO SAY THAT MEN PAID THEIR SHILLINGS TO WATCH TWENTY-TWO HIRELINGS KICK A BALL IS MERELY TO SAY THAT A VIOLIN IS WOOD AND CATGUT, THAT HAMLET IS SO MUCH PAPER AND INK. FOR A SHILLING BRUDDERSFORD UNITED AFC OFFERED YOU CONFLICT AND ART..."

The Good Companions (1928)
JB Priestley (1894–1984)

CHAPTER THREE

CRIME AND PUNISHMENT

Right *The Rover*, January 1939, introducing the character of Cast-Iron Bill (see page 218)

Below Uruguayan captain Jose Nazassi (left) shakes hands with his Argentinian counterpart "Nolo" Fereyra before the final of the first World Cup in Montevideo, on 30 July 1930. Uruguay won 4–2

D.C. THOMSON'S ENTRY INTO THE STORY-PAPERS market meant the Dundee-based publishing giant and its London rival, Amalgamated Press, entered the 1930s going head-to-head for market share. D.C. Thomson, which had entered the sector in the early 1920s with *Adventure*, *Rover* and *Wizard*, added *Skipper* to its roster in 1930 and *Hotspur* in 1933. Eventually, these comics were to become known collectively as the "Big Five", and enjoyed huge success. At its peak in around 1937, *Wizard* reportedly sold over 800,000 copies a week, and a 1940 survey found that the "Big Five" were more popular than any of their competitors among boys aged between 12 and 14. But Amalgamated did not take its new competitor lightly, and responded with new story-papers of their own. *Champion*, launched in 1922 to take on D.C. Thomson's *Adventure*, quickly reached a weekly sale of over 500,000 copies.

The 1930s was a decade of gradual change; in the early years of the decade little in the story-papers changed from the previous ten years. In the real world, football was spreading rapidly across the globe. The first World Cup took place in 1930, played in Uruguay. Thirteen teams took part; nine from South America and four from Europe – the cost

Photo by Keystone/Getty Images

FREE INSIDE DELICIOUS CHEWING SWEET TASTY LICKER TWIST

THE ROVER

Nº 873
JAN 7TH
1939
EVERY
THURSDAY
2º

Above Tubby Ryan leads out the team in *Hotspur* (21 October 1933)

of travel was seen as prohibitive by many of Europe's football governing bodies. In the final, hosts and favourites Uruguay beat Argentina 4–2 in front of a crowd of 93,000 people; no British team deigned to enter. The same insularity was evident in the story-papers.

Many of the football-related stories were traditional crime, mystery and adventure yarns set against the backdrop of the football field. Even in the dedicated sports papers, such as *Sports Budget*, many storylines had only a tenuous link to football. Yet comics including *Triumph*, *Ranger*, *Pilot*, *Champion*, *Startler* and *The Boy's Magazine* continued to reflect the growing popularity of football, with many of their stories based on the game.

Many of *Hotspur*'s football tales were centred on public school life; its Red Circle School stories were "old school" in tone and content. They included such tales as "The Last Minute of the Last Match" – "How a Fourth Former was capped and then clapped by the Red Circle Junior team" (28 April 1934); and "Three Jeers for Captain Ryan" – "When the School Booed its own Football Team" (21 October 1933). *Hotspur*'s other characters included "The Big Stiff", a master with an unconventional approach to

Right "The Big Stiff was a great footer player as well as a great teacher, but the other teachers were shocked when they saw him playing with the boys" – *Hotspur*, 13 January 1934

THE **LAST MINUTE** OF THE **LAST MATCH**

THIS WEEK'S RED CIRCLE SCHOOL STORY

Above Goalmouth action in a Red Circle school tale (28 April 1934)

education and fondness for football. Another unconventional school master was "Burly Brock, The Chucker-Out who Became Sports Instructor at Big School", who appeared in the pages of *Wizard*. A former bouncer, he was "a regular giant of a man, always dressed in a white sweater and a pair of grey flannel slacks", and his love of sport created tension between him and the other staff ("In the masters' common room several of the masters were seated. Through the open window came floating the noise from the playing fields. Mr Gandley, the Fourth Form master, known to the boys as Gandhi, suddenly uttered an exclamation of disgust. Jumping up to the window, he slammed it down. 'Brock has ruined the tone of this school,' he snapped. 'The boys have become a pack of hooligans.'"). It seems in the British public schools at least, from being a noble and manly sport football had become a game for ruffians.

Below There was "a shock for burly Brock" in this yarn that appeared in the pages of *Wizard* (22 April 1932)

The footballers who had to be good at English before they could play for their school team !

SPORTS INSTRUCTOR

BURLY BROCK

UNLIMITED PRIZES OFFERED THIS WEEK!

The MODERN BOY

EVERY SATURDAY
WEEK ENDING 26TH JAN. 1935.
No 364. VOL. 14.

2D

Laughs for the Crowd!

This cover relates to an article by "Well-Known Sports Writer J.T Bolton" on "moments when players and spectators have to laugh at out-of-the-way incidents!" Bolton writes: "One of the funniest things I ever saw in a Cup Final happened when Barnsley and West Bromwich were engaged in a reply on the Sheffield United ground, in 1912. It was a terrific struggle, and in the course of it Dicky Downs, a big strapping full-back of Barnsley, had his foot damaged. He was compelled to go beyond the touch-line for 'repairs', and the first thing the trainer did was take off the player's boot to get at the injured spot. No sooner had the trainer done this than West Bromwich set up a hot attack on the Barnsley goal. Downs sensed that there was a real danger of a goal being scored against his side, so with one boot in his hand he dashed on to the field to help his pals resist that attack."

BARNEY GOOGLE'S GALLOPING GOAL RUSH

The *Startler*'s story "Barney Google's Galloping Goal Rush" (25 April 1931) was typical of the era, combining crime and football with a dollop of humour. It concerns "Fatty Fish" and pals, who get jobs with a catering company selling fish and chips at Wembley in order to get into the Cup final to watch their mate, the eponymous Barney, in action. On the way they encounter a coin counterfeiting scam and, at one point, the villain of the piece manages to steal the FA Cup itself. Naturally, Fatty and friends save the day.

Above and below
Action from the pages of *Startler*

As the competition for readers intensified, so the story-papers' editors looked at new areas to explore, in terms of characters, settings and plotlines. Consequently, stories became more fantastical and the locations more exotic.

Triumph ran a serialised story in 1938 called "Trailed by the Terror Tong" – "They Schemed to Smash the Team", which involved death treats against Gilport Rovers' star player, Chink Conway. "Fang Li, the ruthless leader of the Hidden Hand

Below Chink Conway narrowly escapes death – on the pitch (*Triumph*, 15 October 1938)

Right Sharpshooter 'TEC' Sharp always got his man – or, in this case, ferret

Tong, had warned him that if he scored a single goal for Gilport Rovers this afternoon he would sign his own death warrant!" The Tong – the Chinese and Hong Kongese mafia – were out to fix the match, for… "Just before this afternoon's vital cup match Chink had been offered a hundred pounds by Fang Li if he would sell the match so that the Rovers would be defeated, and he had been warned that exactly three minutes after he had scored a goal for the Rovers he would drop down dead upon the field."

Our hero scored, and the game ebbed back and forth, with Chink conscious of the impending threat and a large contingent of Tong thugs situated behind one of the goals. And as he scored his second… "Goal! G-O-A–" The delighted roar of the crowd ended in a silence of frozen horror. A knife, glinting in the sunlight like a shaft of fire, was flashing through the air from behind the barrier on the left-hand side of the goal – straight towards Chink Conway's head.

"It seemed to the horrified crowd that nothing could save their goal-scoring winger from being murdered in front of their eyes." But Chink manages to

Something flashed in the air. The Terror Tong were carrying out their threat to kill Chink if he scored for the Rovers!

Sports Budget, October 29th, 1932
FAMOUS FOR LONG COMPLETE STORIES
SPORTS 2D.
BUDGET
WANTED
FOR MURDER!
£1,000 REWARD
WILL BE PAID TO
ANYONE GIVING
INFORMATION
THAT WILL LEAD
TO THE ARREST OF
THE FERRET
THIS MAN POSES
AS A FOOTBALLER
T·E·C· SHARP ON THE TRACK OF
The WANTED WINGER
Vol. XVIII. No. 473
EVERY THURSDAY
October 29th, 1932

"What does this interruption mean?" demanded the referee. "Steve Bradshaw mustn't play this afternoon," replied Inspector Collins. "I must insist that he accompanies me to the police station at once. I want to question him about the murder of Bethmann!"

Above and below "The Football Cracksman", aka Steve Bradshaw, has a spot of bother with the law

throw himself against a post to avoid the flying dagger; his life is spared but his shoulder badly damaged. After he has it bandaged up in the hospital he returns to the match; but by now Rovers are losing 3–2. It's too much to bear for our hero; despite his agony he returns to the field – and scores the winning goals!

The players of Farsham Wanderers were subjected to similar threats in "Red Spider's Revenge" (*Sports Budget*, 5 March 1932). They were told to "play to lose on Saturday, or face the consequences". In the pages of **Hotspur**, more skulduggery was afoot. In the serialised story "The Traitor of the Team", the devious and scheming Miles Sweeney is out to destroy Greystone College and the associated Greystone Rangers FC so he can acquire their land for his own profit. His plan? To fill the team's changing room with sleeping gas, thus slowing them down on the field. The plan worked in a trial the week before, when… "Sweeney had caused a number of the Rangers to breathe the gas, with the result that they had only narrowly escaped being beaten by Riverpool United. The crowd had been disgusted at the outcome of the match, and many of them had gone away

NEW FEATURE No. 3.—OPENING CHAPTERS OF EXCITING FOOTBALL YARN

The FOOTBALL CRACKSMAN

declaring that the Rangers had deliberately sold the game." Eventually, his plots were foiled and Rangers prospered. (A football story also called "Traitor of the Team" also appeared in the first issue of **Rover**, on 4 March 1922. There was no link between the two.)

Above Strange goings-on in the pages of *Hotspur*

The "footballers" themselves began to emerge from more diverse and interesting backgrounds than the mill, the factory and the public schools. "Robbie of the Rangers", a serialised story that appeared in **Wizard**, featured a policeman – Bob Robbie (story ran from 5 September 1931 to 2 January 1932). He combined keeping law and order with playing for Chelham Rangers. "'TEC' Sharp – The Football Sleuth" appeared in the pages of **Sports Budget** in 1931. Terence Everard Christopher Sharp was a detective who played for Bilton United.

But not all the new breed of story-paper stars were good guys. Terry Marsden was "The Lifer" in the pages of **Sports Budget**.

Below Why was Standen's star centre-forward playing like a novice? TEC Sharp had the answers (*Sports Budget*, 30 April 1932)

SPORTS BUDGET

THE STAR WHO COULDN'T SHINE ! Tec Sharp and the Bilton goalie were slithering in the mud, leaving Jim Bunn with the goal at his mercy. He lunged out at the ball to send it sailing wide of the post ! Standen's star centre-forward was playing like a novice !

Triumph debuted a new feature called "The Football Cracksman" in its issue dated 6 January 1940. Steve Bradshaw was the star centre-forward for Milton Rovers FC; he was also an ace safe-cracker.

Glamorous footballers in the story-papers were not limited to cons and cops. In the story "Falling on his Footer Feet", *Sports Budget* introduced "Jim Roper, footballer-film-star" who "lives for thrills. The hotter the excitement, the cooler he takes it! Attempts galore are made to upset him but Jim always lands on his footer feet — and comes up smiling for more! He's a 'cracker'."

A later *Sports Budget* character was Dave Denton — "the lad who draws the crowds, star attraction of screen and soccer field". When he's not making pictures such as "Daring Danger" he's an occasional centre-forward with Meldon City FC. Almost contemporaneously *Sports Budget*

Above It was "footer v. film" for Dave Denton in the pages of *Sports Budget*

Below A bitter local rivalry was spiced by the arrival of "The Football Freak", in the pages of *Wizard*

ran the story of Peter Wild, "film star sportsman" (28 May 1938).

The players weren't always the stars of the show. Occasionally, a manager, coach or even chairman took centre stage — and sometimes they weren't even British! An American taking over a top football club? Surely not; the fans wouldn't stand for it! But all involved in Rockvale Rovers ("O.K. O'Keefe of the Rovers", *Wizard*, 13 August 1932) were glad of the intervention of a stranger

Facing page, top O.K. O'Keefe was the original American with designs on an English league football club

Facing page, bottom Another *Wizard* mystery with "The Ninety-Minute Marvels"

Read below what happens when these two teams meet in a league match !

THE FOOTBALL FREAK

who rode into town one day. He tells his story: "'My name's Oliver K. O'Keefe, though the boys generally called me Split O'Keefe, of Great Forks, Arizona, and I want to spend money on this Rockvale football team. I want to help to make it the finest team in the British Isles, and see it carry off the Grand National, or the Derby, or the Boat Race, or whatever prize is played for.'" Warming to his theme he adds: "'I've got five million bucks and nothing to do with it but have fun, and I would get a rare kick out of putting this Rockvale team on the map.'" The story ran for 12 episodes, until 29 October 1932.

A similar thing happened in *Wizard*'s "The Football Freak" (story ran 24 December 1938–25 February 1939): "The crowds of football enthusiasts who were looking forward to watching the matches in the third round of the Football Association Cup little dreamt of the drama behind the two games. These were the two cup-ties which were to be played in the town of Ridlington – a small industrial town in the North Midlands. Ridlington was hardly large enough to support one league team, yet there were two third division sides there – Ridlington Town and Ridlington Panthers. Both these clubs had been on the verge of ruin, owing to lack of support, and then Joe Kerr, a rich American cattle rancher, bought up the Town team, paid off all the club's debts, and got it going in fine

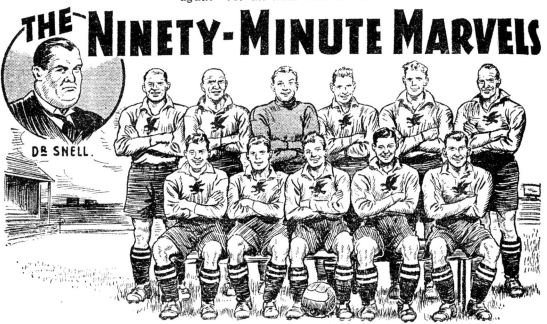

Are YOU reading this astounding story of the man who can make men feel young again—for an hour and a half?

THE NINETY-MINUTE MARVELS

DR SNELL.

ARSENAL'S BIG GUNS: THE HEROES OF HIGHBURY AS SEEN BY JOS. WALKER

THE NO-GOAL MACHINE!

THE YELLOW GOALIE—AND HIS SINISTER INVENTION—Join Forces with Bat Fulger, Andy's Rascally Cousin, to Smash the Wizard Boy Winger.

style with the aid of Johnny Blake, a lad who had done a "freak football" act in a circus. Joe Kerr had bought Johnny Blake to England, expecting that the big league clubs would outbid each other to sign him on. But the managers regarded Johnny's football as freak stuff and showed little interest in him. Joe was so sure that he was right that he bought up Ridlington Town in order to give Johnny a chance of playing in league football, and so amazing was the lad's performance that First Division managers were eager to sign him on now, but it was too late.

"Because of Johnny's wonderful display, Ridlington Town came right into the limelight, and very swiftly the other Ridlington club did likewise, for it was bought up by Seth Modder, another cattle king from America. Seth Modder did not have any real interest in football – he was after Joe Kerr, eager to continue the bitter feud which had existed for generations between

THE NO-GOAL MACHINE GETS 'EM.—Andy saw a knob on the machine and pressed it. The full force of the ray struck his advancing foes.

Above Some folk will stop at nothing to get the right result…
"The No-Goal Machine" appeared in *Boys' Magazine*, 16 April 1932

Facing page Real-life footballers appeared increasingly in the boys' story-papers during the 1930s, and these caricatures of Arsenal players in *Sports Budget* are typical of the style

Above Milton Wanderers players do it for themselves (*Triumph*, 5 January 1933)

Below *Wizard*'s "Robbie of the Rangers"

Far right *Sports Budget* broke new ground with its comic strip-style cover (26 August 1939)

the Kerrs and the Modders. Out in the lonely hills and on the wide ranges in Western America these two families had carried on the deadly feud with guns, but now it was being carried on with football teams."

Another man of mystery was Dr Snell who appeared in *Wizard*'s "The Ninety-Minute Marvels". He was "the man who can make men feel young again – for an hour and a half" (19 August 1939). "For the methods of Dr Snell, the mystery man of football, were amazing the football world". As the story develops it carries a newspaper column that reads: "…ninety-nine out of every hundred football fans were both amused and amazed when they heard that Dr Snell had signed Durward for the Hawks. They knew that to all intents and purposes Durward's football career had finished last season and even then he had hung on long after most professionals retire…

"Millfield gave him a free transfer, just as a matter of form it was thought, since his football career appeared to have ended. Then Dr Snell signed him on for the Red Hawks, and he has played in three matches, each of which has been won by the Hawks. But the amazing part is that Durward has played with the speed and energy of a youngster of eighteen." So what's the secret? As Durward's wife says to him: "'You know what folk are saying – that Dr Snell gives you dope.'" In fact the players were being fed "X23", a drug invented by the fiendish doctor and his partner, now

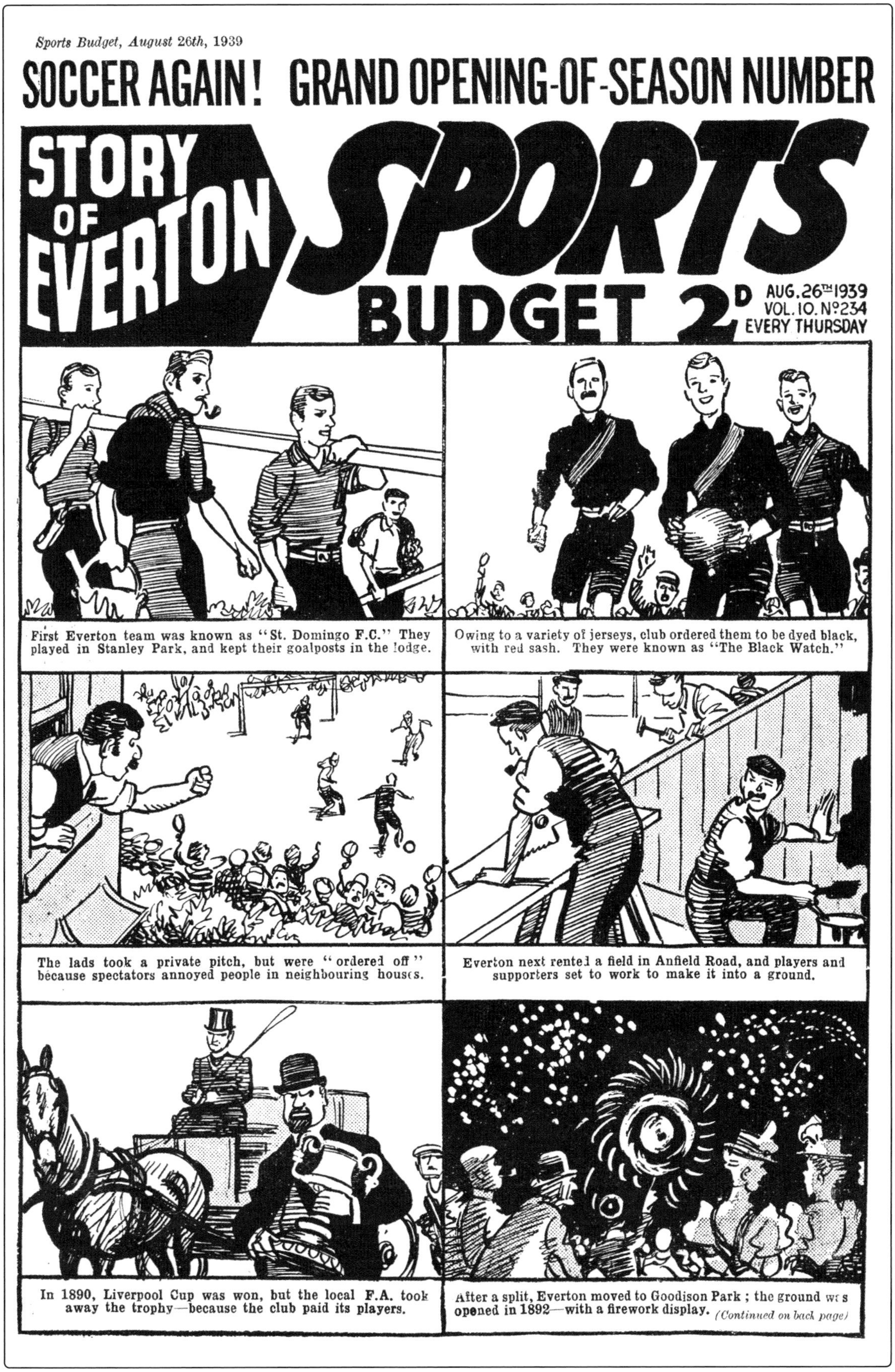
Sports Budget, August 26th, 1939

SOCCER AGAIN! GRAND OPENING-OF-SEASON NUMBER

STORY OF EVERTON

SPORTS BUDGET 2D

AUG. 26TH 1939
VOL. 10. No. 234
EVERY THURSDAY

First Everton team was known as "St. Domingo F.C." They played in Stanley Park, and kept their goalposts in the lodge.

Owing to a variety of jerseys, club ordered them to be dyed black, with red sash. They were known as "The Black Watch."

The lads took a private pitch, but were "ordered off" because spectators annoyed people in neighbouring houses.

Everton next rented a field in Anfield Road, and players and supporters set to work to make it into a ground.

In 1890, Liverpool Cup was won, but the local F.A. took away the trophy—because the club paid its players.

After a split, Everton moved to Goodison Park; the ground was opened in 1892—with a firework display. *(Continued on back page)*

Sensational New Picture-Serial
MYSTERY AT CASTLE GATE
STARTS HERE

"I have made my will, Phyllis," said Sir Walter Regal. "As my adopted daughter I leave the whole of my estate to you, including the Castle Gate Football Ground. I have never told you before, but the ground holds a valuable secret, the clue to which is contained in the will. You can only discover what it is after my death." He smiled mysteriously, then continued. "I'll put the document away now, and get you that book you want from the study."

Nathan Snape, Sir Walter's butler, who had been regarded as a faithful servant for some thirty years, had overheard the conversation. A secret at the football ground? It was the first he had heard about it, despite continually prying into his master's affairs. It might pay him to investigate this strange mystery. Furtively, he followed his master along the corridor and into the study. He saw Sir Walter move into the next room.

mysteriously missing. It was fed to the four veterans in liquid form and made them young again… but the side-effect is death! However, after one fatality and antidote is found and all is well. Story writers were encouraged to let their imaginations run riot. "The No-Goal Machine!" (**Boys' Magazine**, 16 April 1932) was "Another Gripping Footer Yarn of the Boy who is Playing Football for a Fortune". The story's hero, Iron-foot Andy, is thwarted from scoring by a fiendish apparatus which stuns the player as he shoots for goal. As **Boys' Magazine** puts it: "The yellow goalie – and his sinister invention – join forces with Bat Fulger, Andy's rascally cousin, to smash the wizard boy winger."

But perhaps the most bizarre setting for a story was called "Top 'O the Lot" – a "Thrilling Long Complete Soccer & Bridge Building Yarn" (**Sports Budget**, 6 September 1930).

An already common theme that was to become increasingly used in the later story-papers and comics centred on the greedy owner's attempts to either make money out of football at the expense of the team, or destroy the club altogether. In the early days of the story-papers the villain of the peice was the factory- or mill-owner; as the game embraced full professionalism the role was taken by the chairman or owner. "Help the Hire Purchase Soccer team!", which appeared in **Triumph** (5 January 1933), told the tale of third division Milton Wanderers, whose chairman Marcus Crane is attempting to fold the club. Trainer Joe Cobb explains to the players: "'Marcus Crane's a businessman, before being a sportsman,' said the trainer bitterly. 'The tradition of the Wanderers means nothing to him. He is in football for the brass he can make out of it, and also for the figure he can cut in sporting circles.'" For Crane has an

Left *Sports Budget*'s "Mystery at Castle Gate" (starting 22 October 1938) was one of the first illustrated serialised stories in the boys' papers

Right Age is no barrier, *Sports Budget*, 21 February 1931

February 21st, 1931

The TEAM that BROKE INTO ITS OWN GROUND!

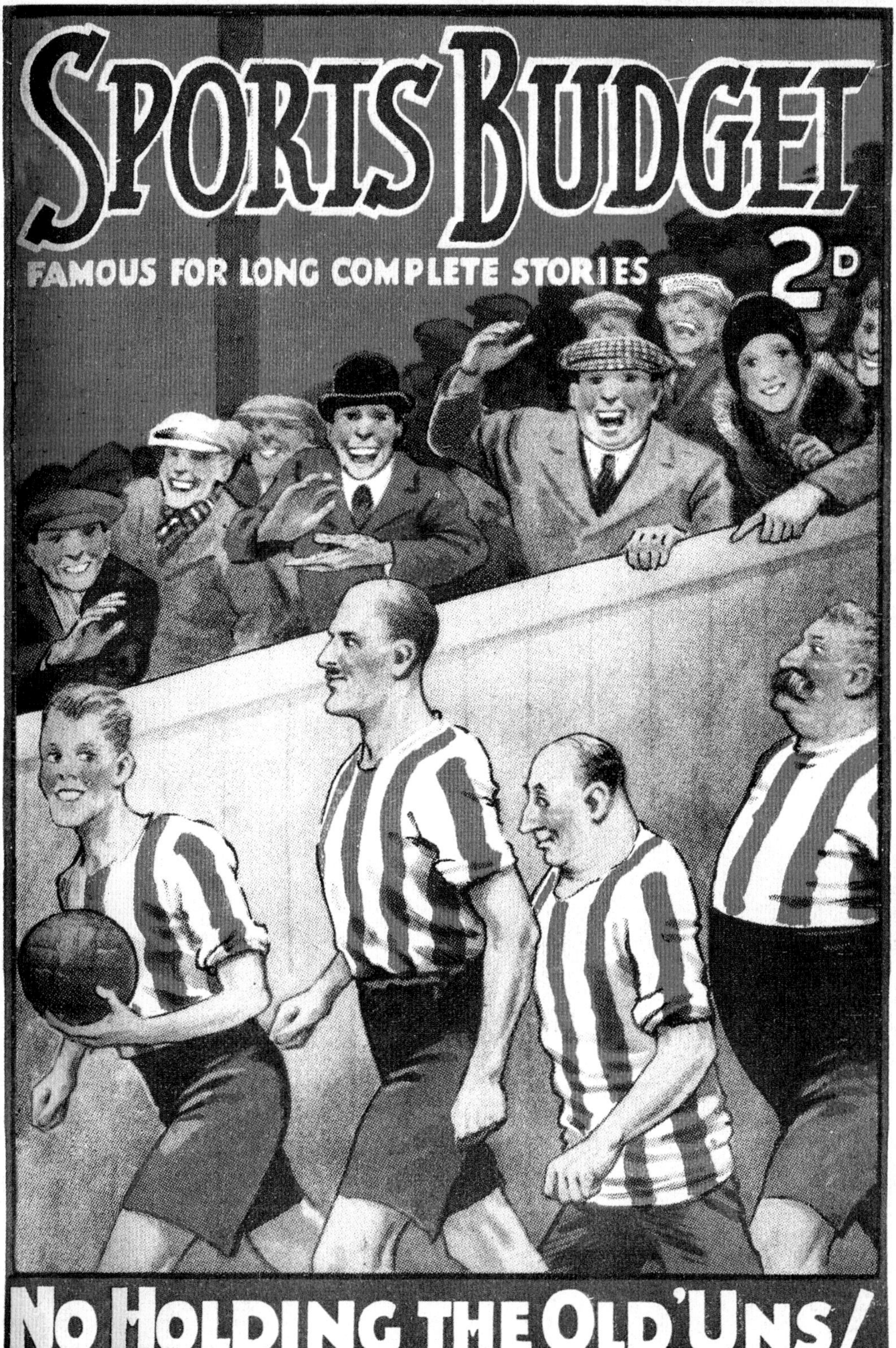
SPORTS BUDGET
FAMOUS FOR LONG COMPLETE STORIES
2D
NO HOLDING THE OLD'UNS!

EVERY THURSDAY

February 21st, 1931

The Wizard Outside-Right Whose One Fervent Wish Was To Be Right Outside the Football Ground! What Was the Strange Plot Behind......

535

The Case of The Frightened Footballer

OUR LONG COMPLETE FOOTER STORY.

Above *The Pilot's* "Case of the Frightened Footballer" involved murder, kidnap and German spies... .

Below "Soccer Soldier" Bert Turner of Charlton Athletic, as profiled in *Sports Budget*

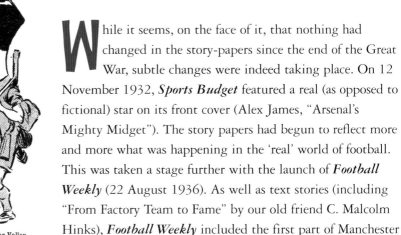

BERT
TURNER
Soccer
Soldier

EVERYBODY knows that South-east London is famous for the presence of Charlton Athletic, who did so much to put first-class football on the map before the War came. And one of the most popular of the Valley favourites was BERT TURNER, captain of Wales.

Bert joined the Army as a young man and spent years out East. As a soldier he won all sorts of honours, played Soccer in China, India and Egypt, and was also capped for the Army at Rugby. Returning home, he played three times for Brithdir, a small South Wales club, and then, to his surprise, he was signed by Charlton. During the seasons that followed Bert Turner filled all half-back positions, and both full-back berths at the Valley. He even tried his hand at centre-forward. But it was as a defender that he won his Welsh international honours.

interest in the Rangers, the Wanderers' arch rivals. As Cobb continued: "'He backed the Rangers last year, ignored us when we needed a helping hand because he was jealous of some of our older directors, who hadn't much brass, but had been with the team from the beginning. Now he's cutting expenses he's wiping us out.'" The solution is simple: the players buy the club on hire purchase.

There's always an answer; no matter how deep the problem and how far-fetched the solution may seem. Club riddled with corruption, from the boardroom to the dressing room? Well, there is "No Holding the Old 'Uns!" – "A Sensational Long Complete Story of a Team of Old Crocks who oust a Club of Crooks and Become a Side of Cracks" (*Sports Budget*, 21 February 1931).

While it seems, on the face of it, that nothing had changed in the story-papers since the end of the Great War, subtle changes were indeed taking place. On 12 November 1932, *Sports Budget* featured a real (as opposed to fictional) star on its front cover (Alex James, "Arsenal's Mighty Midget"). The story papers had begun to reflect more and more what was happening in the 'real' world of football. This was taken a stage further with the launch of *Football Weekly* (22 August 1936). As well as text stories (including "From Factory Team to Fame" by our old friend C. Malcolm Hinks), *Football Weekly* included the first part of Manchester City and England striker Eric Brook's autobiography ("A

Famous Footballer tells his Story"). Interestingly, it also carried a feature called "A Winning Guide to Form", which carried pre-match analysis of all the upcoming Football League games, with score predictions and league and current form tables. Issue 2 (19 August 1936) upped the ante with a free gift of "100 Famous Football Clubs", while Eric Brook confided to readers how in the early part of his career he was "the most miserable man in Barnsley".

Other comics were also beginning to innovate. *Triumph* imported the Superman comic strip from America (starting 5 August 1939); *Sports Budget* had earlier run a "Sensational New Picture-Serial" called "Mystery at Castle Gate" (starting 22 October 1938) and the same paper ran a ground-breaking complete comic strip front cover, "Story of Everton", on 26 August 1939.

Below The *Sports Budget* gears up for war (9 September 1939)

HERE THEY COME, HERE THEY COME—
JOLLY GOOD PLAYERS, EVERY ONE!

FALL IN FOR FOOTBALL!

PETER PARRY'S GRAND COMPLETE YARN OF THE FOOTBALL FUSILIERS

But as the established story-papers looked to get an edge on their rivals with new content and a design innovations, the clouds of war were gathering again over Europe. As had happened a quarter of a century earlier, the focus moved away from the football field and to the theatres of war. Interestingly, a story that appeared in *Pilot*, called "The Case of the Frightened Footballer" (15 February 1936), involved attempted murder and kidnap in a plot that centred on a German spy's attempts to steal blueprints for new British military aircraft and smuggle them out of the country. The plot is foiled by Bill Riley of Brampton Rangers, the "frightened footballer" of the title. *Sports Budget* launched an army-cum-football story, "Fall in for Footer", on 1 September 1938 – readers were invited to "line up for thrills in this grand long complete tale of Army life". The similarly titled "Fall in for Football" appeared on 9 September 1939 ("Peter Parry's Grand Complete Yarn of the Football Fusiliers"); and the same paper's cover on 14 October 1939 crowed that "The Soccer Soldiers are on Parade!"

Paper was quickly in short supply after the outbreak of the Second World War, as had happened during the Great War. But unlike during the previous hostilities, football was suspended immediately war broke out, in September 1939. Many comics and story-papers closed or were amalgamated; those that survived saw their pagination shrink drastically, while others were published fortnightly or monthly rather than weekly. *Sports Budget* was incorporated into *Detective Weekly* on 21 October 1939; and *Triumph* incorporated *Gem* on 6 January 1940 (some 1,711 weekly issues of *Gem* were published over its lifetime). The pair did not last long under the same cover – they ceased publication on 25 May 1940.

Right Footballers go to war – again (*Sports Budget*, 9 September 1939)

Below A true-life story from *Football Weekly* (10 October 1936)

From SOLDIER to SOCCER STAR

By TOM CHEETHAM   Queen's Park Rangers' Famous Centre-Forward.

Sports Budget, October 14th, 1939

IMPORTANT NEWS — SEE PAGE 23

SPORTS
BUDGET

2D

VOL. 10 Nº 241
OCTOBER 14TH 1939
EVERY THURSDAY

THE SOCCER SOLDIERS
ARE ON PARADE!

"THE FIRST SEASON WAS VERY STRANGE. IT WAS QUITE ENJOYABLE BUT A LOT OF THE MATCHES WERE PLAYED IN A HALF-HEARTED MANNER. NO-ONE KNEW WHAT WAS GOING TO HAPPEN IN THE WAR. IT WASN'T EASY TO CONCENTRATE ON FOOTBALL."

Frank Broome, Aston Villa and England (1915–1994)

CHAPTER FOUR

THE GREATER GAME

ON BRITAIN'S DECLARATION OF WAR on Germany, on 3 September 1939, the government was quick to act. "ALL SPORT BROUGHT TO A HALT", screamed a *Daily Mail* headline of 4 September, "Restart When Safe for Crowds". The story continued: "For the moment all sport has been brought to a halt. The concentration of Britain's whole effort on the winning of the war makes its continuance undesired and inappropriate. The Government have let it be known that the assembly of crowds in the open or indoors is at the present time to be avoided, and all events which would attract the public in any numbers have been prohibited."

Thus a season that was only three games old was plunged into confusion; clubs were advised to keep their players "on standby". At the start of the Great War in 1914 football had been allowed to continue; indeed, the 1914–15 season was played to a finish. This continuation caused controversy; many saw the playing of sport while the slaughter in the trenches continued unabated as unpatriotic and inappropriate. No one was able to level similar accusations at the government in the autumn of 1939.

The blanket ban came as a surprise and left many clubs in an invidious position; unlike during the previous war, the professional structure was firmly embedded and clubs had committments to both their players and other staff. According to Jack Rollin, in his book *Soccer at War*, following an emergency meeting of the Football League's Management Committee on 6 September the advice to the clubs to keep players standing by was cancelled and clubs were told to pay their professionals only up to 6 September – although they kept control of the players by keeping their registrations. Also, signing-on bonuses and removal expenses were to be cleared immediately, and injured players were to follow end-of-season procedures when making claims.

ALL SPORT BROUGHT TO A HALT

Restart When Safe for Crowds

FOR the moment all sport has been brought to a halt. The concentration of Britain's whole effort on winning the war makes its continuance undesired and inappropriate.

The Government have let it be known that the assembly of crowds in the open or indoors is at the present time to be avoided, and all events which would attract the public in any numbers have been prohibited.

Future Will Show

It may be possible in due course to minimise or remove the restrictions which have been imposed. Meanwhile, all sportsmen and sportswomen will realise the need for the Government's action.

In view of the fact that since Saturday this country has declared war, the results of League football, racing, and other sports events during the week-end have no significance.

Although the conditions may now be different, the war of 1914-1918 did not prevent the resumption of racing and other sport after a short stoppage. It will be the hope of all that the present interference will be as brief.

Above Paper shortages meant the comics were forced to reduce the number of pages they printed. With such pressure on space, editors concentrated on morale-boosting war and adventure stories. "Breezy Nelson's Dreadnoughts" was one of the few stories with a football theme that was published during wartime. Left *The Daily Mail*, 4 September 1939

No. 1,107. Vol. 43. Every Friday.

Week Ending April 17, 1943.

RED FURY — THE BATTLING BRAVE

THE CHAMPION

AND TRIUMPH

3D

BREEZY
NELSON'S
DREADNOUGHTS

Proposed inter-league games with Scotland and Ireland were cancelled; and, at this stage, season-ticket refunds were not to be given. This hinted at a possible resumption of the game depending on the progress of the war; indeed, the government's stance relaxed very quickly.

Facing page "Breezy Nelson's Dreadnoughts" served their country in wartime while enjoying a good game of footy when the chance arose

But the Football League's Management Committee's diktat had effectively made Britain's professional footballers unemployed. As Anton Rippon wrote in his book, *Gas Masks for Goal Posts*: "As football hung in limbo, the players found themselves in a dreadful situation. The old 'retain-and-transfer' system which was operating in 1939 – and which continued to do so until the 1960s – held all professional footballers in a feudal-like thrall… it's hard to imagine a time when there was a maximum wage and a footballer could be tied to one club for life if that club so wished. That was indeed the case, but now, with a war on, the players were unceremoniously dumped by those same clubs. Their only immediate chance of earning a living was to join the armed forces."

Tommy Lawton, the England international who was playing for Everton in 1939, described the situation in his autobiography, *Football is My Business*: "Then came the war and, with it, the end of my career or so I felt. Surely there

Below International footballers go to war: from left, Joe Mercer of Everton, Matt Busby of Liverpool and Charlton Athletic's Don Welsh, pictured in 1939

Photo by Popperfoto/Getty Images

THE HOTSPUR

Nº 454 — JANUARY 2ND 1943 — PRICE · 2D

couldn't be room for a professional footballer in a world gone crazy? I, of course, being a young, fit man of approaching twenty would go into the services. Meanwhile, in the leisure time I had left I wound up my personal affairs, cursed Hitler and all his rats and occasionally sat down to think of what had been and what might have been."

Facing page Tom Rington, aka The Circus Kid, is on the run – but he can't keep away from the footer field… (see over)

N at Lofthouse was a 14-year-old Bolton schoolboy in 1939, and had recently signed forms with Bolton Wanderers when war was declared. He later recalled: "As I walked through the gates of Burnden Park all the players were lining up in rows on the field. They were disbanding. It was the war."

Thankfully, Lawton was wrong in his view that the conflict would end his career; he played on until the 1955–56 season, having served as an army physical training instructor for the duration of the war. In 1945 he signed for Chelsea for £11,500; he also played for Notts County, Brentford and Arsenal; after playing he managed Brentford, Kettering Town and Notts County. He played 23 times for England, scoring 22 goals.

Lofthouse enjoyed a similarly illustrious career, although he was a one-club man, playing only for Bolton Wanderers. He was also capped 33 times by England between 1950 and 1958, scoring 30 goals.

But in September 1939, the authorities' hard line quickly softened. The ban on sporting activity was lifted outside the major population centres such as

Below Soldiers watch the last game to be played at West Ham United's Upton Park ground in East London as the outbreak of the Second World War stops all league football

Photo by Popperfoto/Getty Images

THE HOTSPUR

N° 455 — JANUARY 16TH 1943 — PRICE 2D

...and the Circus Kid pays the price ("The Secret Round the Circus Kid", *Hotspur*, 16 January 1943)

London and Birmingham; matches were allowed between clubs less than fifty miles apart, with crowds limited to 8,000 in metropolitan areas and 15,000 in so-called 'safer' areas. Football grounds quickly reopened; by the end of September 1939 the 50-mile restriction was lifted and replaced by a "there-and-back-in-a-day" travel stipulation. There was no uplift in fortunes for the players,

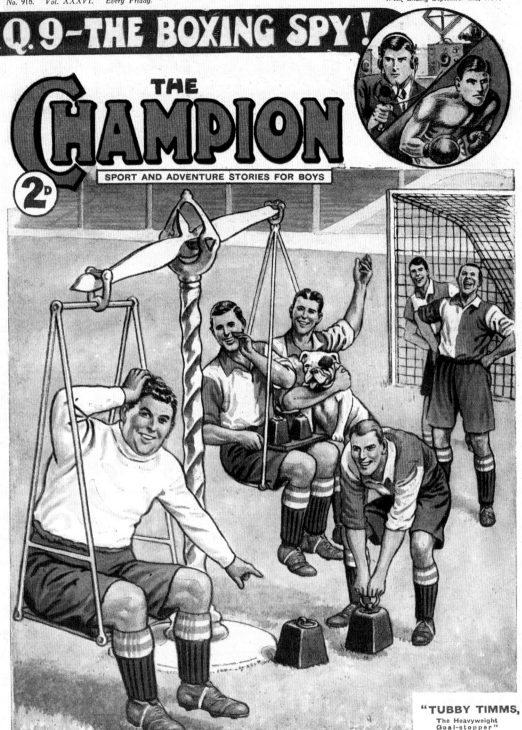

Q.9—THE BOXING SPY !

THE CHAMPION

2ᴅ

SPORT AND ADVENTURE STORIES FOR BOYS

"TUBBY TIMMS,
The Heavyweight
Goal-stopper"

however – they were entitled only to expenses for these wartime fixtures.

A major reason for the government's change of mind was one of worker morale. Critics of the ban said that hard-working factory, dockyard and mine workers needed – and deserved – some recreational time, and football on a Saturday afternoon provided one such outlet. Football boosted the workers'

Above Tubby Timms carried on the story-paper tradition of the larger-than-life goalkeeper

Above Boys were urged to do their bit for the war effort (*Hotspur*, 1943)

spirits, they said, increasing productivity and thus boosting the war effort.

Regional leagues were quickly set up in the autumn of 1939, and clubs were allowed to play "guest" players who may be have been stationed locally for military purposes; travelling was difficult during the early war years and travel was discouraged unless absolutely necessary. The blackout did not help travel, so regional leagues were seen an ideal way for clubs to keep playing – and were keenly supported by the clubs, eager to keep the turnstiles clicking.

However, in the boys' papers there was only one story – the war. Almost without exception editors quietly sidelined their football stories as the characters went to fight. Paper became scarce almost overnight; and boys were urged to recycle their comics for the war effort. Many comics fell victim to this paper shortage. D.C. Thomson's popular comic *Skipper* ceased publication on 1 February 1941; it started out in 1930 as a 28-page publication and was down to 14 pages at the time of its demise. At the outset of war *Rover*, *Wizard*, *Adventure* and *Hotspur*

Right Tom Rington finds the perfect hideaway (*Hotspur*, 16 January 1943)

THEY'RE FOOTBALL DAFT AT HOTSPUR HALL

Above The first comic book football academy (*Hotspur*, 23 October 1943)

were all 24-page publications; all were reduced to 14 pages, not returning to 28 pages until the early 1950s. The four were published fortnightly rather than weekly during the war years and immediately after; *Hotspur* was the first to return to weekly publication, on 11 January 1947.

It was in the *Hotspur* that most football stories could be found, among the tales of Bosche-bashing and battlefield courage and triumph. But the football action was of the domestic variety; and still the public school was the background for many of the stories. These were tales of football, mystery and adventure, shot through with the peculiarly unique mores and characters of the British public school, that had not seemed to have changed for 100 years. So we have the mean, pompous form master whose mission in life is to spoil his pupils' (football) fun; the dashing footballer-hero around whom the story is centred; and the usual coterie of pals, bullies, friendly masters and (often cunning and brutal) public school opponents. The hero is generally encumbered with a disadvantage: he is from a poor background; or is falsely accused of some gross breach of protocol or of some underhand activity; or has in some way besmirched the school's good name; and is so looked down upon. This underdog status, of course, endears him to the reader, who is rooting for our hero to win the day while at the same time being vindicated for his alleged misdemeanours.

Below Readers were urged to reserve their copy of *The Champion* (23 December 1939)

WARNING!

Owing to the War, there is likely to be a shortage of paper. But you will still be able to get your CHAMPION every week so long as you order it in advance. Tell your chums to take this precaution, too ; then fill in the order form given below, and hand it to your newsagent.

"THE CHAMPION"

To....................(Newsagent)

Please reserve a copy of " The Champion" for me every week until further notice.

Name...

Address.......................................

....

"The Secret Round the Circus Kid" (**Hotspur**, story starting 2 January 1943) is a typical tale. The hero is Tom Rington ("The Circus Kid"), who was "a wonderful footballer". He was also "a star performer in a travelling circus", but a warrant was out for his arrest for he was "accused of having assaulted and robbed a man when he had broken out of school on his second night". Having escaped to local woods, where he was living in a tree house, Tom risked everything to return to school to play as the star centre-forward in a crucial match against rivals Suttlebury School. Unfortunately, he was spotted by the player he replaced in the team… "At sight of Tom, Bully Crale's eyes glittered malignantly. He knew how he could get his revenge. He remembered the man who had stopped him a few days before – the man who had said he was a private detective and that he was searching for Tom Rington. He had promised Bully Crale a reward of a pound note if he gave him any information about Tom Rington's whereabouts. The Fourth Form bully did not wait any longer. Grabbing his bicycle, he went scorching to the inn where the so-called detective stayed. He was going to earn that reward of a pound note."

So far, so good… but the plot thickens. "Now the young man who had told him he was a private detective was none other than Oscar Lambert, Tom Rington's cousin. Lambert had expected to inherit John Rington's fortune, but when the old man had died he had left everything to his grandson, Tom Rington, on several rather peculiar conditions. Tom had been more than amazed for he had thought that his grandfather had died years before. The old man was the owner of Woodford School. According to the will Tom was directed to

Right A novel approach to football coaching (*Hotspur*, 12 February 1944)

Below Stan Carter, a new Red Circle School hero (*Hotspur*, 22 September 1945)

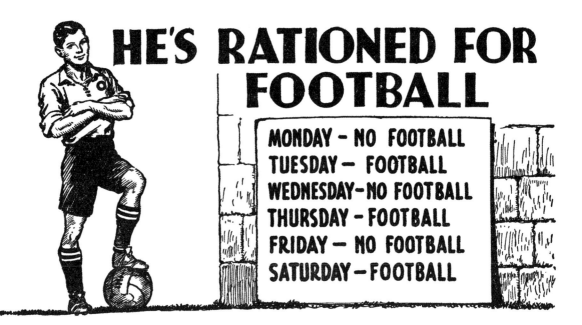

HE'S RATIONED FOR FOOTBALL

MONDAY – NO FOOTBALL
TUESDAY – FOOTBALL
WEDNESDAY – NO FOOTBALL
THURSDAY – FOOTBALL
FRIDAY – NO FOOTBALL
SATURDAY – FOOTBALL

THE PAPER WITH RED CIRCLE STORIES

THE HOTSPUR

Nº 483 · FEBRUARY 12TH · 1944 · PRICE 2D

FOOTBALL FAULTS CURED
AT HOTSPUR HALL. See Page 133.

How Hoppy Hopwood, the famous coach, trains his football stars.

No. 1 (Joe Thomson)—Don't use your hands to stop the ball.

No. 2 (Bill Walker)—Learn to use your left foot.

No. 3 (Alec Watson)—Don't fight on the football field.

No. 4 (Ted Smith)—Always obey the ref's whistle.

No. 5 (Albert Roy)—Don't kick with your toe —use your instep.

No. 6 (Wilf Hutton)—Always pull your weight for the team.

No. 7 (Jack Taylor)—Don't hang on to the ball too long.

Above Up for cups at Red Circle School (*Hotspur*, 22 September 1945)

Below A school inspector with a difference (*Hotspur*, 29 December 1945)

become a pupil of the school. After a certain time he would be given a letter written in Greek. If he succeeded in translating it then Woodford and all it contained would become his property. Now John Rington had had a private room in the school and Oscar Lambert was convinced that the bulk of the old man's fortune was hidden somewhere on the school premises. Being up to his eyes in debt he had decided to lose no time in disgracing Tom. If the boy were expelled from the school then he, Oscar Lambert, would become John Kington's heir, and would become owner of the school. It was because of Lambert's activities that a warrant was out for Tom's arrest. There was no doubt at all that the moment Lambert heard from Bully Crale he would get in touch with the police."

Tom, eventually – depite the plotting of the ever-more dangerous Lambert and his cronies, who attempt to kill him – proves his innocence. The righteous are rewarded and the wicked punished; the winners of the great game are the good guys.

Another regular *Hotspur* story was also set in a public school – but one with a difference. "They're Football Daft at Hotspur Hall" is every sporting schoolboy's dream – a school that is a football academy ("If you can't play football, you can't go to this school"). Owned by "former top football professional" Sam Hopwood, or Hoppy, football was high on the school curriculum. "Hoppy left the lessons to a fine staff of teachers but the most

The centre who played on the touchline

Above Two's company, three's a crowd… a Red Circle football match with a difference (*Hotspur*, 30 December 1944)

important part of the school programme – football – Hoppy looked after himself. If a boy could play football he was welcome at Hotspur Hall. If his parents couldn't pay the usual fees, Hoppy was quite willing to reduce them, especially if the boy's dad was a professional footballer." An interesting comment – as we have seen, professional footballers were effectively thrown out of work at the outbreak of war when the league and clubs tore up their contracts. A story with a similar theme was "Dazzler Drake", which appeared in *Hotspur* just after the war. He was a "football inspector" who's trouble-shooting approach was a forerunner to many characters and storylines that appeared in later comics.

Throughout the war *Hotspur* continued with its famous Red Circle School stories, featuring the adventures of "Rob Roy MacGregor, the Captain of the Home House". "The Captain's Leap" (30 December 1944) was a story of "Queer football – 33 players, 3 goals, no rules and no ref!". This bizarre game is played on a triangular pitch in which the game at times is more akin to the street football played in medieval England.

While shortage and rationing was an everyday reality for the vast majority of people during the war, about the only thing rationed at the Red Circle School was football – for newcomer Stan Carter, that is. In "He's Rationed for Football" (22 September 1945), our hero is allowed to play only on Tuesdays, Thursdays and Saturdays, thanks to a bizarre agreement between his two guardians, his uncles. One an anti-football academic, the other a pro-football sportsman and businessman (Mondays, Wednesdays and Fridays were for extra study). The storyline echoes the age-old debate in teaching circles about whether sport, particularly football, could help or hinder the cause of a good education.

BREEZY NELSON'S DREADNOUGHTS

By Reg Wilson

Above Breezy Nelson leads out his boys in this *Champion* story (3 April 1943). In this episode we meet "the back who biffed the ball like a battleship's broadside"

This theme was repeated in "The Goal that Scored Itself" (17 November 1945). In this episode Red Circle School's quiz teams and football teams take the wrong coaches; the quiz swots end up having to play the cup semi-final; the footer team play the quiz semi-final. How did they get on? The teaser for the following week's story promises: "Two Cup Finals in the next Red Circle story. There are loads of thrills in both!"...

Hotspur's rival, *Champion*, also continued to run football stories during the war years, many of them in a military rather than public school setting. "Breezy Nelson's Dreadnoughts" featured Jack Nelson – a good nautical name – who was based at Ironport Naval Barracks. A "cheerier, more go-ahead fellow it was impossible to meet", and like many a real pro "he had started his career with a professional team just before the war, and was still as keen as mustard on the game". Thus within a week or so of arriving at Ironport he had founded a barracks team, which he had christened the Dreadnoughts. While the stories had a serious side, reflecting the times, they were played for laughs. In the first episode (3 April 1943) a football is hoofed from a practice pitch through the window of a petty officer's office, the feared "Growler". Volunteering to retrieve the ball, "Breezy entered the office. Next moment he nearly burst out laughing. Some of the office ratings were helping the petty officer to his feet, and he presented a most undignified sight. Actually the ball had bounced on the desk, hit Growler in the face and toppled him over the back of his chair. When bouncing the ball on the parade ground, Breezy must have bounced it in some grey paint, for Growler's nose and forehead were battleship colour. The petty officer was in such a state that for a few moments he was speechless. He just glared at Breezy. 'Nelson, you – you were responsible!' he rasped at last. It was typical of Breezy that he steered round the question. 'In a way – yes,' he answered, standing stiffly to attention. 'It was a most unfortunate accident. I –' 'Accident!' raved Growler. 'If I had my way I'd clap you straight into cells! It's time some of you learned there's a war on. I'll see to it that there's no more football during working hours. You'll hear further about this, Nelson. The entire cost of the window repairs will be charged up to you. Now go! Get out of my sight!'" Despite his constant scrapes Breezy always came up trumps, whether taking on the foe on the enemy's side – or on his own.

The story "Fireworks Flynn's Freebooters" also took place against the background of the war. The Freebooters were a struggling team led by the eponymous hero who displayed the traditional characteristics of loyalty, courage, honesty and cheery optimism: "It was hard not to be cheery in the company of Fireworks Flynn, schoolmaster and ex-RAF pilot, who was now directing the fortunes of his footer team." In the story published on 25 March 1944, Fireworks discovers there's a traitor in the team, someone who is the

Below When the quiz team and the football teams get on the wrong buses, this is what happens… (*Hotspur*, 17 November 1945)

RED CIRCLE'S FOOTBALL TEAM GOES TO THE QUIZ MATCH— AND THE QUIZ TEAM LANDS AT THE FOOTBALL MATCH

The GOAL THAT SCORED ITSELF

FIREWORKS FLYNN'S FREEBOOTERS

By Donald Dane

Facing page and above
Fireworks Flynn's Freebooters
stories were full of army and
footer high-jinx (*Champion*,
26 February 1944 and 23 March
1944). See page 218

contact for a German spy. As Chief Inspector Hamish tells our man: "'Someone connected with the Freebooters is in league with Germany, and we must lay him by the heels, now, at once. You're the one person who can help us most. Why, the villain may be out on the field right now. But you must unmask him. This thing has got to be cleaned up before he gets the wind up and vanishes to do damage elsewhere. Now, is there anyone of whom you have the slightest suspicion, anyone who could possibly be the man we want?' Fireworks stared in stupefaction and scorn. A Nazi agent among the Freebooters. It couldn't be." But, undaunted, Fireworks tracks down his man, eventually felling him with a flying tackle in the changing room just before kick-off in a fixture against rivals Elmwood: "It was Bett, one of the reserves who would have played in Fireworks' place. As Fireworks bowled him over, and twisted him into a hopeless ju-jitsu lock, the man cursed and raved in a mixture of English and German. 'Tie him up with towels, stick him in the cold spray, and inform the police,' rapped Fireworks. 'He's given himself away and I'm proud to think he's not a chap I brought into the Freebooters. Now for Elmwood! Come on! The ref's getting impatient.'"

Another *Champion* character who played on throughout the war took a familiar guise – the outsized guardian of the net. In this case it was "Tubby Timms, the Heavyweight Goal-Stopper". In true comic tradition "he weighs 22 stone – but he's worth his weight in goal!". Tubby's adventures with his team mates from Worthsea Rovers involved catching crooks, foiling spies and generally righting wrongs, while beating all-comers on the football field.

No. 1,156.   Vol. 45.   Every Friday.

Week Ending March 25, 1944.

LEADER OF THE LOST COMMANDOS

THE CHAMPION

AND TRIUMPH

3D

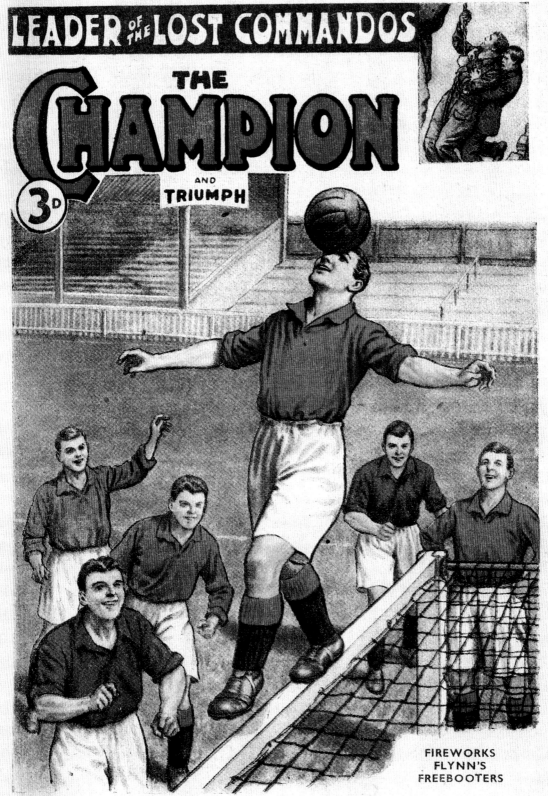

FIREWORKS
FLYNN'S
FREEBOOTERS

TUBBY TIMMS
–THE HEAVYWEIGHT GOAL-STOPPER

Above and facing page Tubby Timms sees the funny side after getting into a fix (*Champion*, 30 December 1939); and he has a novel way of dealing with an opposing player who is getting on his back (*Champion*, 23 December 1939)

Massively popular in the 1930s, *Wizard* steered clear of football stories during the war, focusing instead on the "greater game" that was being played out across the globe. Interestingly, when it returned to sports stories after the war, they often retained a war theme. One example is "The 'Q' Team" (14 September 1946), where readers "Meet the mysterious men who play football as it has never been played before!". Initially set in the Burmese jungle, our heroes keep their hopes and spirits up by playing football – under the watchful eyes of their Japanese guards. It explored deeper, darker themes than standard comic book fare: "A strange factor had helped those British soldiers to withstand the brutal treatment of the Japanese and maintain their morale It was the fact that, among the kits carried by the Japs with their prisoners, there were several footballs. Day after day, for hours at a time, the prisoners had played football. It gave them an opportunity for exercise. It relieved the terrible boredom, and prevented them from brooding. They were, of course, puzzled by the fact that the Japs permitted them to indulge in their favourite sport. But the yellow men had a cunning reason for this. They permitted football because it amused them to watch, and it also gave them a chance to jeer at their captives. Fresh Japanese arriving at the camp were taken to watch the game, their leaders pointing out the stupidity of ball games, saying that this was proof that the power of Britain was fast waning, since these men spent their spare time in playing football instead of improving their minds." The players eventually escape, and, in an act of revenge, steal an idol in the form of a dragon from a nearby temple in a murderous raid led by the band's leader, Ferguson.

"[Ferguson] had crept past the end of the altar, when suddenly the guardian of the dragon turned his head and saw the image had disappeared. The guard's eyes grew wide with astonishment. He opened his mouth to shout, but no sound left his lips. As if impelled by some giant spring, Ferguson lept at his man. His big powerful hands closed around the guardian's throat with terrific strength – abnormal strength created by the knowledge that he would surely die if the alarm was raised. He was positioned behind his victim, who was struggling wildly to get free. The curved sword fell from the guard's hands as he threw them up to tear at the fingers digging with remorseless pressure into his windpipe. With the intuition of despair, Ferguson flung forward his leg to meet the falling weapon and caught it with his bent knee, so that it slithered to the floor instead of clanging down on the stone. Nevertheless, the noise in that vast, empty temple sounded colossal to the sergeant, who expected swift investigation by the remainder of the men. The fear of this gave him even greater strength, and under the awful pressure of his hands the guardian of the dragon ceased to breathe and hung limply in Ferguson's grip. Carefully, the sergeant lowered the lifeless body until it rested on the floor, then he fled on tip-toe – fled into the vast darkness of the night."

But the murder – and the theft of the idol – have no carthartic value for Ferguson. "The cool night air played on Ferguson's face, which was streaming with cold perspiration. His thoughts began to race. What had he gained by his act? His desire for revenge... had not been gratified. True, he had taken something which they worshipped, but now that it was all over, it did not seem to him that he had done much."

This theft comes back to haunt our heroes after they have returned to England as the men from the orient seek to reclaim it. By the time they have reached England bent on retrieving the dragon totem, Ferguson and his compatriots have established a league club, Stockford United: "In the dusk of a Spring evening, there was a re-union of the twelve ex-prisoners. Save that they had lost much of their tan, they looked as they had done when they parted company in India well over a year ago – lean and wiry, full of vigour, and, though still young, their experiences made them older than their years. 'It's fine to see you lads,' said Bob Ferguson. 'I've got something to talk over with you. First of all, though, we'll have a meal.' During the meal they drank a silent toast to their three comrades who had failed to return with them", and Bob informed the assembled company that he had taken over Stockford United and

Tubby Timms didn't worry about the player who had landed on top of him. The 22-stone goalie scrambled to his feet with the chap on his shoulders, and got rid of the ball with a tremendous kick!

The "Q" Team

Above The "Q" Team survived a Japanese prisoner-of-war camp where they honed their football skills (14 September 1946)

Facing page To be part of Sporty Dawson's Cruising School must have been every boy's dream during the dark days of the war. Sporty Dawson was a teacher whose on-board school sailed around the world, giving the pupils exciting adventures in foreign climes

that he wanted them to form the team. The story unfolded over the next 11 weeks to a happy denouement, on 30 November 1946; at the same time, the full extent of the atrocities committed against Allied troops in the Far East were slowly being uncovered.

Many professional players suffered at the hands of the Japanese. In his book, *Soccer at War*, Jack Rollin covers the topic in detail: "Soccer had its share of heroes. They served. Most were unsung. Not all of them came back. They fought through the searing sands of the desert, shivered in the rain, sleet and mud and sweated in the steam heat of the jungle, shoulder to shoulder with clerks, shopkeepers, factory workers and schoolteachers. They could be found in the air over homeland or foreign territory, on and even underneath the high seas. Others were captured and spent the rest of the war in POW camps…" As Rollin writes: "Those who were taken prisoner by the Japanese suffered more than most. Cardiff City had a trio of them: Billy James, Bobby Tobin and Billy Baker, who had four years of ill-treatment. James, who had been in the Royal Artillery, was near blindness through malnutrition."

Emotions were running high, in professional football and the wider world. But while the psychological scars remained, football embraced a bright new dawn, and for the next 15 years entered into a new golden era.

No. 926. Vol. XXXVI. Every Friday. Week Ending October 28th, 1939.

Q.9 - SPY! Meet Him Inside!

THE CHAMPION

SPORT AND ADVENTURE STORIES FOR BOYS

2d

SPORTY DAWSON'S CRUISING SCHOOL

"FOOTBALL FOLLOWERS WHO THINK A HARD TUSSLE BETWEEN FOOTBALLERS MEANS BAD BLOOD ARE WRONG. THE HARDER THE STRUGGLE THE BETTER FRIENDS WE ARE AFTER THE MATCH. THAT IS AS IT SHOULD BE AND IS HOW I HOPE IT WILL ALWAYS BE."

Goals Galore (1954)
Nat Lofthouse (1925–)

CHAPTER FIVE
LET THE GOOD TIMES ROLL

AT THE END OF THE WAR, as society struggled to pick up the pieces and heal the scars of the conflict, football rushed to return to its pre-war glory. While this was driven by the Football League, the clubs found it difficult to keep pace with the League's ambitions. As Anton Rippon observed in his book, *Gas Masks for Goal Posts*: "As football strived for normality, everyone knew that it would not be easy to shake off the effects of war… As they were prone to do throughout wartime, when plans for the 1945–46 season were put forward by the Football League, many clubs had objected. The League wanted to revert to the set-up which had been abandoned in 1939: First, Second and Third Division North and South. The only concession was that there would be no promotion or relegation. Clubs would have a full season in which to settle down before the serious business resumed." But this was too much too soon for

Below After the war there was a huge boom in football crowds – at all levels. The photograph below shows a section of the crowd watching Leytonstone play Newport at Leytonstone's ground in east London, circa 1950 – an amateur fixture

Photo by Evening Standard/Getty Images

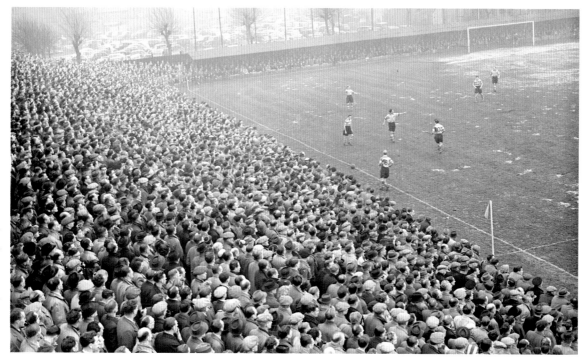

THE TEAM WITHOUT A GROUND

By
Edward Home-Gall

Left Another great goal for 'The Team Without A Ground' (*Champion*, 20 October 1945)

many clubs, especially the smaller ones. Many players were still on active service; Preston North End had 15 players serving abroad and another 22 in the services in Britain. There was some fillip in December 1945 when it was announced that one million servicemen were to be demobbed, including many footballers. But in the meantime managers had to beg, steal and borrow players in order to field a team, and many footballers who were nearing the end of their careers in 1939 suddenly found themselves pressed into "active service" of another kind.

Another problem for the clubs was travel; journeying across England and Wales was a difficult business. Rippon writes: "Clubs, both big and small, argued that the shortage of players and the difficulties of travel and finding hotel accommodation had not been sufficiently eased." Thus a compromise of sorts was reached, for the minnows at least; the lower leagues were subdivided into the Third Division South (South), Third Division South (North), Third Division (West) and Third Division (East).

But despite the clubs' problems, one thing was clear: there was a huge appetite for the game among the general public. Rippon explains: "People flocked to league grounds as never before. True, there had been a boom after the First World War, but nothing compared to this. From 35.6 million in 1946–47, seasonal attendances rose to 41.2 million in the following two seasons, and were still edging 40 million in 1951–52." By comparison, in the season 2007–08, some 29.8 million people attended football matches across all four divisions. Some of the statistics must have made happy reading for the club treasurers. In December 1945, 60,926 turned out for a Merseyside derby at Goodison Park; in January 1946 a second-city derby at Villa Park drew a crowd of 63,820; and at Maine Road in April 1946, 62,144 spectators saw Manchester United play at Manchester City.

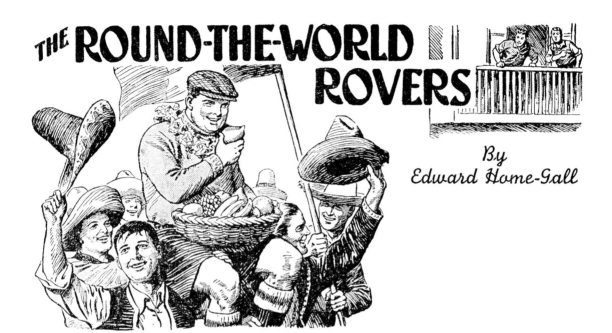

THE ROUND-THE-WORLD ROVERS

By Edward Home-Gall

Above "Podge" Parks enjoys the fruits of his goalkeeping labours in this story from *Champion* (2 August 1947)

Anton Rippon writes: "Charlton's semi-final at Villa Park had been watched by 70,819 spectators. When Derby played at Villa Park in the first leg of the quarter-final, there was a crowd of 78,588 present, still a record for the ground. Some of them had travelled from Derby on the Friday evening and wandered Birmingham's freezing streets in the small hours. Workers at a foundry which adjoined the Baseball Ground had been given permission to take Saturday morning off so they could travel to Villa, but a machine moulder at a neighbouring foundry was suspended for taking time off to watch the match. Sixty of his workmates came out on strike." Derby won the tie, and for the semi-final against Birmingham City some 80,407 fans went to Maine Road, still a record for a midweek match between two English clubs outside Wembley.

The major publishers were keen to tap into this huge swelling of support for football, although they were hampered by tough economic conditions and, specifically, the continued shortage of paper.

And like the Football League, publishers were keen on a return to the pre-war status quo. Football stories immediately after the war changed very little from those that had appeared in 1939; adventure, crime and mystery stories were the mainstays, often coupled with sport, usually football or boxing.

Popular stories in the ***Champion*** included "The Team Without A Ground", which morphed into "The Round-The-World Rovers", both written by Edward Home-Gall, who also wrote for the paper under the pseudonym Edwin Dale. These exotic stories concerned a travelling side, the Roving Rovers, a motley crew led by "Tuffy" Ted Tufton. The format enabled the writer to put the team

Right *Adventure*'s cover shows how much the artist's depiction of the action changed in the 10 years between "The Round The World Rovers" story, above, and "The Guinea-Pig Goalie" (21 September 1957)

STARTING INSIDE—A CHUCKLE-PACKED SPACE STORY!

Adventure

EVERY TUESDAY 3°

No. 1705—SEPT. 21, 1957.

THE GUINEA-PIG GOALIE

1—Lanky Hutton, the star goalkeeper of Redstoke Rovers, was about to start on a new career. Having been deferred until he had fully completed his training as a doctor, Lanky had been called up to do his National Service with the Royal Air Force. It was mainly due to Lanky's skill in goal and his go-ahead tactics as skipper, that the Rovers had been promoted to the First Division. Now, as a new season approached, he was hoping that he would still be able to play football.

2—Lanky duly reported to the Officers' Training Unit which was stationed outside a nearby town, and there began his initial training. Between lectures and "square-bashing", educational film shows and inspections, Lanky was kept very busy as the Air Force changed him from a civilian into an "officer and gentleman." The physical training periods were a part of the course that Lanky really enjoyed and, when he turned up at the Rovers' ground for training, he showed that he still had his old skill.

3—After one training session, when the players had taken their showers and were changing in the dressing-room, Lanky made an announcement. "Pipe down, you rowdy bunch!" he began. "I want to tell you that you won't be seeing me for a few days——" Lanky's next words were drowned in an outburst of cheers and wisecracks. When the noise had died down, Lanky continued. "I'm being posted to my first real job and I won't get back here for a few days, so keep up the training—we'll need it!"

4—On leaving the ground, Lanky walked round to his lodgings where he had been spending the short leave granted to him before going to his new station. There, he collected his bags, loaded them in his pre-war vintage sports car, and began the drive to his new "posting." An hour or so later, he received a smart salute from the service policeman at the main gate of R.A.F. Aldarmoor. The S.P. carefully inspected Lanky's identity card, then directed him to the Officers' Mess. (Continued on back page.)

THE OUTSIDER AT OUTSIDE-LEFT

Below Sam "Inky" Bones impresses his new pals who are The Team Without A Ground (*Champion*, 20 November 1945)

in all manner of circumstances (exotic and foreign) that would have been inconceivable in Britain. The Round-The-World Rovers play matches all over the world, and get into all manner of scrapes, involving revolutions, kidnap and organised crime in the mountains, the jungle and the savannah.

But, ironically, while the game of football was developing at a rapid pace, especially in Europe, the story-papers' characters' adventures were taking place in far-flung and exotic locations, notably South and Central America and Africa. The writers, like the Football Association, seemed oblivious to the footballing revolution that was taking place on their doorstep, in Europe, one which culminated with the end-of-an-era home defeat for the England team at the hands – or feet – of Hungary in 1953 at Wembley.

While the Roving Rovers' players are typical characters from the boys' story-papers (in goal is "Podge Parks, the 18-stone keeper"), they do have a unusual left-back. He is Sam "Inky" Bones, a black man. He is introduced to the Roving Rovers players in the "Team Without A Ground" story that appeared on 20 October 1945: "Tuffy introduced the new player all round, and there were warm handshakes. His name was Sam Bones, better known as 'Inky'. He had a mop of jet-black curly hair and two rolling laughing eyes that were scarcely ever motionless." All took to the new man except for full-back Jack Picard; the two had history. Picard… "turned his back upon Inky and faced Tuffy. 'If you've found a new left-back, and that's him,' he said, 'then you'd better start looking for a new right-back. There's not room in the same team for both of us, so you'd better decide before this afternoon's match which of us you want to keep!' He strode sullenly from the barn. The Rovers watched his departure in silent dismay. Tuffy groaned under his breath. His troubles weren't over, not by long chalks! He had found a new left-back, and now, because of him, he looked like losing their tried and trusted right back." Eventually Picard explains himself. "'Oh, he's a good back all right!' grunted Jack. 'I've played with him in the Army. We were in the same unit in France. It's not his football or the colour of his skin that I object to – it's him. I made a vow once that if I ever met Inky Bones again I'd half kill him. But I'm not telling any tales. If you want to know why I don't like him you'd better ask him!'"

Top left Danny Lee was baffled by the behaviour of some of his team mates (*Wizard*, 5 January 1946)

As the boys' papers evolved into comics as we now know them over the next decade, the supernatural became an increasingly tapped well of stories for editors and writers, but in the main the post-war tales looked to the past for storylines and plot ideas. "The Outsider at Outside-Left", which

Below "The Outsider at Outside Left" proves himself to be the hero of the hour (*Wizard*, 16 March 1946)

The Terrible Secrets of the Vics are Discovered—But is Danny Lee too late to save his Team-Mates?

THE OUTSIDER AT OUTSIDE-LEFT

started in *Wizard* on 5 January 1946, was classic Thirties' fare. It concerned Danny Lee of Longhurst Vics FC, whose mysterious chairman, Sam Weirt, had an "uncanny knack of picking up unknown players who turned out to be exceptional men". But for Danny… "There was something about them which he did not understand, something almost inhuman. They lived, ate, and talked only football. They did not appear to have any outside lives. Now and again he had tried to find out where one or the other had come from before signing up with the Vics, but he had only been met by blank stares and requests for him to mind his own business."

Of course the sinister chairman was the key figure in the mystery; as the story unfurls we find that the Longhurst players are actually star players from other teams who had disappeared and were presumed dead. Each had been given plastic surgery to change their appearance and were drugged with a mind-control agent that made them compliant to the will of the evil Weirt.

Danny eventually solved the mystery, and all ended well: "The captured footballers, most of them too dazed to remember who they were for several days, all recovered, and many clubs which had mourned the loss of their crack performer had reason to thank Danny Lee for his investigations. Men who had been believed dead went back to their overjoyed friends, and in some cases were playing again before the end of the season." The denouement was classic story-book moralising: "Sam Wiert managed to conceal some poison, and committed suicide in his cell." His cohorts…

Below Magic of the cup… the Cannonball Kidd finds out the hard way how tough it is to win an FA Cup tie away at Tegboro' (*Hotspur*, 11 January 1947)

The team that fielded 11 players and 6000 stop-at-nothing supporters

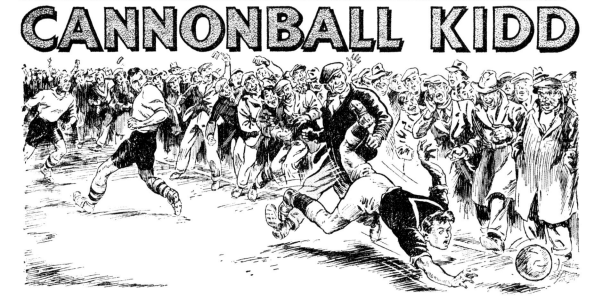

CANNONBALL KIDD

HERE'S THE BIGGEST SENSATION IN FIRST-CLASS FOOTBALL—THE TEAM THAT ONLY SIGNS ON TEEN-AGERS!

TOO OLD AT TWENTY

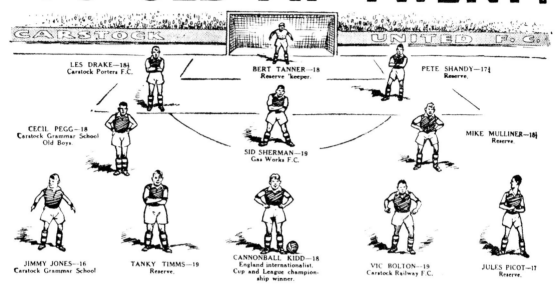

LES DRAKE—18½
Carstock Porters F.C.

BERT TANNER—18
Reserve 'keeper.

PETE SHANDY—17¾
Reserve.

CECIL PEGG—18
Carstock Grammar School
Old Boys.

SID SHERMAN—19
Gas Works F.C.

MIKE MULLINER—18½
Reserve.

JIMMY JONES—16
Carstock Grammar School

TANKY TIMMS—19
Reserve.

CANNONBALL KIDD—18
England internationalist.
Cup and League champion-
ship winner.

VIC BOLTON—19
Carstock Railway F.C.

JULES PICOT—17
Reserve.

"were brought to trial, and told the whole astounding story of the greatest football swindle of modern times. They received life sentences."

Into the 1950s, many of *Hotspur*'s stories continued to be set in a school, although some reflected the wider football world. The Cannonball Kidd (11 January 1947) was a case in point. The hero is schoolboy Billy Kidd, pupil at South Street School – the name suggests a state school rather than a public or private one – who is the star centre-forward of local side Greyport Rovers. His teacher is Jack Raith, also the Rovers' manager. To complicate matters, the school's headmaster, Mr Brasser, is a director of Greyport Select FC, the other first division club in Greyport. "At the start of the war Jack Raith, then the Rovers' centre-forward, and all his team-mates had joined up straight away, and the club had not played in war-time football. On the other hand the Select had kept going and had become very powerful and wealthy. Jack Raith had come back from the war with a limp, due to injury, and taken up his profession as a teacher at South Street School. He had been asked by the principal shareholder of the Rovers to restart the old club. Ten members of the pre-war team had answered the SOS for players. Although in the veteran stage they were as keen as mustard and knew every football wile in the game."

So we have the old and the new; the schoolboy playing with the veterans, the story of many a real-life, wartime and post-war football club. While it is well documented that many a "veteran" turned out for their club in their hour of need

Above You'll never win anything with kids... Billy Kidd and the Bradburn City side, in the pages of *Hotspur* (19 August 1950). The story also made reference to Radwick Rangers manager Ritchie, who appeared in numerous *Hotspur* stories in the 1950s – and beyond

THE TEAM OF THE DOOMED

Above "The Team of the Doomed" in trouble (*Hotspur*, 11 February 1950)

Right Napper Todd was one of the most popular characters in *Hotspur*. Here he was the cover star (4 September 1954)

Below Don't forget that dubbin, boys (*Hotspur*, 11 September 1954)

during the war years and immediately afterwards, the 1939–45 conflict also gave youth a chance. As Jack Rollin recorded in his book, *Soccer at War*, Wolves boss Major Frank Buckley was one of a number of managers who had an excellent reputation for scouting, and blooding, young players. Stan Cullis captained Wolves at 19, and in 1939 Buckley picked two 16-year-old wingers in Alan Steen and Jimmy Mullen for the first eleven. Rollin writes: "Like most groundstaff boys, they were sent home at the onset of war, but several were recalled, found jobs in local factories and given a chance to shine in regional football." Steen and Mullen were almost veterans compared with some who played for the Wolves first team

during the war. Cameron Buchanan was just 14 years and 57 days old when he made his debut on 26 September 1942 against West Bromwich in a 2–0 win. A year earlier Wolves had put out its youngest-ever team, fielding a side at Leicester with an average age of 17. The veteran of the eleven was Derek Ashton, at the ripe old age of 19.

Rollin writes: "Buckley was continually looking for talent and his scouting system still functioned efficiently enough for him to learn of the ability of a 15-year-old called Tom Burden, a London evacuee. He arranged for the lad to have a trial in 1940, but when Burden arrived from Somerset it was snowing hard and the game had to be cancelled. Buckley realised the problems of

"That's the stuff WREN'S DUBBIN keeps boots TIP-TOP"

Get a TIN TO-DAY 7° & 10½°

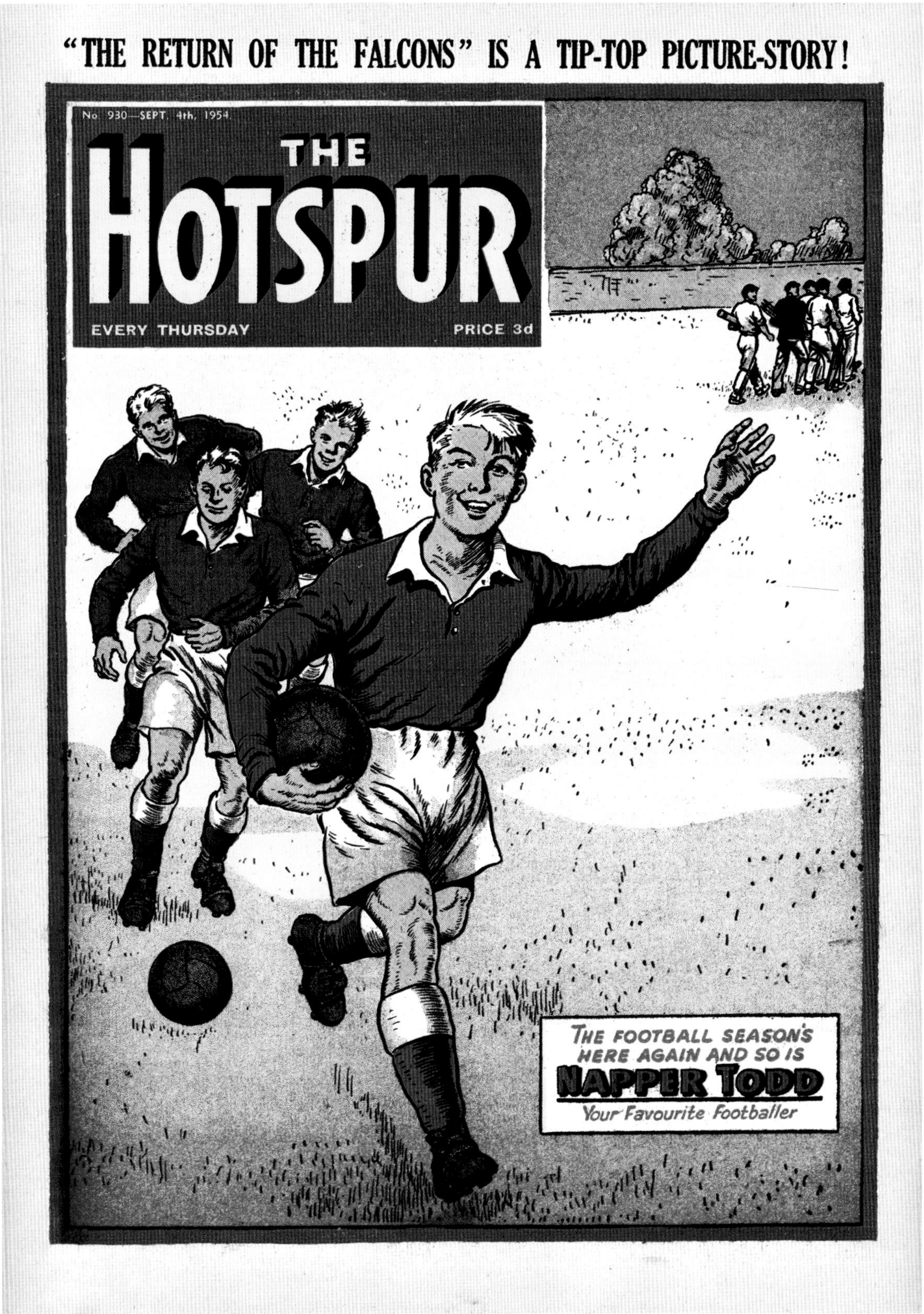
"THE RETURN OF THE FALCONS" IS A TIP-TOP PICTURE-STORY!
No. 930—SEPT. 4th, 1954.
THE HOTSPUR
EVERY THURSDAY
PRICE 3d
THE FOOTBALL SEASON'S HERE AGAIN AND SO IS
NAPPER TODD
Your Favourite Footballer

During the trial game, Donald Wallace never got the ball in a tackle—why did Ritchie sign him on?

trying to get back for another shot so he decided to try the lad at taking penalty kicks and signed him literally on the spot as an amateur!"

A story straight out of the boys' papers; in fact, the schoolboy footballer was a reality, not a comic book fantasy. The Cannonball Kidd's story also hinted at other aspects of the real game. After his team is drawn away in the FA Cup… "Cannonball Kidd could not help looking glum as he heard the news, and Jack Raith gave a shrug. The Rovers would have to travel a hundred and fifty miles to the small northern mining town for the match with the notoriously tough cup-fighters of Tegboro'. Under the new safety regulations the crowd would not exceed six or seven thousand." New ground regulations were brought in as the result of a tragedy that occurred at Bolton's Burnden Park ground on 9 March 1946. An estimated 85,000 turned up to see the FA Cup tie against Stoke City – the ground was reckoned to hold just under 70,000. The result was a catastrophic crush that claimed 33 lives, with more than 500 other spectators injured. A subsequent inquiry identifed the main problems; these were that football grounds did not have official capacities and, importantly, there was no way of knowing when a ground was dangerously full. Measures adopted to tackle these issues included a limit placed on the size of crowds at each football ground (although they were not sufficent to prevent the Ibrox Park tragedy in Glasgow in 1971).

While the Cannonball Kidd was the star of his show, his veteran team mates are important supporting players. Billy is respectful of their experience and knowledge: "As soon as he had finished his tea that evening Cannonball Kidd rushed off to the football ground where Danny the Diddler, Old-Man Dallas, the centre-half, Baldy Brown and Vic Hall, backs, Wheezy Keys and Slinky Harper, wingers, and Frank Fletcher, the keeper and the other players were getting into their training strip…" Billy wanted to tell them that a contact of his had scouted their opposition and knew the way they played: "'Rush tactics, eh? Just what I expected,' murmured the wily old player. 'Well, we shan't waste our breath chasing 'em all over the pitch. The vital spot is just in front of our goal. We'll have a scheme for guarding the penalty box.'"

Facing page Things just weren't falling for "The Team of the Doomed" (*Hotspur*, 7 January 1950)

Tegboro' are eventually overcome (although Greyport Rovers have to beat the crowd as well – some spectators literally tackle Rovers players during the course of the game) and in a glorious season the Football League was won and the FA Cup final reached: "The Rovers had already won the First Divison Championship. That they were in a position to bring double honours to Greyport by winning the cup as well was something of a football miracle. Only at the start of the season had the club been revived after standing down during the war when the players had all joined up. It was Jack Raith, a teacher at South Street School, who had got it going again. At his call the pre-war players, Danny Denton, Old-Man Dallas, Baldy Brown and the rest had rallied round to put in one more season before they hung up their boots. Most of them were on the point of retiring before joining the Forces, but on demob they had agreed to turn out until the club got some young blood. Then Raith found that Billy was a born footballer... the veterans' craft and positional play, allied to the boy's dash, had proved to be a winning combination."

Below Ritchie signs Homer Jones, a farm boy with a rocket shot, pipping his arch rival Henry Granger in the story "The Last of The Rangers" (*Hotspur*, 12 January 1957). It is the tale of a team being rebuilt after an air crash wiped out most of its members. It was published a year before the Munich Air Disaster

Cannonball scored a hat-trick and the Cup was won: "What a great season it had been! Billy hoped he had years of first-class football ahead, but he would never forget the grand time he had had playing with Danny and the other veterans."

Billy the Cannonball Kidd's exploits continued to entertain readers throughout the 1950s, and the emphasis remained on youth. Bradburn City were proof

THE HOTSPUR. January 12. 1957.

A STRANGE WAY TO SIGN A FOOTBALLER! READ ABOUT IT INSIDE.

THE **HOTSPUR**

EVERY THURSDAY　　No. 1053—JAN. 12th, 1957.　　PRICE 3d

that you can win things with kids in the story "Too Old at Twenty" (**Hotspur**, 19 August 1950). The entire first eleven were teenagers, led by the Cannonball Kidd, by now aged 18 and "an England internationalist, Cup and League championship winner". During the story he adds another cup-winner's medal to his collection, "but it was probably the first time that ginger pop was poured into the Cup – a ceremonial actioned performed after the game… none of the lads wanted champagne".

Other stories that seemed fanciful were based on real-life events. "The Team of the Doomed" (**Hotspur**, 7 January 1950) carried the exciting tag-line, "How will the hoodoo on the Rangers affect their new player? He was born on Friday the thirteenth!" The story concerned Radwick Rangers, who had lost their best players and many staff members in a plane crash; the club was said to have been cursed by a gypsy. Forced into making loan signings, Rangers manager Ritchie signs a rather unpromising Scottish half-back, Donald Wallace, known as "Battleaxe". Wallace is warned off signing for Rangers by Scrooby, a journalist with a grudge: "'The Rangers must be the unluckiest team under the sun,' said Scrooby, with the shake of his head. 'There's supposed to be a gipsy curse on the club. They play well, but things keep happening to them.' Wallace was listening with earnest attention.

'Yes, bad luck seemed to dog them,' pursued Scrooby artfully. 'No fewer than ten of their players have received broken limbs since the war.' 'That's bad,' said Wallace. 'But it won't happen to me when I play for them.' Scrooby put on a melancholy expression. 'If you go back into history you'll find out that the club was started on a Friday, and it was also the thirteenth.' He saw Wallace open his eyes wide in amazement. 'What good could ever come of a club that was founded on Friday the thirteenth?' Scrooby asked. Wallace said, 'I was born on Friday the thirteenth.' He

Below Napper Todd, the prodigy of Riverport Casuals, finds his way unexpectedly blocked in a match against Milhouse Avenue (*Hotspur*, 30 October 1954)

yawned and looked out of the window." But Scrooby was persistent: "'I wonder if there is anything in the gipsy's curse?' he asked artfully. Wallace grinned. 'A gipsy cursed me once when I was a kid,' he said. 'Five minutes later I found a threepenny bit in the gutter.'" If only the real-life professionals could demonstrate such sang froid. In 1947, Middlesbrough star Wilf Mannion blamed an FA Cup quarter-final defeat on the fact that "Ayresome Park was cursed by gipsies". Similarly, a party of gypsies were forced to move from the Baseball Ground site when Derby County

Above "He's head and shoulders above everyone else…" Napper Todd nods one in against Mountford Excelsior (*Hotspur*, 10 January 1954)

moved in in 1895. Legend has it that before leaving they put a curse on the ground preventing Derby County from winning the FA Cup. A 6–0 record loss to Bury in 1903 hardly helped matters; when Derby reached the 1946 Cup final some of the players asked for the curse to be lifted. Whether palms were crossed with silver was not documented; in any case Derby ran out 4–1 winners, against Charlton Athletic. In the last minute of normal time in that match something happened that was straight from a comic story; Jack Stamps of Derby's shot was goalbound before, incredibly, the ball burst and dropped at the feet of astonished Charlton keeper Sam Bartram.

Slowly but surely, the comics were moving away from schools-based stories. While the Red Circle School continued to combine footer and adventure action in *Hotspur*, more working-class footballers were emerging as footballing heroes. One was Napper Todd (*Hotspur*, 3 January 1953), an apprentice steeplejack and park footballer with South End Rovers, who play on a kind of make-believe Hackney Marshes ("On football pitches on the Flats, the made up ground by the river at Riverport, on Saturday afternoons, were scores of young footballers"). The trials and tribulations for the players will be familiar to anyone who has played in such circumstances: "On the next pitch, too, an exciting game was taking place. It was a bit difficult to tell which referee was using the whistle." At one point Napper's team attacked… "Sandy got it and kicked it out to Storky. With Napper keeping pace he legged it down the wing

Below "Meet Rocky Rogers, the game's fittest, fastest footballer", who starred in the series "The Cyclone Centre's A Schoolmaster" (cover picture, *Hotspur*, 22 September 1956)

Right and following page
Roy Race in action in *Tiger* (13 October 1956)

and then put over a high centre. Suddenly Napper saw two footballs flying through the air, for the outside-left on the next pitch had made a hash of a corner kick and sent the ball flying towards Napper. Thanks to keeping his eye on the Rovers' ball, he picked it out and biffed it into the goal with his head. But to make absolutely certain, he stuck his leg out and biffed in the other ball as well."

The mid-1950s saw the debut of the most famous comic-strip footballer of them all; Roy Race, known all over the world as Roy of the Rovers. He appeared in the pages of Amalgamated Press's *Tiger* comic, launched on 11 September 1954 with Roy on the cover.

Like Napper, Roy was just an ordinary lad. The creator of Roy of the Rovers was Frank Pepper, who explained the original ideas behind Roy on the Roy of the Rovers official website: "We decided to show an ordinary lad, with talent, with whom the reader would identify, joining a top-class club with long traditions, as a very humble junior and gradually making his way up the ladder, until he became a star. This wasn't as easy as it sounds: in pre-war days none of our footballers ever seemed to live anywhere, or to have any relatives – they just materialised on the pitch on match days and then vanished back into limbo. Done today there'd be no problem: you'd just have him living in a suburban semi with his parents and siblings, but at that time it was unthinkable to have female characters in a boys' paper."

Roy was one of the most enduring characters ever to appear in a British comic; in fact, he outlasted *Tiger*. He was a Melchester Rovers reserve player, first-teamer, captain, player/manager, manager, England international, England captain, Cup winner, European Cup winner... the list is endless. He is the only comic book footballer to have a comic named after him (*Roy of the Rovers* ran from 1976 to 1993) and the expression 'Roy of the Rovers stuff' has passed into everyday usage.

Tom Tully had the longest stint as Roy Race story author. Once described as "the linesman of the Rovers", in an interview for the *Yorkshire Post* in 1979 Tully said of Roy of the Rovers: "The phrase should be in the dictionary. Roy represents something that coloured your life when you were young. He has become something people relate to and use to express themselves. He makes mistakes, feels guilty, loses his temper,

TIGER   October 13, 1956   No. 110

EVERY TUESDAY

DEEP-SEA DUEL WITH A GIANT SWORD-FISH! SEE PAGE 14

TIGER

Incorporating THE CHAMPION

4D.

The SPORT and ADVENTURE PICTURE STORY WEEKLY

Roy of the ROVERS

By Stewart Colwyn

MELCHESTER ROVERS' CENTRE-FORWARD ROY RACE, HAD DEPUTISED FOR THE INJURED GOALIE FOR MOST OF THE MATCH AGAINST WELBECK WANDERERS. ALTHOUGH A LITTLE UNORTHODOX IN SOME OF HIS GOALKEEPING ROY BROUGHT OFF MANY MIRACULOUS SAVES. THE TEN-MEN ROVERS WERE ACTUALLY WINNING, 2—1, WHEN IN THE LAST SECONDS OF THE GAME, WELBECK WERE AWARDED A PENALTY-KICK.

ROY CROUCHED ANXIOUSLY IN GOAL, AS WELBECK'S CRACKSHOT CENTRE-FORWARD STARTED HIS RUN-UP

CAN'T LET 'EM EQUALISE NOW! GOT TO SAVE THIS SHOT—!

A MOMENT LATER, BOOT MET BALL! ROY ANTICIPATED THAT THE SHOT WOULD COME TO HIS LEFT — BUT THE BALL STREAKED TO HIS RIGHT INSTEAD!

ROY'S BEATEN!

BUT ROY WASN'T BEATEN! IN DESPERATION HE FLUNG HIMSELF SIDEWAYS IN A SPECTACULAR, SPREADEAGLED DIVE — AND THEN AN INCREDULOUS ROAR BROKE FROM THE FANS......

SAVED, THE GOALIE!!

HE'S DONE IT! BY THUNDER, ROY'S SAVED IT!

THEN AS THE BALL SPUN FROM ROY'S FINGERS, THE WELBECK FORWARDS POUNDED UP, DETERMINED TO EQUALISE

BUT AT THAT INSTANT, THE REF. BLEW A LONG BLAST ON HIS WHISTLE. THE MATCH WAS OVER — AND ROVERS HAD WON!

PLEASE TURN TO BACK PAGE

CONTINUED FROM FRONT PAGE

THE CHEERS WERE DEAFENING AS THE WELBECK CENTRE-FORWARD SPORTINGLY HELPED ROY TO HIS FEET

GOOD OLD ROVERS!

WELL DONE, RACE. THAT WAS A GRAND SAVE. ALTHOUGH IT ROBBED US OF TWO POINTS

THEN ROY'S PAL, BLACKIE GRAY, AND THE NEW FRENCH RIGHT-WINGER, PIERRE DUPONT, WHO WAS ON A MONTH'S TRIAL WITH ROVERS, RAN UP

BRAVO, ROY!

YOU ARE ZE WIZARD, ROY! ZAT MAGNIFICENT SAVE GAVE US ZE WIN INSTEAD OF ZE DRAW!

PHEW! DON'T PILE IT ON, PIERRE! AFTER ALL, IT WAS YOUR TWO GOALS THAT WON US THE POINTS!

SKIPPER ANDY McDONALD STEPPED BETWEEN ROY AND PIERRE AS THEY TROTTED TOWARDS THE TUNNEL

YOU BOTH DID YOUR PART, FELLERS, AND WE'RE PROUD OF YOU! SO ARE THE FANS! JUST HARK AT THE CHEERS!

GOOD OLD ROY! WHAT A GOALIE!

WELL PLAYED, PIERRE!

UP THE ROVERS—THE TEN-MEN TERRORS!

WHEN THE ROVERS ENTERED THEIR DRESSING-ROOM, THEY FOUND MANAGER BEN GALLOWAY WAITING FOR THEM WITH "SLIM" BARTLETT, THE SECRETARY OF THE SUPPORTERS' CLUB

GRAND GAME, LADS! AND I'VE GOT GOOD NEWS FOR YOU ALL. PIERRE—THE DIRECTORS WANT YOU TO SIGN ON FOR THE REST OF THE SEASON

GOSH! THAT'S GREAT! CONGRATULATIONS, PIERRE!

MA FOI, M'SIEUR GALLOWAY, I AM DELIGHTED! IT IS MY GREATEST AMBITION TO JOIN ZE ROVEURS AND IT IS A GREAT HONNEUR TO BE ACCEPTED BEFORE MY MONTH'S TRIAL IS ENDED!

THEN, AS THE MANAGER LEFT THE ROOM, "SLIM" BARTLETT STEPPED FORWARD

THIS CALLS FOR A CELEBRATION, LADS! AND AS THE SUPPORTERS' CLUB ARE THROWING A PARTY FOR YOU IN THE SOCIAL HALL DOWN THE ROAD, WHAT ABOUT ALL OF YOU COMING ALONG?

WHY, THANKS, SLIM! COME ON, FELLERS! LET'S GET DRESSED QUICKLY!

FINE! THEN WE'LL MAKE IT A WELCOME PARTY FOR PIERRE. DON'T BE LONG!

O.K., SLIM! WE'LL BE THERE AS QUICK AS WE CAN!

COME ON, LADS! LET PIERRE LEAD THE WAY!

THE ROVERS SOON BATHED AND DRESSED, AND EVERYONE WAS IN HIGH SPIRITS—EXCEPT SAM HIGBY, THE RESERVE RIGHT-WINGER, WHO WAS BITTER BECAUSE PIERRE HAD TAKEN HIS PLACE IN THE TEAM

LOOK AT 'EM——MAKING A BLOOMING HERO OF THAT PERISHING FRENCHMAN! BUT I'M POSITIVE HE'S A CROOK, AND THE SOONER I CAN PROVE IT AND GET HIM SLUNG OUT OF THE ROVERS, THE BETTER IT'LL BE FOR ME!

IN NEXT TUESDAY'S "TIGER"—SENSATION AT THE SUPPORTERS' CLUB PARTY

makes errors of judgement, has arguments with his wife and frequently finishes up with egg on his face. But in the final analysis he is thoroughly decent, totally loyal and widely respected."

A nother much-loved hero emerged in the pages of *Wizard* in the early 1950s. While not as famous as Roy Race, Limp-Along Leslie was a popular and enduring character who also rose to the top from humble beginnings. Furthermore, Leslie Tomson had a disability; after a childhood accident he was left with one leg shorter than the other. Despite this, he is able to combine managing a 10,000-acre estate for the Duke of Buckleigh with playing football for Darby Rangers (as an amateur). Furthermore, one of his footballing pals is a gypsy, Ishmael, who was "powerfully built, swarthy-complexioned and wore gold ear-rings". In fact Leslie Tomson pre-dates Roy Race, first appearing in *Wizard* on 27 January 1951. Interestingly, when Leslie Tomson was appearing in *Wizard* in the 1950s, a fellow team member at Darbury Rangers had his own storylines in the comic. Goalkeeper Bernard Briggs also played as an amateur – he "earned a rough living as a general dealer", mainly in scrap metal. He was a "short, powerful man with abnormally long arms" who "had been nicknamed Bouncing Briggs by newspapermen and football fans because of his amazing agility in making spectacular saves". While lacking in formal education, Briggs has a shrewd, sharp mind and, in keeping with tradition, the heart of a lion. He embodies the ethos of the team man; in one story he discharges himself from hospital despite having been buried under a pile of rubble rather than let his team mates down for a big match (17 December 1955).

Below Limp-Along Leslie was one of the most enduring of all the football comic characters. He started in *Wizard* (as seen below, 24 September 1955) and also appeared in *New Hotspur* (1962-74), *Buddy* (1981-83) and *Victor* (1983)

Play to the whistle! The Rangers' dithering defence should be remembering that, instead of appealing wildly for offside against the tearaway winger who's got a clear run in on goal.

LIMP ALONG LESLIE

THE STORIES ARE GREAT—EACH ONE OF THE EIGHT!

While the bulk of the stories in the comics were still text-based, editors were increasingly experimenting with picture-strip presentations. Roy Race in *Tiger* was one of the more sophisticated strip stories at the time; many editors were content to stick to the tried-and-tested one-picture-per-page text story. D.C. Thomson's *Adventure* included a football picture strip story on its cover (issue dated 21 September 1957) with "The Guinea-Pig Goalie" (see page 111). Lanky Hutton was "the star goalkeeper of Redstoke Rovers", called up to do National Service with the RAF. Unlike Roy of the Rovers, the Guinea-Pig Goalie used extended captions rather than speech bubbles. This technique allows for fewer frames per page and seems a poor compromise between the traditional sophisticated text-based stories and the more modern and immediate action-packed picture strips stories with speech bubbles.

"You push the ball too far ahead when you dribble," the trainer told me. So I had to practise with the ball tied to my boot with elastic. Every time I pushed the ball too far—whang!—it came back at me!

Above and following page, How a Soccer Star is Made. "Terry Davis of the famous Upton Rovers" explains some basic skills (*The Champion Annual for Boys*, 1955)

Leslie Tomson and Bouncing Briggs were not the only comic footballers to appear in tandem in the comics. The careers of Nick Smith and Arnold Tabbs of Granton United intertwined on the pages of various D.C. Thomson comics. Nick Smith first appeared in the story "It's Goals That Count" on 29 September

Below Bouncing Briggs (seen here in *Wizard*, 17 December 1955) was the epitome of the tough, working-class footballer – although he insisted on playing as an amateur

IT'S GOALS THAT COUNT

Above Nick Smith's long and varied career was documented in literally hundreds of stories in many different comics. Here he is featured in *Rover* (1 March 1958); he was also in *Hornet* (1965-76) and *Hotspur* (1976-80) among others

1945 in the pages of *Rover*. Arnold Tabbs' back-story was told in *Wizard* (22 January 1955) in "The Blitz Kid". It describes how "when Arnold was a boy, the Second World War was being fought; Britain was being battered by the Blitz… and bombs were raining down on her cities. Alone in the world, Arnold had to face the falling bombs, the raging fires, the tumbling buildings… that was where he got his courage, his determination, his never-say-die spirit."

Hotspur was to launch two other durable and long-lasting characters before the decade was out. Bill Willis, or "Biffalo Bill", was an earth-mover and tree-feller who played for Bramington Wanderers. First appearing on 14 December 1963, he was another footballer from the school of real-life. A giant of a man, capable of astonishing physical feats, he had "a daily feed of pemmican, his favourite grub, which is a North American preparation of meat and fat. It was sent to him by a pal in Greenland." The story was unusual in that it was narrated by one of Biffalo's team mates, Jack Stanton, the inside-forward. Like Roy of the Rovers, the writers created a whole team of characters, whose pen pictures often appeared on the pages. The goalkeeper was Gerald Woodbine, a West Indian; other characters were name-

Right Trainer "Dad" Hammond comes to the rescue when Biffalo Bill's shirt goes missing

Then followed some practice with the Upton Rovers' Special ! I had to shoot balls at the revolving fins and kick 'em on the rebound—straight back at the machine again !

MORE FUN WITH BIFFALO BILL INSIDE — 4 GREAT FREE GIFTS, TOO

THE HOTSPUR

No. 1146—OCT. 25th, 1958. EVERY THURSDAY. PRICE 3ᵈ

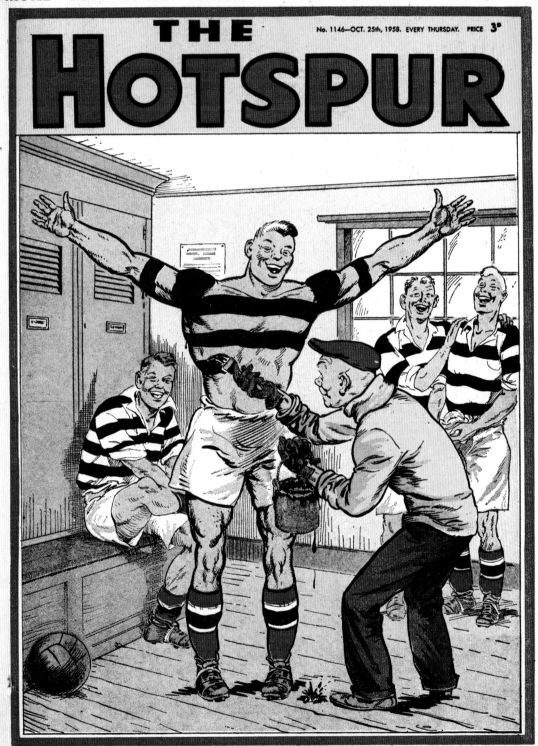

checked during the course of a "match" as the action unfolded. As well as combining adventure and football action, the story was played for laughs. In one episode Biffalo's shirt goes missing just before a match; the solution is to get the trainer to paint the Wanderers' blue hoops onto Bill's torso! (**Hotspur**, 25 October 1958). In the game that follows Bill bewilders opponents who find themselves covered in blue paint as they attempt to tackle the man-mountain ("There was a splodge on the goalie's sweater and Darley had a blue chin. Trevick's nose had changed colour and Hobbins had paint on his hands"). Biffalo's shirt was eventually located; because of its size the "groundsman had thought it was a new flag and put it in the flag locker".

In many ways the story "Dozy Danny", which made its **Hotspur** debut on 5 September 1959, harked back to the boys' story-papers of the 1910s and 1920s, but also reflected the gritty realism of the kitchen sink dramas that were popular in film and literature at the time. The main character was a 13-year-old boy, Danny Lorimer, who lives with a brutal, exploitative stepfather in the grim industrial town of Raddersford. Each day he rises at 4 a.m. to make and deliver coal briquettes. "The boy worked on. He was small, looked about eleven, and had curly black hair. An observer would have noticed that his eyes were quick and alert and his movements quick and deft. Somewhere outside a factory hooter blew. The boy stopped shovelling for a minute and grinned ruefully. 'Six o'clock!', said Dozy Lorimer. 'There isn't going to be much football for me this morning before school!' By half-past-six, however, the one hundred and twenty coal briquettes were made. Danny shovelled some more coal dust into the oven to dry off, then he nipped to the door. In the grey light it was possible to see that Dozy was in a small yard, bounded on one side by a fence that ran alongside the railway, and on the other side by a high board fence with a gate. A small stone-built cottage

Below Dozy Danny has done a day's work before most of his classmates have even had breakfast... no wonder he is always sleeping. But this does not stop him being the school's star player (*Hotspur*, 12 September 1959)

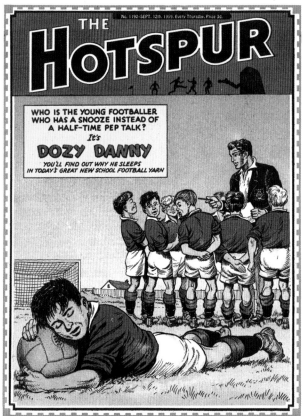

TELL YOUR PALS ABOUT "THE SOAP-BOX SPECIAL"

THE RAGGED ROVERS

Above The Ragged Rovers were "the miser's football club" — chairman Jed Milson would not even buy the team a new kit (*Hotspur*, 28 December 1957)

and three tumble-down wooden shacks were ranged round the yard. Dozy Lorimer went into the third wooden shack and began to groom a tired and sleepy pony there. He chatted to it as he worked. 'Can't be much fun for you, Betsy, dragging that cart round the streets all day long,' he said as he combed the pony's mane. 'I bet the Old Man pushes you about, too!'"

All this before going to school – where he plays football at every opportunity. Not surprisingly, he was prone to bouts of sleepiness, hence the nickname Dozy. Danny's only way out is football, and the story charts his battle to escape poverty and make it in the professional game. It's a theme that is to be repeated in the coming decade.

Other characters also seemed as if they had come from another era – because they had. "The Ragged Rovers" first appeared in *Wizard* on 28 December 1935; the story about Redwood Rovers, who acquired their nickname because "of their shabby appearance on the field and also because of their poor accommodation in the buildings belonging to the ground", also appeared twice as a text story in the 1950s before appearing in strip format in *Hotspur* (12 September 1964). The reason for their strife? A miser of a chairman named Jed Milson, "whose one object in life was to make money, and who never spent a halfpenny if he could help it".

No doubt, as the 1960s approached, many real-life professional players must have felt that Milson was running their club, too. This was still the age of the "retain and transfer" system in which clubs controlled players contracts and their movement between clubs; the players' themselves had no say, or control, over their own careers. But all this was about to alter, and the comics were moving with the times, too, as Britain entered the decade of change.

"YOU CAN DISCOVER MORE ABOUT A PERSON
IN AN HOUR OF PLAY THAN IN A YEAR
OF CONVERSATION."

Plato (427–347 BC)

CHAPTER SIX
NEVER HAD IT SO GOOD

THE 1960s WERE A TIME OF REVOLUTION and upheaval, politically, socially and culturally. It was the decade of The Beatles and Swinging London; the Vietnam War and the political revolutions of 1968; of *That Was The Week That Was* and flower power. Everywhere, barriers were coming down as society transformed from post-war austerity to personal liberation and free love.

There was a revolution happening in football, too; one which was to lay the foundations for the modern game.

Two seismic changes took place in the early 1960s: the abolition of the maximum wage, and the scrapping of the "retain and transfer" system, through which the clubs were able to exert total control over their players and their careers.

Historically, players were poorly treated; wages were low and there was little loyalty from the clubs towards their charges. As Arthur Hopcraft wrote in *The*

Football Man: "Pickings for professional players were meagre... By the mid-1930s a First Division player could not expect to take home more than £12 a week, even with his bonuses for playing in the senior side and for winning a match; a young player, to take the case of Stan Cullis, who joined Wolverhampton Wanderers in 1934, would get a basic wage of £2 10s to £3 in his first two seasons with his club... He was in the Wolves senior side at seventeen-and-a-half and its captain at 19. When he was twenty-two he was not only England's centre-half but captain as well. Yet he was not paid the professionals' maximum wage of £8 in the winter months and £6 in the summer until his third season with the club." Hopcraft cites an interview with Cullis years later when the player recalls his "interview" with Wolves manager Major Buckley. "'He looked me up and down as I imagine a bloodstock owner would look at a

Left Up until the 1960s, football club directors ran their clubs with an iron fist – and had done since the game went professional. This *Football and Sports Library* cover (issue 338, 1932) graphically demonstrates the point. **Above** *The Hornet* was one of a number of comics launched in the early part of the decade

Right Bobby Smith in profile, from the "When He Was a Boy" section of *Victor* (12 December 1962)

racehorse. He said, 'Stand up.' He tapped me on the chest and said, 'What have you got there?' I didn't know what he meant. I thought he must meant something about my clothes. He said, 'Are you frightened?' I said, 'What of?' He said, 'Of getting hurt.' I said, 'No.' That was all he said to me. He had some words with my father which I couldn't hear, and I was a professional footballer.'"

The maximum wage continued right up until the 1960s. In the 1950s, the Football Players' Union put increasing pressure on the football authorities to, among other things, abandon the maximum wage. This the authorities subbornly refused to countenance; instead, the rate was increased to £14 (1951), £15 (1953), £17 (1957) and £20 (1958).

The players made further wage demands in 1960 but the crunch came in 1961. On 14 January, the now-renamed Professional Footballers' Association, led by Jimmy Hill of Fulham FC, used the threat of a strike during a series of protracted and highly publicised negotiations with the Football League. Finally, the league caved in, abolishing the maximum wage and increasing the minimum wage to £15. John Macadam, a writer on the hugely popular and influential magazine *Charles Buchan's Football Monthly* – it sold 125,000 copies a month in 1959 – wrote: "What struck me most forcibly was the youthful vigour of Jimmy Hill, and by severe contrast, the advanced age of his opponents." In

Below Jimmy Hill, President of the Professional Footballers' Association, talks to members of the press at St Pancras Town Hall, London, in January 1961. The topic in question is the threatened football players' strike

Photo by Douglas Miller/Keystone/Getty Images

The story of the football mad lad whose Yorkshire grit took him to the top line of football fame!

Bobby SMITH

WHEN HE WAS A BOY—

BOBBY SMITH, CENTRE-FORWARD OF TOTTENHAM HOTSPUR AND ENGLAND, WAS BORN IN THE LITTLE YORKSHIRE MINING VILLAGE OF LINGDALE.

Bobby's enthusiasm for football began at an early age. After school he could often be seen playing in the street.

THERE'S BOBBY AT IT AGAIN.

IF HE DOESN'T PLAY FOR ENGLAND ONE DAY, I'LL EAT MY HAT!

Every Saturday he went to the local ground to cheer on his team.

SHOOT, TOMMY, SHOOT!

HOPE HE DOESN'T TURN ROUND!

When Bobby couldn't afford a ticket, he found other ways of getting into the game . . .

once with disastrous results.

OUCH, MY KNEE!

To this day, he has a scar on his left knee to remind him of his escapade.

When Bobby left school he became an apprentice blacksmith in a local pit.

NOT LIKE THAT, LAD. IT'S NOT A FOOTBALL BOOT YOU'RE PUTTING ON!

I WISH IT WAS A FOOTBALL BOOT. I'D RATHER BE PLAYING FOOTBALL THAN WORKING HERE!

One day he narrowly escaped death when part of the tunnel roof caved in.

LOOK OUT!

PHEW, THAT WAS CLOSE.

137

New continental football boots only 12'6

What a bargain! Only 12/6 for the
football boots of the year!
In light flexible plastic
with reinforced toe-caps,
foam-cushioned insoles
and nail-less studs.
They're real goal-getters
in the same continental style
worn by top-scoring European stars.
Available sizes 1-8. Black only.
Get yours today!

CUT OUT
THIS COUPON NOW!

Please send me_____pair/s of continental
football boots, size/s_____
I enclose a cheque/postal order for_____
NAME_____
FULL POSTAL ADDRESS_____
_____
_____COUNTY_____

To: Slipper Supplies Ltd., Fisher St., Blackburn, LANCS.

Above What the upcoming footballer was wearing on his feet (advertisement
in *Hotspur*, 9 December 1961)

Right "Hurry of the Hammers" in action in *Hurricane*

the same magazine, with devastating insight, the Wolves player Bill Slater said: "It will be only a matter of time before a number of really outstanding clubs emerge and a Premier, or Super League, establishes itself."

Players soon felt the benefit of the scrapping of the maximum wage, Hill's Fulham team-mate Johnny Haynes becoming the first to earn £100 a week. And for professionals everywhere, more good news was just around the corner. In 1963, the High Court ruled that the hated "retain and transfer" system operated by the Football League was an unjustifiable restraint of trade. The case had been brought against Newcastle United by player George Eastham, and, as Arthur Hopcraft described, "the effect… was to make every professional player a free agent, just like a journalist or insurance salesman, able to negotiate his pay and length of service with a club, subject only to the contractual conditions which protect employer and employed against unreasonableness from each other." Hopcraft succinctly sums up the case: "George Eastham had found himself in a position common to many footballers. He was a brilliantly gifted forward, of the thoughful kind the game calls a 'schemer'; he was an England international. He was the key figure in Newcastle United's forward line, but he and the club management fell out, and he asked for a transfer. The club declined to give him one, put him on its list of retained players at his old wage and that, as far as the rules of the League went, was that. The iniquity of the 'retain-and-transfer' system was that the clubs were wholly in control. If Newcastle had decided to pay him only the minimum wage of £8 a week Eastham would have been forced to stay with them unless he could persuade the League

Ride with **BLACK AVENGER!** SEE INSIDE!

25th JULY 1964   EVERY MONDAY   6D

Hurricane

COMPANION PAPER TO *VALIANT*

"HURRY" OF THE HAMMERS!

'HURRY' CANE, A YOUNG CENTRE FORWARD WHO IS TRYING TO JOIN THE MIDLANDS FAMOUS "HAMMERS"—HAMMERSFIELD TOWN F.C.—IS PLAYING IN A TRIAL MATCH AT THE CLUB. HE HAS SCORED TWICE AND THE RIVAL CENTRE HALF, MIKE JOSSER, DELIBERATELY FOULS 'HURRY' AS HE SHOOTS HIS THIRD GOAL...

AAAGH! MY KNEE!

HURRY'S SHOT WAS ONLY HALF POWERED—

HURRY LAY FOR A MOMENT, AGONY SPEARING INTO HIS KNEE—

I'VE GOT TO GET UP AND PLAY OR I'LL FAIL THE TRIAL!

GOOD—LOOKS AS IF HIS KNEE WILL BE CROCKED FOR THE REST OF THE GAME!

HURRY'S KNEE ALMOST GAVE WAY AS HE STOOD UP—

ARE YOU ALL RIGHT, CANE? YOU LOOK PALE!

I—I'M FINE. JUST SHAKEN!

HARD LUCK YOU MISSED YOUR HAT-TRICK, BUT THERE'S STILL TIME!

HURRY'S RIGHT WINGER SENT OVER A HIGH IN-SWINGING CORNER—

HURRY WENT UP FOR IT—

TERRIFIC HEADER! AND IT'S THERE! HURRY'S HAT-TRICK!

NO WONDER THEY CALL HIM HURRY INSTEAD OF HARRY!

Above Legge's Eleven in European action in the *Valiant Annual* 1968

Management Committee to intervene under an appeals rule. He appealed and the Management Committee decided it had no cause to intervene. The acrimony between the player and Newcastle's management developed. Eastham did not play football for a year. Backed by the PFA he began the legal action which eventually freed all players from a system described by Eastham's counsel in the trial as being like the bartering of cattle and a relic of the Middle Ages."

In the comics, the players began to play with a swagger too, for a quiet revolution was taking places within their pages, with the emphasis slowly switching from the collective to the individual. In the first few years of the new decade little changed from the 1950s, except that more picture stories were being produced rather than text-based ones. By the end of it, the comics had undergone a radical overhaul, in look, content and attitude.

There was certainly plenty of pages to accommodate the new breed of players (and the old ones, too). While the 1950s had seen a number of comic mergers, such as *Tiger*'s subsuming of *Champion*, the early 1960s saw a rash of new launches. D.C. Thomson launched *Victor* in 1961 and *Hornet* in 1963; sandwiched in between, Fleetway/IPC, which had taken over the Amalgamated Press stable, launched *Valiant* (1962). Fleetway/IPC also launched *Hurricane* in 1964. The first issue of *Valiant* carried no football stories; bizarrely, the free gift advertised on the cover was "Football League Ladders" (a gift that was to crop up time and again in various comics over the next 20 years). Indeed, the only football-related feature in the first issue was "Soccer Roundabout", a digest of interesting facts and fun. Possibly *Valiant*'s best-known football story was "Legge's Eleven", the story of Ted Legge's exploits with Rockley Rangers, a small Fourth Division club in the north of England (first appearance 26 September 1964). Billed as "Britain's Strangest Soccer Team", the team included monocled Lord Darcy Lozenge, fiery Welshman Griffith Jones, sophisticated Frenchman Pierre Gaspard, the tearaway twins, Les and Ron, Chubby Mann, Nippy Norton, bespectacled Algenon Simms, hard man Badger Smith and bearded Scot Angus MacPhee.

*V*ictor and *Hornet* were much more football-orientated. *Victor* ran text stories alongside comic strips in its launch issue, with "Come Away the United" its first football story. It featured circus showman Sam Barnham, who spots that one of his circus performers, Jim Daly, has real footballing talent. Sam buys a football club, Kegford United, and signs Jim up. His faith is rewarded when the lad scores a last-minute winner on debut. Further glory awaits; Kegford win the cup at Wembley (12 May 1961) with Jim scoring a hat-trick; Sam's masterplan of playing seven backs and no goalkeeper pays off!

As the decade progressed *Victor* carried an increasing number of comic strips in place of text stories, which had the effect of rejuvenating many of the established, older characters. For example, the comic gave a new lease of life to "Gorgeous Gus", who had appeared in text-based stories in the 1950s in *Wizard*. He was to become one of the most popular characters in *Victor*, with the comic strip format perfectly suiting the humour his exaggerated aristocratic persona generated. Gus, or more correctly The Earl of Boote GBE, DSO, MC, buys struggling Redburn Rovers and immediately signs a number of England internationals to boost the club's fortunes (9 September 1961). He also upgrades the ground, with workmen "erecting an addition to the stand, a

Below Gorgeous Gus as he first appeared in *Wizard* (18 November 1950)
Following page Gorgeous Gus in new-look comic strip format in *Victor* (9 September 1961)

Jeepers! A footballer with his own dressing-room, creases in his shorts, a valet to attend him! Ah, but this is no ordinary footballer, boys! This is

GORGEOUS GUS

The footballer who had his own dressing-room—and a butler!

luxurious one-man dressing room, fitted with the latest devices and richly furnished. This ornate building was promptly nicknamed the Royal Pavilion." Out of this changing room, just before the start of the new owner's first match in charge, emerges Rovers' new centre-forward – Gorgeous Gus himself! While generally idling around the pitch during the game looking bored, much to the chagrin of the crowd, Gus somehow manages to score two (literally) net-busting goals. After the second one goes in Gus asks to leave the field – with 20 minutes still to go in the match – saying to the referee: "… I crave permission to retire. My presence is no longer necessary."

Redburn eventually win the league. Gus scores a hat-trick in the final match of the season, the championship decider, having missed the first half when his car broke down – he hires two cart-horses to pull him to the ground (28 October 1961). Gus's extraordinary feats continued to enthrall. As league champions, Redburn are invited to enter the European Cup (31 March 1962). In the first round Redburn win the away leg, with Gus netting five goals in five minutes. They reach the final, to be played at Hampden Park; unfortunately, Gus has a prior arrangement, a meeting with the King of Norvania at Holyrood. He plays the first five minutes and is then whisked away by helicopter. The king is informed of the situation during his meeting with Gus and gives him permission to return to the game, so Gus arrives back at Hampden by helicopter at half-time. Redburn are 3-1 down but with Gus back in the team they win 4–3.

Issue 81 of *Victor* saw the re-appearance of The Goalmaker (18 September 1962), a story that was first in *Wizard* in 1948. As with Gorgeous Gus, the yarn was

Below The Goalmaker, a footballing tale of the supernatural (18 September 1962)

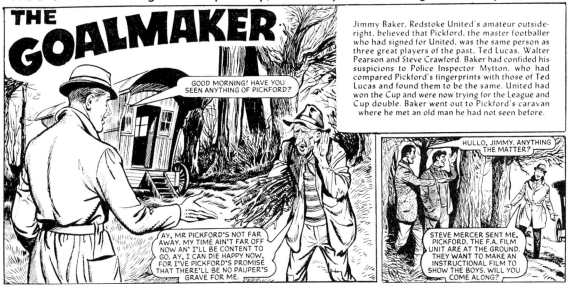

The Goalmaker plays the game of his life as United go all out to win the vital match that could clinch the League Championship, and complete the League and Cup double!

Above *Jag*'s Soccer School was designed to help readers improve their game with tips and hints on how to play (25 January 1969)

perfectly suited to the comic strip format, combining football and intrigue in a supernatural thriller about "a master footballer with a spine-chilling secret". It opens thus: "On the moors outside Redstoke stood a gipsy caravan. Beside it, a man called Pickford was displaying his amazing mastery of football." Pickford is muttering to himself as he juggles a football: "Ball control is the most important thing in football. All the great teams through the years have known that." Hanging in Pickford's caravan are photographs of three football teams: Prestford Wanderers in 1887, Rimthorpe Albion in 1912 and Lingbury Rovers in 1937. In each photograph is an inside-right who looks remarkably like Pickford... In the first episode, the gypsy heads off to Redstoke United's ground where he watches the team lose 1–0. "'Get five new forwards, United!'" yells a frustrated fan at the end. Pickford is more pensive: "'No. They need a goal maker. That will be me!'" After the match Steve Mercer, United's manager, and trainer Gil Thornton, head off to try to sign inside-right George Stretton from Manford Arsenal, who has been put on the transfer list. But the pair's race to get to Stretton before any other clubs beat them to it is thwarted by a gypsy caravan blocking the road – driven by Pickford. As the pair try to pass Pickford warns them: "'Don't sign on George Stretton. The poor chap will be dead within ten days!'" Having been delayed Mercer and Thornton just miss out on signing Stretton, and curse Pickford, vowing revenge. But sure enough, in his first match for his new club, coincidentally against Redstoke, Stretton has a heart attack and dies on the field. Later, Pickford turns up at Redstoke's ground demanding a trial. Mercer agrees, instructing his players to rough Pickford up; but the gypsy's brilliant display in the trial means the club has no option but to sign him up. Pickford becomes "the goalmaker" for Redstock United, where his similarities to the stars of the past does not go unnoticed. It seems as though Pickford is the incarnation of the dead footballers.

The story comes to a climax in issue 100 (19 January 1963), when Redstoke

Below The Goalmaker, a.k.a. Pickford, in action (19 January 1963). See page 218

Rovers equalised just before half-time. On the resumption, United had another bit of bad luck . . .

FOUL!

WHAT A LUCKY GOAL! THAT BLOOMING BALL BENT BACK!

IT'S GOALS THAT COUNT

Your old favourite, Nick Smith, returns in a great new football story of the club that had loads of money, a super ground, a poor team and no support!

win the league and Cup double. Pickford dies on the pitch and his body is claimed by mysterious "People of the Phoenix".

Victor was an immediate hit with readers; its mix of comic strip stories and features on real footballers (its "When he was a boy" section featured the likes of Spurs' "Bobby Smith – the story of the football mad lad whose Yorkshire grit took him to the top line of football fame" (22 December 1962), proved a winning combination in the early part of the decade.

Hornet, too, was an immediate hit. It also featured some old friends, with the scrap-metal dealing "Bouncing Briggs" (in issue 1, 14 September 1963), and Nick Smith, from the "It's Goals That Count" series, "transferring" from *Wizard*. Bernard "Bouncing" Briggs, it seems, had become an even better player than he was in the pages of *Wizard*; he achieves the ultimate goalkeeping feat by going through the entire season with Blackton Rovers without conceding a goal! Searching for a new challenge, Briggs later signs for Bradstoke Town FC, the worst club in the country (3 October 1964). Briggs's arrival sees gates increase from 2,000 to 8,000, and remarkably under Bernard's captaincy the

Above The ubiquitous Nick Smith bangs in another yet goal (*Hornet*, 31 December 1966)

THE LEFT-FOOTED CHICKEN

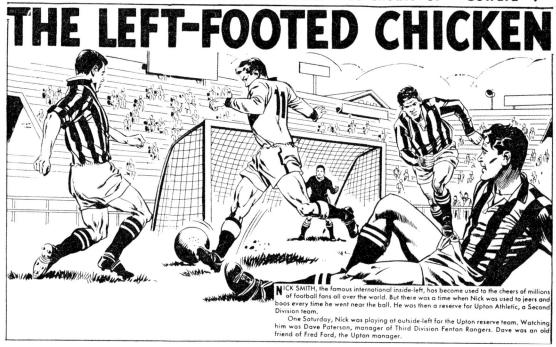

NICK SMITH, the famous international inside-left, has become used to the cheers of millions of football fans all over the world. But there was a time when Nick was used to jeers and boos every time he went near the ball. He was then a reserve for Upton Athletic, a Second Division team.

One Saturday, Nick was playing at outside-left for the Upton reserve team. Watching him was Dave Paterson, manager of Third Division Fenton Rangers. Dave was an old friend of Fred Ford, the Upton manager.

This and facing page It's Goals That Count... Nick Smith in action in the stories "The Left-Footed Chicken" (above); "The Goalie's Name was Muggins" (below); and "The Seven Men of Bellford" (opposite)

club reach the semi-final of the FA Cup (21 January 1965). He also proved something of a sporting all-rounder, also playing cricket and rugby.

Meanwhile, Nick Smith, international inside-left, has been transferred from his old club, Stonebury Arsenal, to Chidsea (and from the pages of late-1940s' *Rover*). Chidsea have managed to just avoid relegation for the past four seasons; Smith is the man to turn around the club's fortunes by bringing in his friends, including Arnold Tabbs (5 December 1964). For the first time Nick Smith's adventures were in comic strip format; and the character was to become one of the most popular and durable for the remainder of the 1960s (and beyond).

In 1965, Nick became player-manager of Third Division strugglers Kingsbury Rovers, although he has to part company with close pal Arnold Tabbs (1 January 1965). Life is very different for Nick in the lower reaches of the Football League; on his first day in charge he finds the players warming up for the new season by starting a card school in the dressing-room. Nick has his work cut out, but gradually transforms a team of no-hopers into a team of fighters – helped by the signing of one Arnold Tabbs! As a player-manager Nick Smith was years ahead of his time. During Rovers' cup run he enlists the help of Sir Henry

Tuxford, "the famous scientist in charge of the Atomic Research Station near Kingsbury. Sir Henry's hobby was football…" (10 July 1965). He tells the football manager: "'I've watched five of your recent matches, and at each of them I plotted a graph. The striking thing is that the graphs of the five games showed an astounding similarity. And from them I was able to construct the general graph you see on the wall.' He continues: 'As you can see from the graph, you start strongly then you are pressed back. As the interval draws near, you seem to find a fresh lot of steam, and give your opponents a hammering. After half-time you are on top form for a while, then you slump, but not badly, and have recovered by three-quarter-time. Then you suffer a dreadful drop, to come back with a vengeance at the approach of time.'" Smith is astounded and intrigued: "'Gosh, this is near the mark. I can see where Hamborough scored their goal – and where we put on the pressure that led to ours!'" Armed with the professor's statistics, progress for Kingsbury Rovers is assured – 35 years before Prozone was invented.

Nick Smith's "career" generated a huge number of stories. His back-story was the theme for many of the comic's football stories. Three such tales appeared in December 1965: "The Seven Men of Bellford" (4 December 1965); "The Left-Footed Chicken" (11 December 1965); and "The Goalie's Name was Muggins" (18 December 1965). "The Seven Men of Bellford" went back to Smith's earlier footballing days when he played for Bellford United. The team endured a disastrous run of bad luck and injuries; the ref accidently "headed" a goal for the opposition and in the next fixture Bellford's injury jinx struck again and the team had to play the second half of a crucial relegation battle with just seven men!

"The Left-Footed Chicken" also harked back, to a time when as a young inside-left for Upton "Nick was used to jeers and boos every time he went near the ball". The reason, as explained by Upton manager Fred Ford: "'Smith is good all right but he'll never play in the first team. He just doesn't have the heart.'" As the game progresses Ford adds: "'He's afraid of taking a hard knock. They call him 'chicken' here.'" But during the game Nick gets a blow on the head and is concussed. When he returns to play he tackles like a demon. It transpires that

If you get into the penalty area with the ball and the goalie's running out, don't just blaze away and miss. Lob it over his head so that it drops into the net.

Above If you want to be a pro... Learn to Play the Roy Race Way, from the *Roy of Rovers Annual* 1962

Right The Scarlet Hawks were "The Team of the Doomed" (8 January 1966)

he shied away from tackles because in his early days during a match he had gone in hard on an opponent and broken his leg.

"The Goalie's Name was Muggins" featured a mysterious goalkeeper who came to the rescue of Brendon Rovers; he was really world-famous ballet dancer Ernesto Palladino, playing under an asssumed name to protect his anonymity. All these retrospectives were complete stories, as was "The Winger from Pit 19" (1 January 1966). It told the sad tale of Joe Devitt, a young miner who played just one game for First Division Hillstock Rovers. Having had a successful trial Joe is picked for the first eleven but is involved in a mining cave-in, damaging his leg. He plays in the game, scoring the winner, but in the process further damages his leg. Told by the club doctor he will never play again, he says: "'I don't care. I've had my day in the sun. I've played for Rovers.'" The story is a poignant reminder of how fragile the career of a professional footballer can be.

Two aspiring footballers from vasty different backgrounds featured in **Hornet**, "The Wonder of Winter Island" (4 January 1964) and "No Game for Jimmy" (5 September 1964). In the former, young Gordon Jones, growing up on Winter Island, had a burning ambition to be a footballer. Gordon retrieves a hamper which washes up on the shores of the island containing football kit and balls. Despite the fact Gordon's strict father refuses to allow him to play – "Winter Island people must work" – Gordon teaches himself to play football. When a volcano erupts on Winter Island the residents are evacuated to England, and Gordon is seen practising by Walter Harrow, manager of Third Division Portsea. Knowing a good PR opportunity when he sees it, Harrow invites him to sign, and Gordon sees his first football stadium on his 16th birthday.

Gordon is invited to sign on to the ground staff of Everley Rovers; he helps

THE TEAM OF THE DOOMED!

The Scarlet Hawks have the strangest strips in soccer—but it cost the lives of eleven men to get them!

THE SCARLET HAWKS, THE FAMOUS FIRST DIVISION CLUB, HAVE ONE OF THE MOST UNUSUAL STRIPS IN SOCCER—A WHITE SHIRT WITH THE DESIGN OF A LARGE, FLYING HAWK ON THE CHEST. BUT IT WAS NOT ALWAYS SO. AT ONE TIME THEY ONLY WORE A SMALL BADGE. THE CHANGE CAME IN SEASON 1935–36 WHEN THE HAWKS WERE INVITED TO PLAY DIE FALKEN, THE CHAMPIONS OF GERMANY. AT THAT TIME, GERMANY WAS RULED BY ADOLF HITLER, LEADER OF THE NAZI PARTY. HITLER WAS TO BE AT THE GAME...

LOOK, THEIR BADGE IS THE SAME AS OURS, ONLY BIGGER.

YES, DIE FALKEN MEANS 'THE FALCONS' IN ENGLISH. LOOK OUT, HERE COMES HITLER!

THE HAWKS WERE PRESENTED TO HITLER BY BILL TOFT THEIR CENTRE-HALF AND CAPTAIN.

THEN, OUT OF SIGHT OF THE CROWD...

AAGH!

GOSH, SOMEBODY HAS TRIED TO ASSASSINATE HITLER! THEY MUST HAVE USED A SILENCED RIFLE!

YOU SAW NOTHING, UNDERSTAND? NOTHING!

BILL WAS CALLED TO TOSS UP WITH CARL HESSEN, THE GERMAN CENTRE-FORWARD AND CAPTAIN.

HESSEN LOOKS WORRIED. I WONDER IF HE KNOWS ANYTHING.

BILL LOST SO JOCK WATSON KICKED OFF FOR THE HAWKS, WHO IMMEDIATELY ATTACKED DOWN THE LEFT.

WE'VE SCORED WITHOUT A GERMAN PLAYER TOUCHING THE BALL, YET THERE ISN'T A MURMUR FROM THE CROWD. I'VE NEVER EXPERIENCED ANYTHING LIKE IT BEFORE!

them win the Youth Cup. Eventually he plays for the first team, helping Everley to win the FA Cup and the European Cup.

In "No Game for Jimmy", orphan Jimmy Brewster wants to play football but has to help his evil uncle delivering groceries. Enter "the amazing mysterious Crutchy Martin", an invalid who works as a nightwatchman and also watches football. He decides Jimmy has a special talent – after watching him deliver newspapers, Crutchy takes Jimmy under his wing. When Jimmy's uncle discovers he has been playing football he carries out an earlier threat and sends him to an orphanage. Fortunately, thanks to dedicated coaching and encouragement from Crutchy, Jimmy develops confidence in his game and signs for a professional club. The final twist is that Crutchy is in fact Grant Martin, the only Englishman to have played for Madrid All Stars.

One story, "The Hoodoo at Number Nine" (24 January 1964), a story of the Scarlet Hawks football club, is reminiscent of the Derby County versus Charlton Athletic Cup final of 1946, as mentioned in the previous chapter. The Hawks are cursed by a gypsy, the ball bursts twice in the match, a spectator stops the ball crossing the line and a goal goes in off the referee!

The Scarlet Hawks reappeared in *Hornet* in a complete story called "The Team of the Doomed" (8 January 1966). Set in pre-war Germany, the team is

Right Dozy Danny in comic strip format (*New Hotspur*, 10 September 1960). See page 218

Below Stan Rankin scored "The Goals That Nobody Cheered" (*Hornet*, 16 December 1967)

invited to fly to play Hitler's favourite team, Die Falken, in a game exclusively for the Fuhrer's entertainment. During the course of the game the German captain informs the Hawks that if they win, they will be killed, along with the players of Die Falken. The Hawks make a dramatic escape. This "Team of the

NOW IS MY CHANCE TO SCORE IF I CAN BEAT THE 'KEEPER TO THE BALL.

Doomed" is in no way related to the team of the same name that appeared in *Hotspur* a decade earlier.

Not all the new comics were a roaring success. *Hurricane*, launched on 29 February 1964, lasted just over a year before being merged with *Tiger*. Its one notable story was "Hurry of the Hammers" (4 July 1964), about Limstone Youth player Harry Cane who went on to sign for the famous Hammersfield Hammers. It was notable only in that it was an exact reprint of the artwork from the first Roy of the Rovers story, published some 11 years previously. Only the names were changed.

While some of the newcomers were shortlived, long-established *Hotspur* – renamed *New Hotspur* from 24 October 1959 – continued to prosper, adapting to the changing times with the introduction of more and more comic strips. The progress of Dozy Danny (see previous

DOZY DANNY

DOZY DANNY LORIMER, a fifteen-year-old Mancaster schoolboy, was in his second year as an English boy international footballer. Dozy got his nickname from his habit of snatching "forty winks" whenever he could

Wembley The English Schoolboys were playing a Spanish Schoolboys team

Because of his age this would be Dozy's last School international. He raced in on the Spanish goal

—and scored a great goal!

Among the huge crowd were several senior football club managers

HIS SECOND GOAL! DOZY IS THE BEST BOY CENTRE-FORWARD I'VE EVER SEEN.

YOU'LL BE AFTER HIM, I SUPPOSE! YOU WON'T GET IT ALL YOUR OWN WAY, PAUL. I WANT HIM, TOO!

Dozy was superb. His football brain tied the Spanish defence in knots.

WHAT A SAVE! DOZY GAVE HIS INSIDE FORWARD A GREAT OPENING—HE SHOULD HAVE SCORED.

LOOK! DOZY'S FOLLOWING IN. HE'LL GET IT!

Dozy, as good with his head as with both feet, thumped the rebounding ball past the helpless 'keeper to complete his hat-trick.

GOAL!

When the game ended. Dozy exchanged shirts with the Spanish captain.

THANKS FOR A GREAT GAME!

HELLO, LORIMER. I'M PAUL HEADLEY, MANAGER OF LONDON ALBION. YOU PLAYED A FINE GAME, SON.

THANKS, MR HEADLEY. I'VE SEEN YOUR PICTURE OFTEN, AND I'VE SEEN THE ALBION PLAY AT MANCASTER.

chapter) continued in picture strip format (10 September 1960). Now 15, Danny is an established England schoolboy international, his habit of nodding off now caused not by a vicious stepfather but by his devotions to his study.

But nothing is straightforward for our Danny. He is finally offered professional terms with Mancaster United on his 17th birthday and he accepts, providing he is allowed to continue studying (26 August 1961). Unfortunately, no sooner is the deal agreed than the ground burns down. The directors and half the players, who are attending a meeting, are killed. The ground staff boys are dismissed as a cost-cutting exercise by the new chairman, Amos Carter, but Danny promises: "'The United will rise again someday, and when it does I'll be around ready to play.'" Life seems to have come full circle for Dozy when he gets a job making coal briquettes, but things look brighter when he is invited to play in a youth team with his friend Lampy Flack, who he is in business with. While playing in the game he is seen by Liverport Rovers and invited to attend a trial. Work and studies mean he arrives tired and fails to impress. The drama continues. Danny gets another chance when spotted by First Division Brummagen City. Again he performs badly, but is offered a second game. However, this fixtures clashes with a college game, and he chooses to play for the educational establishment. Eventually, he is invited by Mancaster Rangers to play in a charity game against Mancaster United. He is offered terms by Rangers but returns to Mancaster United despite Amos Carter's presence. Lampy also signs, and both are picked by England Under–23s. Finally all comes good; Danny passes his exams, and on the last day of the season United win 9-0 to avoid relegation. Life is never dull for Danny.

As well as Dozy Danny, two other *Hotspur* heroes' adventures were given a new lease of life when their stories were produced in comic strip format. "Biffalo Bill" – "the biggest bloke in football" – got a fresh start (14 December 1963). He gets his big break by filling in for a practice match – "'A game? But this is a

Right Hotshot Hawkins
(*Hotspur*, 30 March 1963)

Below Dozy Danny gets a taste
for the big time (*Hotspur*,
10 September 1960)

THE BOMBER THAT DROPPED A FOOTBALL BOMBSHELL ON HAMPDEN PARK.

HOTSHOT HAWKINS

HOTSHOT HAWKINS, a brilliant young English footballer, played for the Italian club, Torina. He was also an apprentice locksmith at Torina Locks. Torina were due to play Bruntfield Hotspur at Hampden Park, Glasgow, in the final of the European Cup, but on the day of the final, Hotshot had been set a test by the Locksmith's Union!

HERE COME SIGNOR GRANDI, THE FOREMAN, AND SIGNOR FRANCHI, THE MANAGER. THAT'S MY TEST FINISHED, BUT I'LL NEVER GET TO GLASGOW.

COME ON, HOTSHOT. WE'VE NO TIME TO LOSE.

I'LL SEAL YOUR APPRENTICES TEST IN THE BOX, HOTSHOT. BEST OF LUCK IN SCOTLAND.

I CAN'T GET TO HAMPDEN IN FOUR HOURS!

THIS ISN'T THE WAY TO TORINA AIRPORT? SIGNOR FRANCHI!

THAT'S BECAUSE WE'RE NOT GOING THERE, HOTSHOT.

Later.

'GOOD LUCK, HOTSHOT.

THE ITALIAN AIR FORCE!

IT WILL BE AN HONOUR FOR ITALY IF TORINA WIN TODAY. THE AIR FORCE WILL TAKE YOU TO GLASGOW. IT'S ALL ARRANGED!

WE ARE OVER PRESTWICK NOW, SIGNOR HAWKINS.

TWO HOURS, FIFTEEN MINUTES! SOME GOING!

THIS HELICOPTER WILL TAKE YOU TO RENFREW, WHICH IS MUCH CLOSER TO HAMPDEN.

I'M BEGINNING TO BELIEVE I'LL PLAY AFTER ALL.

THAT'S HAMPDEN DOWN THERE. SORRY I CAN'T DROP YOU ON THE PITCH!

NEVER MIND. WE'VE GOT FORTY-FIVE MINUTES BEFORE KICK OFF!

A MOTOR CYCLE WILL BE QUICKER THAN A CAR. THE ROADS ARE JAMMED—HALF OF SCOTLAND IS TRYING TO GET TO HAMPDEN.

HERE YOU ARE HOTSHOT, WITH TWENTY MINUTES TO SPARE!

THANKS A LOT, MATE. I HOPE THE RUSH WAS WORTH IT.

MEET LESLIE TOMSON, A YOUNG LAME LAD WITH TWO BURNING AMBITIONS—TO PLAY FIRST-CLASS FOOTBALL AND TO TRAIN A CHAMPION SHEEPDOG!

LIMP ALONG LESLIE

GOOD GIRL, LIZA, STAY THERE!

LESLIE TOMSON, an orphan lad of 14, lived with his uncle and aunt, Mr and Mrs Dan Smith, at a farm near Dalestone, in the Lake District. An accident in infancy had left Les with a short left leg, but that didn't stop him from practising football. He had uncanny ball control and spent every spare minute with a football.

Watching intently was Liza, one of the sheepdogs.

Les could trap the ball from any angle.

I'D BETTER GET MY CHORES DONE BEFORE UNCLE AND AUNT COME HOME. I'VE GOT PLENTY TO DO.

Les did his full share of jobs on the farm. His lameness was no handicap to him.

Leslie's own bedroom was like a sports' gallery. There he displayed the medals, caps and honours won by his father, the late John Tomson, who had been a star player for the famous Rangers.

JOHN TOMSON'S GENIUS AND GENERALSHIP GIVE RANGERS VICTORY.
HE PLAYED SUCH A SUPERIOR BRAND OF FOOTBALL THAT HE WALKED THROUGH THE GAME.

THE NEWSPAPER CUTTING SAYS HE WALKED THROUGH THE GAME. IF I CAN MAKE THE BALL DO THE WORK, MY BAD LEG WON'T AFFECT MY GAME.

SOME DAY I'LL DO WHAT MY FATHER DID! I'LL PLAY FOR THE RANGERS AND TRAIN A CHAMPION SHEEPDOG!

A week later, Les had started supper with his aunt and uncle, when his cousins, Edgar and Fred Smith, came in from their work.

TAKE THEM DOWN TO THE RIVER!

LIZA'S DEAD, DAD! WHAT'LL WE DO WITH HER PUPS? THEY DON'T LOOK ANYTHING WORTH TO ME!

YOU CAN'T DO THAT! LIZA'S PUPS ARE THE LAST OF SKIPPER'S STRAIN—

YOU MIND YOUR OWN BUSINESS, LES! WE CAN'T AFFORD TO KEEP WEAKLINGS—THEY'D BE A BAD ADVERTISEMENT!

First Division team – but we're one short! You can join in!'" – while carrying out repairs with two fellow workmen at the ground of Bramington Albion. Curiously, Biffalo's surname changed from the 1950s' Willis to the 1960s' Bradley, and the team are now Albion rather than Wanderers; other than that, the stories are pretty much identical.

Limp-Along Leslie's return to *New Hotspur* (1 September 1962) represented the first time his adventures were represented in comic strip format. But his ambitions had not changed: "'Some day I'll do what my father did. I'll play for the Rangers and train a champion sheepdog!'"

He manages to secure a trial at Danbury Rangers, but the childhood accident that left him with a short left leg leads Richard Strake, the club's manager, to doubt that Leslie can make it to the top. Disappointed, Leslie has a trial with Dalestone and District School Association, impresses, and is selected to play. At the same time he gets a job working for Major Keene, the owner of one of the largest sheep farms in the district, following a second place in a sheepdog trial, and he is offered the chance of a job in Australia. His performances for Dalestone School put him back on Danbury Rangers' radar and he is offered a trial. Boss Strake admits: "'I've been a fool not to have recognised your ability. I've never seen a better inside forward play than I saw today. You're not going to Australia Les! I'll see to that! I'm going to keep an eye on you – and one day

Left *New Hotspur* welcomed an old favourite with the first comic strip outing for Limp-Along Leslie (1 September 1962)

Below Biffalo Bill's first comic strip story (14 December 1963)

155

Above New signing Algernon Simms enters the field of play in Legge's Eleven (*Valiant*, 12 December 1964)

Below Iron Man Martin of Brenton Albion (*Jag*, 1 February 1969)

you'll play for Rangers like your dad.'" And his dream comes true; he plays for Rangers against Tottenly Hotspurs and scores the winner in his first game.

As well as the reappeareance of many an old favourite, there were plenty of new characters, too. Hotshot Hawkins (6 October 1962) was spotted by Nat Allison, a football scout employed by First Division club Brunton City, not on the pitch put in a public park, performing acrobatics on the crossbar. Young Hotshot was unorthodox in his goalkeeping, too; the youngster played an unorthodox game using his head and feet to defend his goal rather than his hands. He is offered a trial at City, whose owner also owns Brunton Locks. By coincidence Hawkins is an apprentice locksmith, and this allows him to continue his apprenticeship. But Hotshot fails to impress at Brunton City and is rejected; then by chance he plays centre-forward for the Brunton Locks team and scores four goals. Interestingly, Hotshot's next club is in Italy – thanks to scout Allinson, he goes to play for Italian club, Torina. In the real world Manchester City's Denis Law had been transferred to Italian giants Torino in 1961, while Jimmy Greaves joined AC Milan in the same year. Both had short, unhappy spells on the continent, but Hotshot Hawkins had better luck; he scores against Roma in 10 seconds, going on to complete a hat-trick. He scores another hat-trick in a European Cup tie as Torina progress and at Hampden Park in the European Cup final he nets six times!

While the comics slowly morphed throughout the 1960s, becoming more picture strip-dominated as the decade progressed, the past was frequently mined for suitable storylines. One such, "The Team from Nowhere", appeared in *Victor* on 20 February 1965. It was similar to many stories that had previously appeared, involving the Corsairs: "They don't play in a league. They are a private team belonging to Mr Betram Zeff. He built the stadium and found all of the players. None of the players had been heard of before Mr Zeff found them, and they are beating all of the best teams in the world." In fact, in Zeff's laboratory, his sidekicks Orr and Kinley have developed a machine which can transfer skill from one man to another. Kidnapping quality players, he transfers their skills to vagrants, to create his wonder team. In the denouement, Zeff's scheme is uncovered and he commits suicide (17 April 1965).

While the comics subtly reflected what was happening in the wider football world, in 1966 they showcased an event like never before. The World Cup in England attracted the comic's attention like no previous football event. The traditional free gifts included "World Cup Scorebooks" and "World Cup Badges" and wallcharts galore. International football was in the spotlight in a big way; and the comics, as always, took a novel approach. In *Victor*, football's favourite aristocrat Gorgeous Gus turned his attention to the big event. The

Above Advertisers were keen to tap into the growing readership of the boys' comics, as this advert for the RAF shows (*Hornet*, (3 December 1966)

World Cup is discussed thus: "The way the preliminary contests will be arranged, it is possible that Scotland, Russia, West Germany and Italy, all capable of winning the trophy, could be drawn to play one another. So three top countries could be eliminated while Korea or Egypt could get through to the final competition. The arrangement is ridiculous" (21 May 1966). Gus is offered a "backdoor" route to Jules Rimet glory when he unexpectedly becomes king of Gannet Island following the death of his uncle. Gus immediately registers Gannet Island with FIFA and enters the World Cup. Gannet Island are drawn in the qualifying rounds against Albavia, Danemark and Tyrolia, and qualify for the finals – where they lose to England in the final. That "World Cup Final" took place in the issue dated 30 July 1966 – the actual day England won the World Cup at Wembley.

And Legge's Eleven, in *Valiant*, were also seeing international action – in 1966 they played and beat the Brazilian "World Cup" holders, Grazia.

In *Hornet*, our old pal Nick Smith turns his attention away from domestic football. Not to the World Cup, though; Granton United, as English First Division champions, had gained admission to the newly formed "World League", which included clubs from Brazil, Germany, Hungary, France, Austria, Spain, Russia, Uruguay and Scotland (14 May 1966). During the close season the directors of Granton had given the club's cheque book to manager George Coker, and told him to spend what he needs to. Coker then shells out £500,000 in filling his all-international team with soccer stars. The players brought in included Nick Smith and Arnold Tabbs, who both had many England caps.

But mystery surrounds Granton's goalkeeper, J.P. Sedley, an amateur who was unknown before the start of the season. Nick and Arnold are convinced he is Roger Crogden, a half-back who played for Manford City and England before the war. In the final, Granton beat German side Wassen to win the World League. In the course of the match Sedley receives a bang on the head, and his memory returns; he is Jack Dellard, an England centre-forward.

Nick Smith must surely have been the most travelled football player in comic history. He turns up again in the story of a club that has loads of money to spend and a super stadium, but the team is poor – and it has no support (31 December 1966). Blackford is a rugby league town, with no interest in football. However, the England international is approached by Sampson P. Brill, President of the Vanex Corporation of America, who is opening a factory in Blackford. He wants to make Blackford one of the best-known towns in England, and having a top football team is part of the strategy. Brill buys Second Division Blackford Wanderers and signs Nick as player-manager. Naturally, Nick signs up his old mate Arnold Tabbs. In addition to recognised players he also signs various sportsmen including a cricketer, a rugby player and a boxer.

Drawn in the cup against non-league Mottisford, Nick Smith's task is not made easier by a serious injury list. For "Mottisford's goalkeeper is West Indian. He claims he can put a jinx on opposing teams – and the two previous clubs they have played against have had players

Right Our old friend William "Fatty" Foulke makes a welcome appearance on the cover of *Valiant*

Below If You Were Ref… what decision would you give? *Roy of the Rovers Annual* 1962

6: FROM A HARD SHOT THE BALL STRIKES THE UNDERSIDE OF THE CROSSBAR AND BOUNCES OUT. THE FANS YELL "GOAL!" WHAT DO YOU THINK?

FREE INSIDE— LEAGUE LADDER TEAM CARDS

VALIANT

6ᵈ

COMPANION PAPER TO *Hurricane*

EVERY MONDAY

THE GREATEST...

3rd OCTOBER, 1964

A WEEKLY SERIES OF
STARTLING WORLD RECORDS

FOOTBALLERS

THE OLDEST PLAYER IN FOOTBALL TODAY IS THE LEGENDARY STANLEY MATTHEWS! NOW IN HIS 50th YEAR, STAN JOINED STOKE CITY AT 15 AS GROUND-BOY BEFORE MOVING TO BLACKPOOL TO PLAY THE GAME OF A LIFETIME AND WIN A COVETED CUP-WINNER'S MEDAL IN 1953. HE PLAYED 84 TIMES FOR ENGLAND (INCLUDING WARTIME), AND IS NOW BACK WITH STOKE—TRULY THE GREATEST RIGHT WINGER OF ALL TIME!

THE MOST HIGHLY-PAID FOOTBALLER IN THE WORLD... SCORER OF OVER 700 GOALS FOR CLUB AND COUNTRY... "BRAZIL PLAYER OF THE YEAR" SIX TIMES IN SUCCESSION! THIS REMARKABLE ACHIEVEMENT BELONGS TO ONE PLAYER — EDISON ARANTES DE NASCIMENTO — BETTER KNOWN AS THE FABULOUS "PELE" OF SANTOS AND BRAZIL! TO DATE, HIS PRESENTS FROM ADMIRERS INCLUDE FIVE CARS AND SEVERAL HOUSES!

WEIGHT 22 STONE... HEIGHT 6 FEET 3 INS! THAT DESCRIPTION MAKES WILLIE FOULKE THE BIGGEST FOOTBALLER EVER! ALWAYS KNOWN AS "FATTY", THIS GIANT GOALKEEPER REPRESENTED ENGLAND IN 1897, WON CUP MEDALS WITH SHEFFIELD UNITED IN 1899 AND 1902... AND NATURALLY WAS A BIG FAVOURITE WITH THE FANS!

© Fleetway Publications Ltd., 1964

A JOLT FOR JOHNNIE FROM BOBBY MOORE

JOHNNIE CAN'T KEEP GOING

PETE ALWAYS BEATS YOU, JOHNNIE!

HEY, FELLOWS – IT'S BOBBY MOORE

WHAT'S THE TROUBLE, JOHNNIE. OUT OF SHAPE?

I DON'T KNOW–JUST DIDN'T HAVE ANY WIND!

IT'S THOSE FAGS, JOHNNIE. I TOLD YOU A MILLION TIMES

DON'T YOU SMOKE, MR. MOORE?

CIGARETTES, EH? NO WONDER, WORST THING YOU COULD DO

NOT ME, JOHNNIE. THEY GET YOUR WIND AND CUT YOUR STAMINA. YOU ASK ANY ATHLETE

TAKE A TIP FROM ME THE BEST WAY TO "QUIT" SMOKING IS NEVER TO START

BOBBY MOORE – ENGLAND & WEST HAM STAR

Inserted by The Ministry of Health

Above Star players – including England captain Bobby Moore – advertised everything from football boots to bubble gum to anti-smoking campaigns (*Hornet*, 6 March 1955)

Below Stan Rankin in action in "The Goals That Nobody Cheered"

carried off with serious injuries." But Wanderers win the day, with Blackford going on to win the Second Division and the FA Cup. Arnold Tabbs is as busy as Nick Smith – at this time he is appearing in two serials in the same comic, also featuring in "The Blitz Kid".

As the 1960s progressed, many of the comic strip footballers began to reflect the flamboyance and flair of the real-life footballers who were grabbing the headlines. A new breed of players – sometimes called misfits, sometimes called rock 'n' roll footballers – were illuminating the game with their brilliance, epitomised by the likes of George Best, Rodney Marsh and Frank Worthington. They brought a new attitude to the game, elevating skill, flair and originality above the traditional virtues of running and tackling. Love them or hate them, football fans could not ignore them. One story that reflected this new breed of players was *Hornet*'s "The Ball of Fire" (2 September 1967). Fans nicknamed Wally Brand "The Ball of Fire" because "for setting the game alight, there was no one like this brilliant, controversial, goal-grabbing England centre-forward". Bought by Brickley Albion for a record fee, Brand is his own man and does things his way – including skipping training when he feels like it. But this does not mean he is afraid of hard work; Brand is often on the training ground practising his skills long after his team mates have gone home.

Another controversial figure was Stan Rankin, who appeared in "The Goals That Nobody Cheered" (16 December 1967). As centre-forward of Hampton Town, Rankin made the headlines when in a match against Bramley Albion he accidentally kicked Jeff Westwood in

THIS IS MORE LIKE TEAM-WORK.

the head in a goalmouth scrimmage. Westwood dies, but the coroner clears Stan of any blame. Tragically, the following week, in a match against Castleford United, Rankin is involved in another collision and Morrison, the Castleford goalkeeper, also dies. The crowd react badly on hearing the news and the board sack him. But Rankin is determined to clear his name and prove himself the most brilliant goal-getter in the game. Eventually, using money from a property sale, he buys the majority shareholding in Hampton and makes himself player-manager. Despite scoring twice in a 2–0 win in in his first game in charge, the fans refuse to cheer Rankin.

His problems get worse. Jim Westwood, the brother of Jeff, plays against Hampton Town and collapses on the pitch, with Rankin accused of injuring him deliberately. It transpires that the goalie had an infection, and only a stadium announcement stops a riot.

Rankin is a marked man – every time Rankin goes near a goalkeeper he is accused of unfair play. Eventually, an FA inquiry into his style of play clears him of the death of the two goalkeepers, and Rankin is offered a fresh start with the opportunity to play in Italy. While there he stages a charity match with Italian champions, Coletta, with the proceeds going to the families of the two keepers.

Below The Mystery Man at Inside-Left in action, in the pages of *Victor*

From the kick-off, the City launched an attack.

JUST MADE IT.

I HOPE SPARKY'S NOT TOO FLUSTERED AFTER HIS RUSH ON TO THE FIELD AND CAN DO SOMETHING WITH THIS PASS.

WELL DONE, SPARKY. YOU NEVER WASTE CHANCES TO SCORE.

Shortly before half-time, with the City still leading 1-0, Buster Hardy tried to stop a German attack.

DRAT IT! THERE GOES THE EQUALISER!

AL KATRAZ JOINED IN THE ARGUMENT!
AND IF YOU'VE ANY IDEAS ABOUT PLAYING THIS GIPSY KID... FORGET 'EM! THE STATE HE'S IN WITH ALL THIS FORTUNE-TELLING STUFF, HE'D BE A BIGGER DANGER TO US THEN GLENKIRK!
THAT'S JUST WHERE YOU'RE WRONG, CHUM! YOU SEE, I'VE MANAGED TO SORT OUT RAVEN'S PROBLEMS..!
TRIUMPHANTLY, BALDY EXPLAINED HOW HE HAD RESTORED RAVEN'S CONFIDENCE, WITH THE HELP OF THE PHOTOGRAPHS!
SO EVEN THOUGH LARRY VINCENT MAY BE THE FAIR-HAIRED EVIL-BRINGER, HE AIN'T GOT NO POWER OVER ME! OI AIN'T A-FEARED OF 'IM NO MORE!
THAT'S IT, RAVEN ...YOU TELL HIM!
B-BUT, I...I...!

Above Raven on the Wing in another confrontation with his nemesis, Al Katraz

Right The Football Family Robinson were cover stars in the short-lived *Jag*

While the "outsider" was not a new character – in fact, the character-type dates from the earliest boys' story-papers – there was certainly many variations on the theme in the 1960s. Two of them were Raven on the Wing (***Valiant*** 1968–72) and The Mystery Man at Inside-Left (***Victor***, 1 October 1966). Raven was a mysterious figure whose trademark was playing in bare feet. A gypsy, he was discovered by Baldy Hagan, manager of Highboro United, a struggling First Division team with a losing habit. Hagen was sent by Highboro chairman Sir Mortimer Child-Beale to disperse a gypsy tribe camping on Noakes Heath, the team's training ground. There Baldy sees a barefooted boy scoring goal after goal, to the wrath of his mates. Baldy saves the boy from his bullying Uncle Joe and gives him a trial in a third-team game. "'Swipe me, if it ain't a bare-footed wonder', they sneered, but the Lengro lad was soon a brilliant left winger."

"The Mystery Man at Inside-Left" was "the thrill-packed story of Midford City's inside-left, Sgt "Sparky" Morton, and the secret he holds which makes him the target of a deadly spy ring". A James Bond-type figure, one moment he is saving the life of a colleague; the next he is playing for Midford City, the Football League champions, against the German champions Munsterhaven in the European Cup. After the game Morton meets with the mysterious, deerstalker-wearing Colonel Lockwood, who asks Morton to forego his demob and stay with the service. Lockwood explains: "'Your football can be used as a cloak to conceal

JAG

29th MARCH 1969
EVERY SATURDAY

7ᴰ

Australia 10c; New Zealand 10c; South Africa 10c; Rhodesia 1/0d; East Africa 1/0d; West Africa 1/0d; Malaysia 40c; Barbados 25c; Canada 15c; Denmark Kr. 1.85; Finland FM. 60; Germany DM. .55; Greece Dr. 4; Guyana 25s; Holland Fl. .65; Italy Lire 120; Malta 9d; Norway Kr. 1.25; Portugal Esc. 5 00; Sierra Leone 10c; Spain Pes. 10; Sweden Kr. .75 inkl. moms; Thailand Bahts 2.25; Philippines Pesos .50.

THATCHEM UNITED, A STRUGGLING CLUB IN THE FOURTH DIVISION, WAS OWNED AND RUN BY FRED ROBINSON AND HIS FAMILY. THE CLUB NEEDED ONLY TWO POINTS FOR PROMOTION, BUT WAS TRAILING 0–1 IN A HOME MATCH AGAINST RELEGATION-CANDIDATES, KNIBSWORTH. THEN THE VISITORS FELL BACK ON DEFENCE...

FOOTBALL FAMILY ROBINSON

HALF-TIME CAME WITH THATCHEM STILL A GOAL DOWN. MA ROBINSON GAVE THE PLAYERS THE ROUGH EDGE OF HER TONGUE.

THE ROBINS OPENED THE SECOND HALF WITH TACTICS THAT MADE THEIR SUPPORTERS IMPATIENT...

CONTINUED OVERLEAF.

your real job from the spies who are interested in Project X. Will you help us and your country? You have the reactions which the job demands.'" Comes the reply: "'Since you put it that way, Sir, all I can do is accept. It looks as if I'm going to have a very interesting life from now on.'"

Sparky eventually wins a rare honour among the comic footballers – the OBE. He is awarded the gong after foiling an Eastern European plot to plant atomic bombs in selected sites in Britain and Europe (7 January 1967). Sparky survives several assassination attempts, while at the same time winning the FA Cup with Midford City and scoring the winning goal in the European Cup final.

By the late 1960s, the established comics had an iron grip on the market. Even the comic-publishing giants had no guarantees of success with new launches. A case in point was Fleetway/IPC's *Jag*, which was launched on 4 May 1968. A million miles away from the comics of the previous decade, this tabloid-sized publication used garish colours and, stylistically, borrowed heavily from the American comics. The first issue included "Bobby Moore's Book of the FA Cup", and the comic placed heavy emphasis on real footballers, with features including "Star Team" and "Story of a Star". However, the

Below Hurricane "Haddie" Hadley combined a career as a deep-sea fisherman with net-busting goal-scoring for Barmouth United in the pages of *Hornet*

Above Some people are on the pitch... crowd trouble for the Football Family Robinson (*Jag,* 1 March 1969)

writing was on the wall when *Jag* reduced its paper size (although it upped its pagination) on 22 February 1969; indeed, the last issue appeared on 29 March 1969, when it was merged into *Tiger* to become *Tiger and Jag.*

But *Jag* did bequeath one funny, irreverant and original football story – "Football Family Robinson". It centres on Thatchem United, a struggling Fourth Division football club whose players (all members of the Robinson family) have two jobs because the club is unable to pay their wages. The club is also run by the Robinson family, but wealthy businessman Max Sharkey wants to buy United, knock it down and build a supermarket. He offers the Robinsons £10,000, which they reject, and so Sharkey threatens open war. Thatchem sign a number of players with various talents as they battle for points and to stave off Sharkey. The Football Family Robinson transferred to *Tiger* when *Jag* ceased publication, and in the 1970s moved to the *Roy of the Rovers* comic.

Some of the most popular football characters from the 1970s had forerunners in the 1960s comics characters. "Haddie" (whose first appearance *Hornet* was on 3 February 1968) was a prototype "Hot Shot" Hamish. Hurricane "Haddie" Hadley was a deep-sea fisherman who became the new hope of Barmouth United as a net-buster with a rocket shot. Billy Binns was a character who started out in *Boys' World* in 1963 before moving to *Eagle* in 1964, to feature in a standard schoolboy adventure called "The Boys of Castleford School". However, it was soon changed to "Billy Binns and his Wonderful Specs". Billy is the biggest duffer at sports – until he gets given a new pair of glasses, which have mystical powers. They change the weedy lad into Castleford's sporting star – and it's impossible not to draw comparisons with the legendary Billy Dane of "Billy's Boots" fame, That story launched in 1970 – a decade that was to provide exciting times for football comic fans.

"HE DAZZLED ON HIS DEBUT AT 17, TOOK THE BREATH AWAY WITH HIS SUBLIME GOALS, AND ALWAYS LIVED HIS LIFE AS HE PLAYED THE GAME: ON HIS OWN TERMS."

James Lawton tribute to Peter Osgood
(*The Independent*, March 2006)

CHAPTER SEVEN

THE HARD MAN AND THE FANCY DAN

IF THE MODERN ERA KICKED OFF IN THE EARLY 1960s, when footballers won their freedom from the straitjacket of ball-and-chain contracts and the maximum wage, it was to be a decade before the ramifications of these fundamental changes would be fully felt. For it was in the 1970s that the leading footballers began to reflect their new-won freedom by expressing themselves on the pitch, putting the emphasis on flair and skill instead of the thud-and-blunder that had been the hallmark of the British game since the war. Supremely talented players such as Alan Hudson, Tony Currie, Frank Worthington, Rodney Marsh, Peter Osgood and Duncan McKenzie, while highly individualistic, saw it as their sworn duty to entertain the crowd. Each knew only one way to play; it was their way, and it was the right way. And they

Photo by Evening Standard/Getty Images

weren't going to listen to anyone, anyone at all, who tried to tell them differently, or tried to make them alter their style of play.

Their spiritual leader, the shaman for this group of mavericks, was George Best, the Northern Irishman who weaved his magic for Manchester United from 1963 to 1974. The Best legend does not need retelling here, but amidst the tales of the booze, model girlfriends and high living, his footballing achievements are sometimes overlooked. Making his first-team debut at the age of just 17, Best went on to win two League Championship medals and the European Cup in 1968, the same year he was named European Footballer of the Year. He was described by Pele as the best footballer in the world – the salute Best himself most treasured. Best's *annus mirabilis*, 1968, marked the point at which real-life football caught up with the comics. Georgie Boy actually did what the characters in the

Left Football takes on a glamorous style, with Alan Hudson of Chelsea in action against wild-child Stan Bowles of Queen's Park Rangers. The match took place on 19 October 1973. **Above** *Scorcher* was the UK's first dedicated football comic. It appeared in January 1970 and gave us stories such as "Billy's Boots" and "Bobby of the Blues". *Scorcher* presented a new, more aggressive illustrative style and a more realistic approach to storylines comics had been doing for 80 years: the mazy dribbling, the fierce shooting with right or left foot, the subtle passing, the predatory goal-scoring.

From beginning to end, Best made people sit up and take notice. Pat Jennings, the legendary Spurs, Arsenal and Northern Ireland goalkeeper, recalled the day he and Best made their international debuts. It was a wet evening in April 1964 when two teenagers pulled on their international jerseys for the first time for a match against Wales at Swansea. The conditions were terrible, the pitch soggy. At 18, Pat Jennings was just one year older than Best. He recalled: "I was just coming out of the third division with Watford when I got capped – I hadn't come up against George with Manchester United. That was the first I had really seen of him, even though there had been a few headlines in the papers before that." Although Best did not get on the scoresheet in the 3–2 win, his undoubted skill, balance and athleticism were there for everyone to see. "As soon as I saw him, I knew that this was a special talent," Jennings recalled. "It was a real wet night on a boggy pitch and he was just skating over the top of the ground. You knew that this was somebody special, even at that age."

Right "The Lost 47 Minutes" was among a number of storylines that explored the use and misuse of science (*Wizard*, 28 August 1971)

Below Lord Rumsey's Rovers represents a clash of the old and the new, with the old-school father relying on the efforts of his "beatnik" son to save the family pile (*Score 'n' Roar*, 19 September 1970)

On his death in November 2005, Richard Williams, writing in the *Guardian* newspaper, described the impact Best had had. He wrote: "Best was the first footballer of any consequence to grow his hair long and to choose his clothes at the boutiques that sprang up around the country in imitation of Carnaby Street and the King's Road. Off duty, he usually seemed to have champagne in his hand and a model, an actress or a Miss World – sometimes all three – on his arm.

The ghostly faces that haunt Len Bowman.

19 FOOTBALL SPECIAL

THE LOST 47 MINUTES

LEN BOWMAN of Fourth Division Bandfield United had discovered that his new soccer skills had been stolen for him from other players by Doctor Breck's electro-hypnosis. One other person, ex-reporter Tim Kent, knew of the great soccer robbery but he had been imprisoned by Doctor Breck. But Len's conscience started to trouble him and he began to see the ghostly faces of the players whose skills he had stolen.

No! Let me go! Leave me alone! I don't want your skills anymore!

Doctor Breck took charge of his creation—

His nerve has cracked! Seize him, Argon! Quickly, or my work will be ruined!

At the doctor's laboratory—

Let me go! I don't want to be the perfect soccer player!

I fear all is lost, Master. What will become of us?

Silence, fool! I've prepared for such an emergency!

Let me go! I've had enough of this! You're crazy!

My work nears completion! You'll not destroy my dream!

What are you doing, Master?

It's the final transference Argon. I, Doctor Breck, shall take control of the mind and body of Len Bowman.

I fear this thing you do, Master.

Imbecile! It only takes 47 minutes for the transfer. Throw the switches.

No! Arrrrgh!

No! Let me out of here!

WZD 28.8.71

171

STARTS TODAY, Joe Packer's fight to climb the football ladder.

POOR YOUNG JOE

JOE PACKER'S fifteenth birthday was a great day for him. He left school and got a job as an errand-boy with a local grocer, and he scored a hat-trick for Hornford Boys' Club. That hat-trick was watched by Fred Grimes, who called himself a soccer scout . . .

Grimes did not scout for any particular club—

That you, Mr South? Fred Grimes here. Listen, Mr South, I got a boy here...

You need an agent, Joe. Somebody who will fix you up with a top club, somebody like Harvey South.

South's an agent. Handles footballers, boxers, television stars, cricketers, pop stars. Lots of top clubs in the First Division get their lads from South.

Who's he?

Just a minute, Joe. I'd like a chat with you. Come into the cafe there and bring your pals...

I never knew it was done like that. How do I get to meet this Mr South?

Four hours later, Joe Packer was in London with Grimes.

HARVEY SOUTH ENTERPRISES

Come on in, Joe. We've arrived.

Mr South's secretary is expecting you.

Cor! This is just a receptionist! This is some place!

Stone the crows! This carpet's a foot thick!

I told you he was class, son.

WZD 3.10.70

"His behaviour incurred the disapproval of his elders, notably that of Bobby Charlton, United's totemic forward, who saw the world through the eyes of a more strait-laced generation. Charlton also believed that Best's self-indulgence extended to a habit of hanging on to the ball too greedily and neglecting opportunities to enable others to score goals for Matt Busby's magnificent team.

"Best scored 178 goals of his own for United in 466 appearances and could claim to have been at least the equal of any footballer born in the British Isles. For sheer sleight of foot he was perhaps matched in the world game only by Diego Maradona. From his United debut in 1963, at the age of 17, Best's unstoppable dribbling blended with Charlton's surging runs and Denis Law's cold-eyed finishing to make the team the biggest draw in English football. Together they brought Old Trafford out of the long depression engendered by the 1958 Munich air crash, winning the league championship and the European Cup and inspiring Busby to rechristen United's home ground the 'Theatre of Dreams'.

"The way Best played football was certainly the stuff that dreams are made of. Around the country, in tenement alleyways and on recreation grounds, young boys grew their hair and practised their close control in imitation of Georgie Best."

But like Best, the flair players of the 1970s were constantly at loggerheads with authority, and the more they insisted on doing it their way, the more entrenched the establishment became against them. Alan Hudson and Peter Osgood are cases in point. Both sublimely gifted and with monumental

Left Poor Joe Young fought to climb the football ladder (*Wizard*, 3 October 1970)

Below "Bobby of the Blues" was a 1970s flair player who reflected the changes going on on the pitch in the pages of the ground-breaking *Scorcher*

confidence in their own ability, they won just a handful of England caps between them. Both made their name at Chelsea, but fell out with the club's management for refusing to toe the line and were placed on the transfer list in the same month, January 1974. Within a month, Hudson had joined Stoke City for £240,000, his career with Chelsea over at the age of 22. Osgood's Chelsea career was longer – he started playing for the Stamford Bridge outfit in the 1965–66 season – but he too left the club at the peak of his powers, when in March 1974 he was transferred to Southampton for a club-record £275,000.

Osgood's early playing career could have been lifted out of the pages of the football comics. In his book, *The Mavericks*, author Rob Steen describes a goal the 17-year-old Osgood scored against Burnley at Turf Moor. "Gliding across the muddy morass at Turf Moor, a gazelle on skis, Peter evaded four challenges before rounding off a solo sally of such outrageous panache that even the Burnley keeper, Adam Blacklaw, applauded him to the centre circle."

But the players' problems extended beyond club football. Owing to a ban from international football after refusing to tour with the England Under–23 side, Alan Hudson didn't make his England debut until 1975. Don Revie, the England manager who had replaced Osgood's nemesis, Sir Alf Ramsey, could not ignore Hudson's sparkling performances, and called him up for a game against world champions Germany. He starred in the 2–0 victory at Wembley, and then

Right Another case of the appliance of science in the pages of *Wizard*. The Red Rangers relied upon the strange theories of their directors

Below *Scorcher*'s Cannonball Craig was another footballing wunderkind. His secret? Grandpa's bubble-and-squeak!

NEXT INSTANT, AS CRAIG LET FLY... THE WORLD SEEMED TO EXPLODE!

OH, M-MY STARS! WHAT'S HAPPENED? HOW DID I..? GRANDPAAAA!

BWAAM!

WHOMP!

Bad passing puts Penstone Rangers in trouble.

THE RED RANGERS

THE famous scientist Sir Herbert Foster had inherited First Division Penstone Rangers Football Club. Sir Herbert decided to run the club himself, using his own unusual ideas. Now Sir Herbert and directors, Nathan Lewis and Humphrey Warden were watching the Rangers play Hullboro'.

That was a bad pass by Harris!

Aye, it's so murky out there. It's difficult to distinguish one team from the other.

It'll be worse at Ironfield next week. It's always smokey and grey there.

Then we'll have to do something about it.

You'll not be able to change the atmosphere, Sir Herbert.

No, but we can make our players more easily seen.

Oh, what a pass back! Straight to our striker! He must score!

Great save!

That's the final whistle. A goalless draw was a fair enough result.

The Rangers' players did not see Sir Herbert for the rest of the week. He spent the time in his laboratory. The weather continued to be dirty and did not look good for the game at Ironfield.

On Saturday as the players waited for the coach to take them to the station, Sir Herbert arrived carrying a large parcel.

Come with me, Murray. I want you to try on the new strip I've had made.

But we don't need a new strip, we've got about six sets already!

WZD 5.6.71

OUR JACK'S NOT NORMALLY AS SLOW AS THAT!

I DON'T THINK HE'S TOO HAPPY ABOUT HIS RIGHT FOOT!

Above Jack Chelsey's sister Pat expresses her concerns

Below Jimmy Chelsey of City has no problem scoring. The Chelsey brothers' stories – Jack of United and Jimmy of City were intertwined in the novel *Score 'n' Roar* comic

in the 5-0 destruction of Cyprus. Before the Germany game, according to Rob Steen, Revie "had prefaced his third game as national manager by taking [Alan] Ball and Alan [Hudson] aside for one of his more inspired pep talks. 'I'm sick and tired of seeing continentals come here and take the mickey out of us with their skills. Go and take the mickey out of the Germans. Be cocky, be confident. Show me you're the greatest.' 'It was music to my ears,' Alan told the press. 'Alf Ramsey used to drop people for being too cheeky.' In the seventh minute, Alan brought off a one-two with Ball, sending Mick Channon clean through only for the Southampton striker to be brought down. From then on the new kid ran the block, directing a 2-0 victory. The notices were rhapsodic. 'The memories of Raich Carter and Wilf Mannion stirred again,' reported David Miller in the *Daily Express*. 'At the heart of the Germans' destruction stood the languid, hip-shrugging Hudson, commanding the Wembley stage with classic skills and razor perception.'" Yet despite this performance, these were the only two England caps won by Hudson. (Typically, Hudson was later to say that he had won only one England cap – he considered Cyprus such poor quality opposition that the cap did not count.)

Osgood fared only marginally better, winning four England caps. In spite of his talent and goalscoring prowess, Osgood's England career was surprisingly limited, with England manager Alf Ramsey disapproving of his playboy lifestyle. A member of the 1970 World Cup squad, Osgood made just two substitute appearances, against Czechoslovakia and Romania.

THEN HE DREW AWAY FROM HIS OPPONENT WITH A TERRIFIC BURST OF SPEED!

THE RINGHURST DEFENCE IS OVER-STRETCHED!

JIMMY DREW THE GOALKEEPER OUT OF POSITION AND LET FLY!

IT'S THERE!

CITY ARE ONE UP!

A GREAT GOAL, JIM!

Above Castleburn City's manager explains to Jimmy why he is exactly the right sort of player for his club (*Score 'n' Roar*, 19 September 1970)

In the comics, too, the players were beginning to do it for themselves. And there was plenty of opportunity for them to strut their stuff, as IPC in particular put more and more emphasis on football in its comics. Indeed, in 1970 it broke new ground with the launch of not one but two football-only titles. It was the first time the publishing giant had produced a comic – or comics – centred on a single theme. While in these titles – *Scorcher* and *Score 'n' Roar* – it was football, single-theme comics were seen as the way ahead by the publishers, and many more were launched in the 1970s and 1980s.

IPC's two ground-breakers, the aforementioned *Scorcher* and *Score 'n' Roar*, were highly influential comics that launched a range of characters who would eventually outlive the comics that created them.

Scorcher, the better-known of the two, was launched on 10 January 1970. Its free (rather unoriginal) gift was "A great soccer wallchart" and the comic trumpeted that it was "A super new paper for all football fans!" While breaking the mould, it could not quite abandon the text-based story; the tale "The Goal Thief" ran across two pages. Featuring profiles of Jack Charlton and Dave McKay, it also carried a "Big Match Preview" (Southampton versus Everton) and the back page was devoted to a selection of club badges. "Know-All" was "Soccer's Mister Big-Head! See if you can catch him out…" Readers were also urged to "Challenge Your Chum – to quiz football", a game in which a counter was advanced up the pitch towards the opponent's goal with each correct answer given. "Goal Post" was the comic's letters page – in issue 1, Derek Smith from Chatham in Kent asked: "Could you tell me the name of the famous footballer who runs a fish and chip shop?" The answer is "George Curtis, Coventry City's star defender. He's always been partial to fish and chips and last year he opened a shop of his own in Coventry. His wife runs it while George is playing and training." *Scorcher*'s "Team of the week" in the first issue put the spotlight on The Hough Secondary School, Wilmslow, who share a page with Celtic, the week's nominated team in the comic's "Roll of Honour" feature.

But the bulk of the new publication is devoted to comic strips, and here for

the first time we meet an impressive array of characters. "Royal's Rangers" charts the progress of Caxton Rangers, under the managership of Ben Royal; Kangaroo Kid is the boy from the outback who is a wow with Redstone Rovers, who discover him while touring Australia; "Byrd of Paradise Hill" covered familiar ground with its tales of a footballing school master; while "Sub" was a comedy strip about the exploits of a football duffer who is always warming the bench.

Of more interest are the four other strips that appeared in that first *Scorcher*. "Paxton's Powerhouse" was the story of "the ruthless soccer dictator who vowed to build a team of world-beaters!". The near-psychotic Vince Paxton's brutal methods get results, but his fiery temper makes him virtually unemployable. His solution is to take over a lower-league club and drive them to the top – helped by a secret weapon, Professor Zarron, the inventor of machines that can turn even average footballers into "power men".

Bobby of the Blues also made his first appearance in the first issue of *Scorcher*. He is a centre-forward blessed with the outrageous skills of a Peter Osgood. Bobby, who plays for "world-famous Everpool Rovers", is possessed of a silky touch and goal-scoring prowess that make him the target of every hard man in the business.

"Lags Eleven" centres on a group of inmates at Bankhurst Prison, led by Willie Smith, also known to his pals as "Brilliant Genius". His masterplan is to

Above Another cunning plan... form a football team and break out of prison! "Lags Eleven" was an original *Scorcher* story that combined football and prison life. Did the inmates of Slade Prison borrow this idea?

Below Can a scientific approach beat natural talent? Paxton's Powerhouse are about to find out in *Scorcher*

Speech bubbles (part of image): "HE'S A *STRIKER*, NOT A *'KEEPER*... BUT JUST LOOK AT THOSE SAVES!" / "WATCH AND LEARN FROM HIM, BOY, AND YOU'LL *HELP* TO KEEP REDSTONE ON TOP!"

Above *Scorcher*'s Kangaroo Kid was raised by a herd of kangaroos – and had kick to match. Original storylines were still around in the 1970s

set up a prison football team as the cover for an escape plan. Witty and sharp – the title itself is a neat pun on a strip called "Legge's Eleven" that had appeared in *Valiant* in the 1964 – "Lags Eleven" sees Brilliant run rings around his arch enemy, the martinet prison officer "Bad News" Benson. The ruse is devised in the first episode, and explained to Brilliant's pal, "Nut-Case": "'That is the plan, Nut-Case. We form a prison football team... You'll play in it! I'll play in it!' 'I like football! I got sent off once for hitting the ref! 'Ow do we escape, though?' 'When you play football... you play home and away games, right? Well, when we play our first away game, Nut-Case, we'll vanish... like snow in summer!'"

Lags Eleven" proved an extremely popular strip; some observers believe that the character of bank-robbing Brilliant was based on Peter Sellars, and that of Bad News on Lionel Jefferies. Judge for yourself.

But while the prison team became a hit with readers, the most popular and enduring story from *Scorcher* concerns the soccer adventures of young Billy Dane. A keen football fan, Billy, who lived with his gran, was a complete duffer until he found an old pair of boots once owned by legendary footballer "Dead-Shot" Keen. The boots were imbued with mystical powers, for whenever Billy put them on he found he could play as well as old "Dead-Shot". From being a laughing stock to hero of the school team, Billy's boots propelled him through numerous adventures. But there was always danger around the corner; his hapless gran frequently threw the old boots out, and often Billy was forced into impromptu games – without his boots. Such was the popularity of "Billy's Boots" the story was transferred to *Tiger* in 1974 when that title subsumed *Scorcher*; later it was to appear in *Eagle* and finally, in 1986, in the **Roy of the Rovers** comic.

Such was the huge and immediate popularity of **Scorcher**, publishers IPC decided to chance their arm with the launch of a second dedicated football comic, also in 1970. **Score 'n' Roar** appeared on newsagents' shelves on 19 September, with the promise of "Two great football comics in one!" (and *Shoot*-syle Football League ladders as a give-away). In a novel piece of marketing, **Roar** was indeed a 16-page pull-out comic in the middle of **Score**; each had its own front cover.

Score kicked off with "Jack of United", the story of Jack Chelsey, a cultured centre-half with Castleburn United. In a parallel story in **Roar**, Jack's brother Jimmy was the star centre-forward for United's arch rivals, Castleburn City. While the stories sat separately there were numerous connections between the two, with many scenes taking place in the family home. And of course there was the occasional Castleburn derby, when the brothers faced each other. These invariably ended with honours even between the two teams and the Chelsey brothers. Interestingly, the "Jack of United" and "Jimmy of City" stories made much of their family life; for added spice sister Pat was a United fan and younger brother Clive a City fan.

Below The "Lags Eleven" team performs well above expectations

Right A unlikely hero makes his debut. Billy Dane and his "magic" boots arrive, on the pages of the first issue of *Scorcher* (10 January 1970)

Other stories in **Score** included "Cannonball Craig", whose secret was "the bubble-and-squeak that gave him a dynamite kick"; and Lord Rumsey's Rovers, the tale of an aristocrat who had fallen on hard times and is forced to form a football

MEET THE LAD WHO WAS CRAZY ABOUT FOOTBALL – BUT COULD NEVER GET A GAME!

FROM NOW ON, I'LL BE WEARING FRISBEE'S GEAR, BOTH ON AND OFF THE FIELD. ALL I'VE GOT TO DO IS LOOK SMART, AND I'LL COLLECT FIFTY QUID A MONTH! NEAT, EH?

Above Nipper Lawrence, a new style of superstar. See page 218

Below The original owner of Billy's Boots, "Dead Shot" Keen, takes an interest in Billy's progress and prowess. See page 218

team to protect his stately pile. The latter was played for laughs, his Lordship's beatnik son – a star footballer – being saddled with some particularly 1970s vernacular.

In another league altogether, literally and metaphorically, was the story "Nipper". The eponymous hero was an orphan whose mission in life was to clear the name of his late father, who was (wrongly) accused of swindling money from his employer. To do this he had to raise enough money to hire a lawyer; hence his desire to become a professional player with local side Blackport Rovers. Nipper, meanwhile, who lived on his own with his pet dog, Stumpy, had to juggle school work, playground politics, work and dodging his legal guardian, the criminal and bully Nat Munger, while trying to fulfil his footballing dreams. The story's hallmark was its gritty realism, typified by its strong dialogue and made flesh by the dark and brooding black-and-white illustration.

Roar comic, as well as being home of Jimmy of City, also featured "Peter the Cat", the story of young goalkeeper extraordinaire Peter Swain; and "Mark Your Man", about "the policeman who joined a First Division team to catch a master crook". "Phantom of the Forest" was an updated take on an old-fashioned theme; a supernatural thriller about an old-time footballer – J.R. Phantom – whose ghost stalks the corridors of Rustford Forest. Legend has it that Phantom will be

IN THE STANDS, DEAD-SHOT KEEN HIMSELF WAS WATCHING...

COME ON, YOU SOUTHERN BOYS!

I'LL GET MORE FILM OF THE GAME THIS HALF, DEAD-SHOT!

BE SURE TO GET PLENTY OF YOUNG *DANE* IN ACTION!

brought back to life if a football on show in the club museum ever bursts; and some of the club's young players, hearing the story, break into the museum and kick the old football around (26 September 1970). The ball is punctured, and Phantom is released and made flesh… and his task begins: "'These conceited young oafs shall know what it means to play football like men!'" he vows.

But with *Score 'n' Roar* it seems IPC over-estimated the market; despite the undoubted quality of the comic(s) the title was to last just 35 issues. On 3 July 1971 it merged with *Scorcher*, to become *Scorcher and Score*, the *Roar* title disappearing. Jack of United and Jimmy of City survived the merger, as did Lord Rumsey's Rovers and Nipper.

In Dundee, D.C. Thomson responded to IPC's launch of *Scorcher* by resurrecting an old title of its own – *Wizard* – and by increasing the football content in its established titles. The new-look *Wizard*, for its re-appearance on 14 February 1970, was branded a "Football Special" and "The two-in-one picture story paper", and included both text and comic strip stories. The comic mixed stories with features on real players, such as "My Home Team", and Peter

Above For every flair player there was a hard man waiting… brute force appears to be the order of the day in stopping the mercurial Nipper Lawrence

Below Peter the Cat believes he is not appreciated (*Score 'n' Roar*)

A GREAT NEW SOCCER STORY STARTS TODAY!

SCORE 'n' ROAR

**EVERY MONDAY
24th APRIL 1971**

4ᴾ

TOP SOCCER STARS IN COLOUR IN OUR PICTURE GALLERY!

TRY OUR FOOTBALL QUIZ – INSIDE!

PETER THE CAT GETS KIDNAPPED

JIMMY of CITY – *INSIDE!*

© IPC Magazines Ltd 1971 Australia 12 cents, New Zealand 12 cents, S. Africa 12 cents, Rhodesia 13 cents, East Africa 1/25, West Africa 1/3, Malaysia 60 cents, Malta 1/-

25 FOOTBALL SPECIAL

THE BOY FROM WINTER ISLAND

Neither Pedro nor I, played in the first match, I wonder if we'll improve the teams performance today

SIXTEEN-YEAR-OLD Gordon Jones from Winter Island in the South Atlantic had been signed by First Division Everley Rovers. Pedro Alvarez, a youth from a circus had also joined the Rovers.

Gordon who had developed a deadly accurate cross formed with Pedro, who was strong in the air, a high scoring partnership for Everley's Youth Team.

The Youth Team were about to play Darnley in a Youth Cup Quarter Final replay.

Facing page *Score 'n' Roar*, a new style of comic combining the best of live action and innovative comic strips

Left *Wizard's* Gordon Jones made the long trek from the South Atlantic to England to find football glory

Below "Coote's Crocks" was yet another football story from the pages of *Wizard*

Osgood is profiled in the first issue. The new-look **Wizard** carried a host of football stories, including "The Fiery Man at Number Six"; "Simple Simons" ("The Worst Centre in Football"); "Arnie's Army"; "Poor Young Joe"; "The Red Rangers"; "The Lost 47 Minutes"; "The Lost Years of Lonely Martin"; "Coote's Crocks"; "Away Went Kelly"; "Shinguard Smith"; "Scrappy"; and "The Boy from Winter Island".

While many of these stories covered familiar themes, "The Fiery Man at Number Six" was a more modern tale, featuring a footballing rebel called Joe Greer and charting his struggle to reach the top against all the odds (the story later appeared in **Victor**). Joe plays for Langdale Rovers, but following a rash of disputes he is moved on to Oldboro United in the Third Division (24 June 1978). Constantly picked up for petty mistakes, he disagrees with the captain, Roper, who is a blustering bully and a windbag, and he falls foul of the ultra-conservative manager, disagreeing with the too-rigid tactics. The team want to win at all costs and will resort to clogging, but this is not Joe's style and he endeavours to introduce a more stylish type of play. Two players,

COOTE'S CROCKS

LUSHAM YEOMEN, a struggling football side, depended on the money from a fund controlled by whoever was in charge of the Lusham military museum. The Yeomen's latest game against Stockley was going badly—as usual.

Stockley have scored again. Now the riots going to start. Mr Mayor, I think you and the directors should retire to a safe place.

Footballers! They're a bunch of blooming cripples. Come on, mates, let's show 'em what we think.

Yeah! Let's tear down the goal posts.

HEAR THAT, STUMPY? THEY'RE GOING TO TAKE SOME TEAM PICTURES! YOU CAN BE IN 'EM AS OUR MASCOT!

Priddy and Cutler, are both determined to be the leading scorer, and this leads to more problems for Joe.

There's a shock in store when Ernest Joiner, the chairman of Oldboro, steals the gate money and disappears, meaning the club has to fold. Joe goes back to watch Langdale, and while there sorts out some fighting among a group of yobs. He is invited back to Langdale on trial and impresses; his form is such that he gets the chance to play for the first team. Unfortunately, the crook Joiner turns up, insisting he owns Joe's registration and refusing to allow him to play for Langdale. However, Joe spots a loophole in the deal that means he can play for

The vet told Scrappy that during the fight, one of the louts must have kicked Scruffy. The brave dog had fatal internal injuries.

I've lost my dog, my home, my sport, my old headmaster who liked me. It's my "O"-level year and I've joined a senior team. I should be on top of the world, but it seems I'm all alone again!

Langdale. He is still the same Joe, but during one game he holds the side together and against all odds, a player short and with an injured player soldiering on, he drives the team to victory. It is apparent to the manager that Joe is the one the rest of the players turned to when the going got tough and he is made captain of Langdale because he is an inspiration.

The character returns in the story "The Jinx of Joe Greer" (23 December 1978). In this tale Joe has suffered a head injury that gives him occasional fits of blindness, a situation he keeps a secret from the directors and the players. These fits occur at the most inappropriate times. Manager Pascoe is injured in a car

Top left and above right
A footballer's best friend... Nipper Lawrence with Stumpy, and Scrappy with Scruffy

Right Scrappy, a boy alone, overcomes the trials of life and becomes a top-class goalkeeper. A similar storyline, Tuffy, formed the basis of a popular strip in *Buddy* in 1981

Facing page Joe Greer had a troubled life after "killing" two goalkeepers, overcoming blindness and ineffectual management. But he manages to make Langdale Rovers a success, in both *Wizard* and *Hotspur*

STARTS TODAY — Another great story with your best pal—Scrappy!

JOHN SMITH, known to everyone as Scrappy, was playing goalkeeper for Foster's College against a local amateur side, Wigton Wanderers, on the day before the new term started.

Come on, Wanderers! Get stuck into those College creeps!

Scruffy, the dog that Scrappy had saved from drowning, watched as Scrappy held the Wanderers at bay.

Boo! Foul! Fix that dirty keeper, Wanderers!

Mr Pitt-Watt, the new headmaster, spoke to Dr Collins, the retiring head.

I'm surprised that Foster's should play soccer. You can see the sort of people it encourages, Dr Collins.

THE FIERY MAN AT NUMBER SIX

JOE GREER, a hard-tackling left-half was signed by First Division Langdale Rovers. Joe made a sensational start in the Reserves, being sent off by his own captain. On Monday morning—

Funny, I haven't been summoned to the boss, Mr Pascoe, about Saturday's affair with Roper.

After training, Joe bought a paper.

No further action, eh! We'll see about that. I'm going to see Pascoe.

NO FURTHER ACTION TO BE TAKEN BY LANGDALE OVER NEW BOY GREER'S SENDING OFF

This statement is not good enough, Mr Pascoe. I consider that my side of the affair should be made known.

You're a real fiery man aren't you, Greer? Well you've got to learn that Langdale Rovers don't air their troubles in public.

I wasn't the one who was dirty on Saturday! It was Roper! He sent me off because I objected to his fouling the young winger.

We know that, Greer. We don't like Roper's kind any more that you do. He's on the transfer list and you're in the first team.

The following Saturday—

Look at me, Joe Greer, dressed up like a tailor's dummy in the Rovers' blazer. Hello, someone at the door.

Roper! Clear off! I've nothing to say to you.

You've finished me in football and pushed yourself up the ladder! I'll fix you!

A few moments later—

Mr Greer! Stop it! Stop it! Oh, my furniture! I'm going for the police.

WZD 13.3.71

crash and the directors appoint Major Norland, an underperforming, opinionated character who tries to implement unworkable plans on the team, changing their style of play. When the club starts to play badly Norland accuses the players and transfer-lists all of them. Norton's incompetence forces him to resign; Joe becomes player-manager and leads the team to the League and Cup double. His blindness problem is revealed and he goes into hospital just as Pascoe returns to the club to take up his managerial position.

The character Scrappy had parallels with *Score 'n' Roar*'s Nipper Lawrence; the title character is a 15-year-old schoolboy who lives rough, with his dog Scruffy his only companion. Scrappy, so called because he lives in a scrapyard, is a boy with no name and uncertain origin. Constantly pursued by the authorities, he lives by his wits. A young lad of enormous integrity, he has a desire to learn and creeps around under the floorboards of Fosters School to achieve his ambition. He makes friends with some of the boys and enemies of others. Instrumental in starting a Fosters football team he proves to be an outstanding goalkeeper. Through thick and thin he strives to gain entry to Fosters. His persistence eventually pays off; he gains entry to the school and helps them win the cup.

A different type of story entirely was "The Lost 47 Minutes". It featured a poorly performing Fourth Division club, Bandfield United, who are approached by the strange Dr Franz Breck, who says that he can give the club the perfect player. Dubious, the directors humour him and allow him one week to make one of their players a star – which he does. The transformation is achieved by a sort of hypnotic transference of ability from one player to another, which takes 47

Right "Play Till You Drop" from the infamous *Action* comic, which caused questions to be asked in parliament and managed to offend Mary Whitehouse

Below "Paxton's Powerhouse" prepares for an evening kick-off in the pages of *Scorcher*

In our next issue-the bloodsucker digs deep into Alec's pocket!

Suddenly, Froyd was there, silencing everybody with his stare.

YOU WILL GO OUT THERE AND PLAY IN AN EIGHT-A-SIDE GAME. YOU WILL PLAY ONE BACK, THREE HALF-BACKS, FOUR FORWARDS...

IT'S UNCANNY! SUDDENLY, THEY'RE ALL AS QUIET AS MICE. WHAT ABOUT ALL THE QUESTIONS THEY WERE GOING TO ASK!

THE EXTENSION IS COMPLETE! THE WORKMEN MUST HAVE WORKED ALL NIGHT, AND THAT'S NEVER BEEN KNOWN BEFORE! WELL, LET'S GET ON WITH THE TRIAL.

YOUNG JIM PARTRIDGE COULD BE A GREAT PLAYER. WE MUST NURSE HIM CAREFULLY. NOW FOR HIS PASS....

Jim's pass reached Mike, and then . . . .

HEY! WATCH IT, KORNER! ARE YOU TRYING TO KILL ME OR SOMETHING? IT'S ONLY A PRACTICE.

After the practice . . .

THEY'LL HAVE TO DO FOR A START. JIM PARTRIDGE AND ALAN KORNER WILL COME WITH ME, HOLLINS.

ABOUT JIM AND KORNER, MISTER FROYD. CAN I PUT YOU WISE TO A FEW THINGS THAT YOU SHOULD KNOW?

Above Never trust a man named Froyd. More mind-bending shenanighans from the pages of *Wizard* ("Behind the Crimson Door", January 1970)

Below The East Mound Mob played for the Slatepool City Junior team – they were "crack footballers of 12 and 13 who were already being groomed for professional soccer" (*Scorcher*)

minutes. His fee…total control of the club. A sceptical reporter tries to find out the truth as the doctor continues to give the player more and more skills, thus turning him into the best player in the world.

Wizard's stories, too, often had a strong element of sci-fi or the supernatural. "The Voice that Ran the Rangers" centred on the tribulations of struggling Blackton Rangers. The team's fortunes take a bizarre twist when the manager takes a mysterious phone call advising him on team selection. Unimpressed by the stranger's continued interventions, the manager eventually rips the phone out of the wall – but that does not stop it ringing once again…

Matching IPC wallchart-for-wallchart, *Victor*'s giveaway on 17 January 1970 was a "Week by Week Record of all Football Leagues". The stories relied on the tried-and-trusted formulas that had served it well. In "Behind the Crimson Door", a new manager takes over at Manton City, the team bottom of the first division – and his first step is to sack 10 of his first-team players (17 January 1970). The new manager, Sinton Froyd, orders an extension to be built on the

MEL'S LET FLY WITH A GREAT SHOT!

'E'S SPOT ON! IT'S A GOAL!

YA-HAA-AAA-'POOL!

TSK, TSK! WHAT'S THIS?

stand, fitted with a crimson door. The mystery deepens when new players arrive at Manton, their old clubs appearing to have let them go for very small, if any, transfer fees. These players seem to change their style of play after meeting Froyd behind the crimson door. Soon the secret behind the crimson door is revealed: Froyd is using hypnotism and a strange range of machines to programme players. His plan is eventually undone, and Froyd is exposed and dies when his machines explode.

Victor also continued to run complete, one-off stories. In "The Player with the Dirty Face" (9 January 1971), Burnham manager Bill Powell receives a call from one Arnold Parry, offering a young amateur player for trial – his son George. But boy performs badly and is regarded as unsuitable. Later, Powell spots a group of miners having a kick-about and, impressed by one lad, he invites him to Burnham for a trial. The boy, with the coal dust and grime washed from his face, turns out to be George Parry, who, without his overbearing father's involvement, is a good player and signs for the club.

Stablemate *Hornet* similarly stuck with the tried-and-tested. "Bailey Mends Broken Men" (28 February 1970) is typical fare. It is the last game of the season and Grangeford Rovers are playing Burton Athletic. With 10 minutes left, Len Brown, Rovers' young centre-half and captain, who was recently capped for

Below "The Player with the Dirty Face", a case of "if at first you don't succeed, try again" (*Victor*, 9 January 1971)

 IS YOUR ANKLE ALL RIGHT?

IT HASN'T HURT ME IN THE LEAST.

Above In "Bailey Mends Broken Men", new-age healing comes to the aid of injured Len Brown (*Hornet*, 28 February 1970)

Below, both pages "Hot Shot" Hamish in action. Hamish made his debut in *Scorcher* (25 August 1973)

England, breaks his ankle in a tackle. The club organises prominent surgeon Sir Nigel Lane to help with Len's recovery. Unfortunately, Sir Nigel, who is believed to be the only man capable of helping Len, is killed in a car crash.

Then, while Len is watching a game, a stranger approaches him, saying: "'My name is Bailey, just Bailey. I will be back in a few days to help with your recovery.'" The mystery man appears to have healing hands, and soon has Len out of his wheelchair and walking on sticks. Bailey, it transpires, is in fact Sir Nigel Lane; the person killed in the car crash was a hitchhiker. Following the crash he had lost his memory and it had only recently returned.

"The Amazing Mister Cedric" (11 December 1971) features Vic Wallace, who works for Ajax Electronics, a company that manufactures television sets, computers and similar hardware. Vic supports Renfield Rovers, but they didn't give him much to cheer. The Rovers were in the Third Division and heading for the Fourth. Vic needs to do something to help, so he runs tests on a new Computer for Electronic Direction of Received Information, model C – or Cedric for short. On a whim he programmes in all available information on Renfield, including press reports and player statistics. At a board meeting the directors discover that their attempts to attract a new manager have resulted in no applications. They do, however, receive strange instructions from Cedric. The board implements the instructions and the team improves so much that Cedric is offered the job as manager by the board, who do not realise he is a computer.

Old friends continue to appear in the pages of **Hornet**, too, with Nick Smith and Arnold Tabbs combining in many new adventures (and some old ones, too).

In 1973, a strapping Scottish centre-forward made his debut in the pages of

POOR WEE WALLIE... I WISH THERE WAS SOME WAY WE COULD HELP HIM...

HEY, THAT BALL AND NET...I'VE GOT AN IDEA!

WE'LL TIE THIS PIECE OF STRING TO WALLIE'S TOOTH AND THE OTHER END TO THE BALL-CARRYING NET...

I GET IT! THEN HAMISH HITS HIS HOT-SHOT AT THE BALL... AND OUT COMES THE TOOTH!

OKAY, LADS...HERE I GO! HOLD TIGHT, WALLIE...YE WILLNA FEEL A THING!

R-RIGHT YE ARE, H-HAMISH!

Scorcher (issue dated 25 August). He was to become one of the best-known footballers from the comic pages, with his trademark, net-busting sharp shooting, and his name was Hamish Balfour – or "Hot Shot" Hamish. A gentle Hebridean giant, Hamish was brought from his remote island home to play for Princes Park under manager Ian McWhacker. Like Biffalo Bill before him (in the pages of *Hotspur*), Hamish could not find a shirt that would stretch over his massive torso, and the terrifying sight (for defenders and goalies) of Hamish charging down the pitch was matched by the devastating power of his shot. His goals transformed the fortunes of Princes Park, turning a struggling Second Division side into Scottish Cup winners and European contenders.

Hamish moved to *Tiger* when that title incorporated *Scorcher* in 1974, and in 1985 moved to Roy Race's dedicated *Roy of the Rovers* comic. That launched on 26 September 1976 and became the home for many comic-book footballing superstars when, as the market declined, comics were closed down or merged with other titles.

Roy of the Rovers' legendary cast included Kevin "Mighty" Mouse; Johnny Dexter ("The Hard Man"); Gordon Stewart ("The Safest Hands in Soccer"); Jorge Porbillas ("The Kid from Argentina"); and David Bradley ("Millionaire Villa") to name but a few. Kevin Mouse was a one-off; a rotund, bespectacled medical student who looked like he had wandered onto the pitch straight from a sci-fi convention. Mighty Mouse played for First Division Tottenford Rovers when not working at St Victor's Hospital. Despite his shambling gait, Kevin was surprisingly agile and quick off the mark; he also possessed a fearsome shot that baffled opposition keepers as it boomeranged into the net.

Johnny Dexter was an archetypal 1970s tough guy who added steel to Melchester Rovers when he signed for Roy Race's team from Danefield United. Despite his fiery temper, Johnny played a hard but fair game. As a young player Johnny was constantly in trouble off the pitch as well as on it. Johnny courted controversy and was a tabloid newspaper target – the press has a field day when he gets arrested for brawling after angry fans pick a fight with him in a bar. But Dexter sees the error of his ways and, a reformed character, he becomes skipper of United and a role model.

A more conventional player was Gordon Stewart, the "goalkeeping equivalent of a brick wall", according to an article in *The Observer* entitled "The 10 best comic book footballers" (30 November 2003). It added: "On his day, which was nearly every time he pulled on a pair of gloves, nothing could get past Gordon Stewart in *Roy of the Rovers*. No matter the placement, power or trajectory of a shot, when Stewart was between the sticks for Tynefield City, he was unbeatable. If luck was needed, Stewart had that covered, too, courtesy of his mascot Fred – a toy skeleton that he kept in his glove bag. He died in a plane crash off the coast of Brazil in 1982, but the Stewart name lived on through his son, Rick, who played in goal for his father's arch rivals Tynefield United."

The Observer also listed David Bradley in its top 10; he featured in the story "Millionaire Villa": "In a storyline that long predated Roman Abramovich's arrival at Chelsea, rich-kid David Bradley went one step further by giving Selby Villa £2 million to guarantee himself a place in the team. He was completely useless, of course, and consistently held the team back with his inept displays. Bradley... used his wealth to force the club to accept his baffling schemes. On one occasion, Bradley insisted that the entire team played an important cup tie in the new boots that he had bought them. None fitted properly and, 90 blister-inducing minutes later, Selby were out of the cup."

One *Roy of the Rovers* story that captured the moment was "The Kid from Argentina", which appeared in 1979. At that time Argentinian footballers were the flavour of the month, with Ossie Ardilles and Ricky Villa having signed for Tottenham Hotspur in a £750,000 deal after Argentina's win in the 1978 World Cup. Manton County followed the North London club's lead by signing Jorge Porbillas for £350,000. However, County manager Bert

Above Kevin "Mighty" Mouse, a hero for both Tottenford Rovers and St. Victor's Hospital. He obviously used the same training regime as Billy Bunter

Right A powerful *Valiant* front cover (13 December 1975) featuring a determined Dave Brady

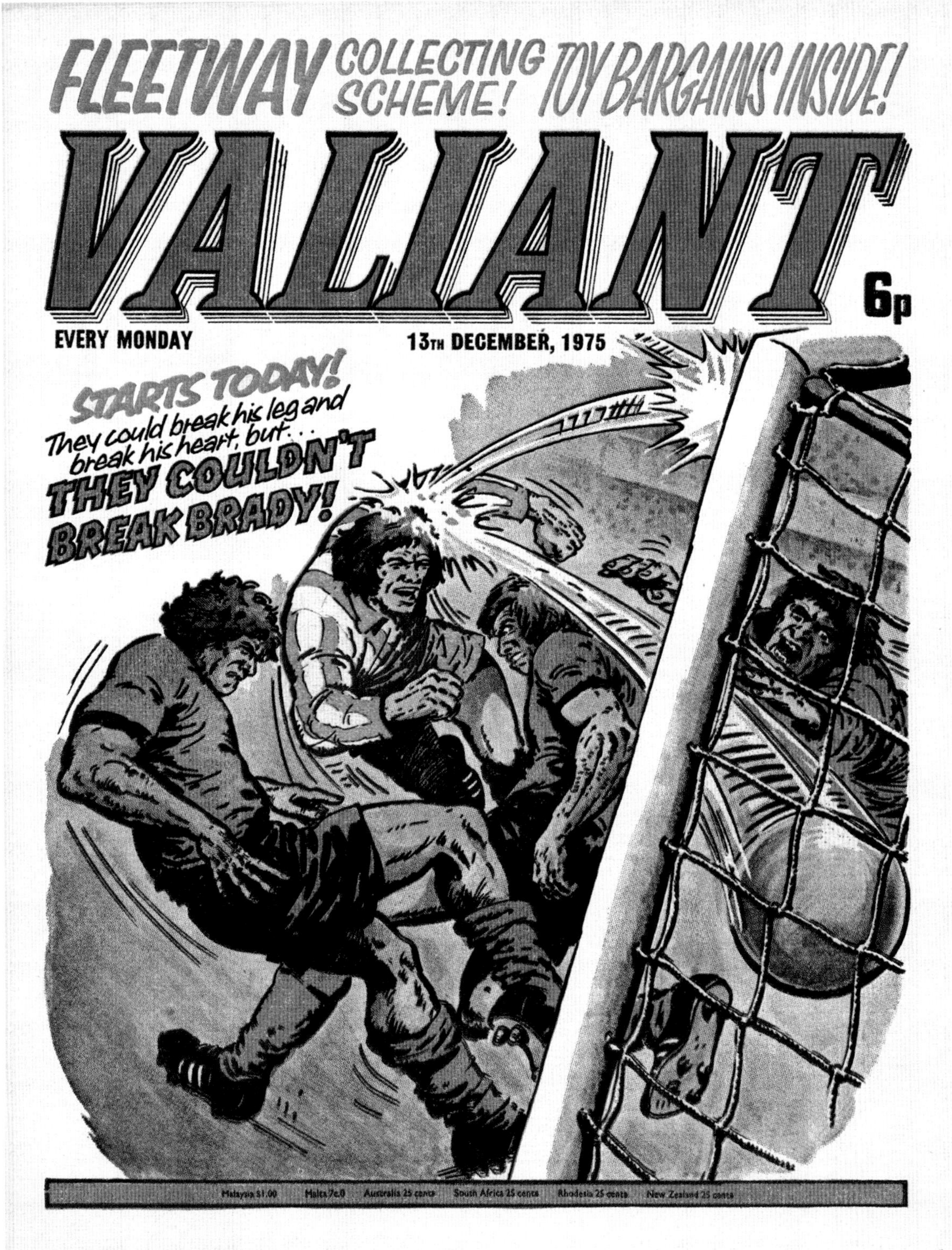
FLEETWAY COLLECTING SCHEME! TOY BARGAINS INSIDE!
VALIANT
6p
EVERY MONDAY
13TH DECEMBER, 1975
STARTS TODAY!
They could break his leg and break his heart, but...
THEY COULDN'T BREAK BRADY!
Malaysia $1.00 Malta 7c.0 Australia 25 cents South Africa 25 cents Rhodesia 25 cents New Zealand 25 cents

Trubshawe inadvertently signed up the wrong Jorge Porbillas; instead of the World Cup winner he had recruited a skinny 15-year-old kid!

Another of football's great individualists appeared in IPC's *Valiant* in 1975. "They Couldn't Break Brady" (13 December 1975) told the story of Dave Brady's courage and determination to play again after breaking his leg. Star inside-forward Brady was written off by First Division Kingston City after the injury, told that his career is over. Despite this he is invited to play for Fourth Division Burford City, and he jumps at the chance even though Burford can only offer him £30 a week. The Burford chairman believes that signing a star of Brady's calibre will have a beneficial effect on the gates – he is right – although he does not expect him to last the season.

Brady performs well in the first game, but finishes the match in agony from the old injury and his doctor advises him that one more knock could cripple him permanently.

It seems he is beaten, and Brady returns to his home town to a job working with his father in the mines, but soon realises he needs to be playing football. He would have to change his playing style from an attacking midfielder to an organising midfielder. Burford release him but relent when they discover First Division Millburn United want to sign him, and try to retain Brady, hoping to earn a transfer fee. The scheme does not work and Brady signs for Millburn.

Brady's new way of playing ensures he stays injury-free, and eventually

Below Storylines moved into the digital age, with a computer that picks football teams. That would never happen, would it? "The Amazing Mister Cedric" (*Hornet*, 11 December 1971)

Millburn win the League Championship. As he declares at the end of the story:
"I've shown them they couldn't break Brady."

Another **Valiant** story that ran concurrently with "They Couldn't Break
Brady" was "The Lout That Ruled the Rovers" (20 December 1975). It
concerned Alf "Monty" Montgomery, who had been a player with Mudville
Rovers until the chairman banned him from the ground for life. Now he ran a
seafood stall outside the ground.

Rovers, unfortunately, had plummeted from the First to the Fourth Division
in three seasons, and Monty's business had suffered due to reduced crowds. One
Saturday afternoon when things are particularly bad, Monty bunks into the
ground to watch the match. Unable to contain his frustration at the team's
ineptitude, he runs onto the pitch and sticks the ball in the back of the net,
much to the crowd's amazement. Not surprisingly, the police escort him out and
the club's directors confirm his life ban.

But fortune is about to smile on our hero. Monty receives a message asking him
to visit a solicitor, where he is informed that Sam Barton, a previous director of the
club, has died and left Monty a majority shareholding in Mudville Rovers. Monty
takes over and appoints himself manager, much to the chagrin of the board.

Slowly Monty pulls the club's fortunes around, although not without a
struggle. At one point the directors make Monty responsible for the club's debts
and he struggles to make ends meet; he has to have a blanket collection at half-
time to pay an electricity bill so a game can be completed.

Above "The Lout That Ruled the
Rovers" was every supporter's
dream – the chance to run your
own football club (*Valiant*,
20 December 1975)

CAN LAMPTON PULL IT OFF? SEE NEXT WEEK!

But *Valiant* was soon to be merged. After 713 issues *Valiant* joined with *Battle*, in October 1976. It wasn't the only comic to close during the 1970s. In that same year *Hornet* ceased publication; launched in 1963 it closed on 7 February 1976. *Rover* had shut down three years earlier, the last issue being published on 13 January 1973, when it joined forces with *Wizard*. But the combined *Wizard & Rover* title did not see out the decade; it folded on 24 June 1978. Nevertheless, as older, more established titles closed, upstart titles were launched to take their place. Two of these stand out from the crowd; IPC's *Action* (launched on St Valentine's Day, 1976) and D.C. Thomson's *Scoop* (first issue 21 January 1978). Both broke new ground; indeed, *Action* was probably the most controversial boys' comic ever published in the UK. Graham Kibble-White takes up the story in his anthology, *The Ultimate Book of British Comics*: "At the end of 1975, [IPC editorial director John] Sanders formulated the idea for a new project (working titles: Boots and Dr Martens) which would appeal to streetwise kids who had forsaken comics. It would be modern, edgy and – again – overseen by [*Battle* comic co-creator Pat] Mills. The *wunderkind* appointed the former *Lion* editor, Geoff Kemp, to actually edit the comic, and the two put together something that screamed of contemporary culture… 'You've never seen stories like these before!' ran the promotional pull-out featured in the likes of *Buster*, et al." An understatement, as Kibble-White expounds: "Issue one of 'the sensational paper for boys!' gave some small indication of the furore that was to follow.

Facing page "Look Out For Lefty" and the *Action* comic incident that upset both Mrs Whitehouse and Football League Secretary Alan Hardaker

Below Wally Brand is England's centre-forward and captain of First Division Brickley Albion in *Hornet* (21 March 1970)

'*Action* is deadly!' ran the editorial. 'You are about to experience the toughest stories ever – Fast! Fierce! Fantastic!'." More understatement. In April 1976, in an echo of the "penny dreadfuls" of 100 years earlier, the *Sun* called **Action** "the sevenpenny nightmare"; and the *Daily Mail* was soon to get in on the act, too. Its objections to **Action** were directed at the comic's football story, "Look out for Lefty". It was an unconventional football strip based on the adventures of Kenny Lampton, a working-class teenager whose powerful left-foot gave him the nickname of "Lefty". The strip included scenes of football hooliganism, and Lefty was far from being a role model for Britain's impressionable youth. The *Daily Mail*'s flames of fury were stoked by a particular episode when Lefty's girlfriend, Ang, throws a bottle onto the pitch, aimed at an opposing player. As Kibble-White writes: "Lefty himself was seen to be endorsing her actions, declaring, 'Good ole Ang!' The [*Daily Mail*] brought in Football League secretary Alan Hardaker to exclaim: 'It really is appalling that there are people so brainless as to sell comics to children with stuff like this inside them. The man responsible ought to be hit over the head with a bottle himself.'"

Facing page Before the term "mercenary" was used to describe the modern footballer, Jon Stark had created an original payment structure for his involvement. Interestingly, he was described as "the footballer of the future"

Below Ben "Leiper the Keeper", a new style of goalkeeper from "This Goalie's Got Guts". He appeared in the pages of *Scoop*

By now Mary Whitehouse's National Viewers and Listeners' Association was piling in, along with a group called "The Delegates Opposing Violent Education". But it was threats from W.H. Smith that caused the title to be pulled; or rather rumours that the retailing giant was considering banning **Action** from its shelves. Its publication was halted in October 1976; when it returned to the shelves in December of that year it was a watered-down version and the comic was never the same again. It was incorporated into **Battle** in November 1977.

While *Scoop* was not exclusively a football comic, the emphasis was very much on the people's game. It certainly reflected the glamour of the time; the likes of Kenny Dalglish, Glenn Hoddle, Paul Mariner and Peter Barnes were all signed up to provide regular contributions. The comic was chock-full of features, player profiles and competitions, and its large-size format certainly helped it

Ben is soon in action.

OOOOH! BAD LUCK, ROVERS— KEEP AT 'EM!

Great save, Ben! Now get it together, City— don't make him work TOO hard!

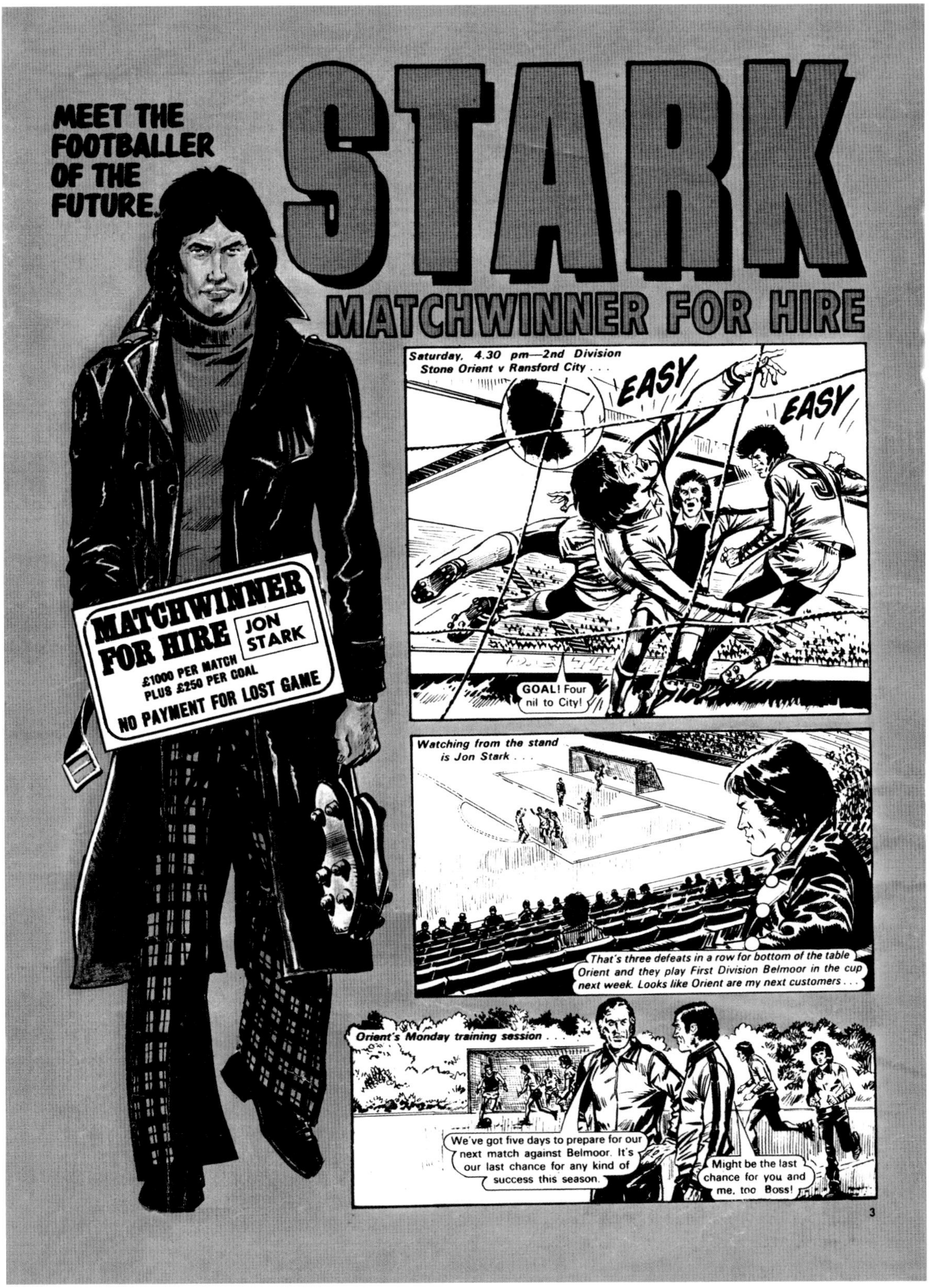
MEET THE FOOTBALLER OF THE FUTURE...
STARK
MATCHWINNER FOR HIRE
MATCHWINNER FOR HIRE
JON STARK
£1000 PER MATCH
PLUS £250 PER GOAL
NO PAYMENT FOR LOST GAME
Saturday, 4.30 pm—2nd Division Stone Orient v Ransford City . . .
EASY
EASY
GOAL! Four nil to City!
Watching from the stand is Jon Stark . . .
That's three defeats in a row for bottom of the table Orient and they play First Division Belmoor in the cup next week. Looks like Orient are my next customers . . .
Orient's Monday training session . . .
We've got five days to prepare for our next match against Belmoor. It's our last chance for any kind of success this season.
Might be the last chance for you and me, too Boss!
3

make a splash. *Scoop* was also the title that gave us "Stark – Matchwinner for Hire". Did we "meet the footballer of the future" when we first encountered Jon Stark? For here was no ordinary, run-of-the-mill professional; he advertised his services to whomsoever was prepared to pay his fee – "£1,000 per match plus £250 per goal – no payment for lost game!".

Much to the disgust of club officials – "it's freedom of contract that's to blame!" one huffs – and to the delight of readers, Stark flitted from club to club, earning his corn. In issue 1, Stark turns out for Stone Orient and earns himself a cool £1,500 by scoring twice in a 2–0 victory over Belmoor. In a story with a continental touch (25 March 1978), Stark manages to play for both sides in a two-legged UEFA Cup tie between Leclerc and Dubois. Such is his mercenary instincts he even plays against doctor's advice, and ends up being crippled during one match (8 April 1978). But there's no keeping a good man down, and Stark returns to action in August 1978. While he was undoubtedly *Scoop*'s headline act, there was a fine footballing supporting cast. "The Boss" was player-manager Joe Judd, who signed up for Italian side FC Malino. He has his work cut out dealing with fiery-tempered players, match-fixing and the team's coach crashing on the way to a match (the brakes had been tampered with). Judd's star player is kidnapped (15 April 1978); Malino suffers an outbreak of hooligan violence; and when a knife-wielding thug tries to attack a player on the pitch and is shot dead by a sniper, the ground is threatened with closure. Judd then gets kidnapped at gunpoint, finally being released as the first series ends

Below King Rudolph Maximillian Rantzberg IV of Moravia was the blue-blooded star of "King of Football" (*Scorcher*, 15 May 1971)

STARTING TODAY: *Penton Rovers have a second-rate ground and a third-rate team! But things change the day they become—*

STEELMAN'S ELEVEN

The town of Penton had two football teams, second division Penton Orient and struggling fourth division club Penton Rovers. Rovers, nicknamed the Ragbags, had an ancient ground which had been left to the club in a will. Now Rovers were playing Denfield Athletic in a league match . . .

THIS IS PATHETIC TO WATCH!

THE LAST TIME I COME TO SEE THE RAGBAGS.

But the Denfield supporters were having the time of their lives!

GOAL NUMBER FOUR!

WHAT A MASSACRE.

Centre-half Tom Brown was captain of the Rovers.

DENFIELD ARE ALL OVER US. WE'RE A LAUGHING STOCK.

(13 May 1978). Not surprisingly, our man is keen to return to England, which he does when the story kicks off again in December 1978.

Another hugely popular *Scoop* tale was "This Goalie's Got Guts". It was the story of Ben "Lieper the Keeper", who turned out for Fourth Division Mancastor City when he wasn't training to be a student doctor. Ben needs two incomes because he has vowed to pay off his father's debts, but the unsympathetic attitude of the hospital authorities makes life awkward for Ben.

Scoop could also lay claim to launching the prototype "fantasy football", with its "Inter City Superleague"). Participants were asked to predict the scores of games between 12 fictional representative sides consisting of players from around each region. So, for example, "Thames Southern", with players from West Ham, Chelsea, QPR, Crystal Palace, Fulham, Millwall, Charlton Athletic, Orient, Wimbledon, Reading, Brentford and Gillingham, might "play" against "Pool City", with a side selected from players from Liverpool, Everton, Wrexham, Southport, Crewe, Tranmere and Chester. The "match" results were then predicted by *Scoop*'s computer, and points awarded to those readers who had made the correct forecasts. League tables were combined on the basis of the computer's results.

But despite its star names, excellent football-related features and memorable comic strip characters, *Scoop* lasted only until 1981, when it was merged with *Victor*. It was a sign of the times; for, as the 1980s approached, the writing was on the wall for the boys' comics.

Above Penton Rovers, nicknamed the Ragbags, are in trouble… until Professor Blanchard introduces them to Stanley Steelman, a robotic humanoid who the professor has designed and built, programming him with all available data relating to football. After that, success is guaranteed… (*Victor*, 14 January 1978)

"EVEN WHEN YOU'RE DEAD YOU SHOULDN'T LIE DOWN AND LET YOURSELF BE BURIED."

Gordon Lee, former Everton manager (1981)

CHAPTER EIGHT
THE FINAL WHISTLE

BY THE LATE 1970s, consolidations, mergers and closures were increasingly frequent occurrences – and in the 1980s the boys' comic virtually disappeared. The closure/merger list reads for the period 1974–1993 reads: *Lion* 1974; *Hornet* 1976; *Bullet* 1978; *Wizard* 1978; *New Hotspur* 1981; *Scoop* 1981; *Buddy* 1983; *Champ* 1985; *Tiger* 1985; *Valiant* 1986; *Victor* 1992; and *Roy of the Rovers* 1993.

D.C. Thomson continued to try to find new ways of invigorating the market. In 1981 it launched *Buddy*, which it claimed was for "boys who like action, adventure and sport!". It mixed comic strip and real-life action with features including the "Buddy Super Personality", which in the first issue (14 February 1981) featured Andy Gray, printed in two colours over two pages. *Buddy* also featured some old favourites, including Limp-Along Leslie, and some new characters, including a caravan-dwelling, football-mad orphan called Tuffy. The story bore similarities to Scrappy, which appeared in earlier *Wizard* comics.

Below Joe Judd in action in the *Scoop Sports Annual* 1983. Judd was the star player and manager of Westhampton Wanderers, where he did things his way

Like Scrappy, Tuffy's only friend is his dog and his story is reminiscent of a Victorian "potboiler". Tuffy is forced to eavesdrop on lessons at Fosters school in an effort to get educated, even joining in a kick-about with the pupils. Impressing them with his goalkeeping skills, he is invited to play for the school team and to attend lessons. But Tuffy is eventually sent to Rampton House, a home for juveniles. He performs well in the football trials, dispossessing the school bully of his place, and Rampton reach the Council cup final, where they beat Tuffy's old school, Fosters, 2–0.

But things were about to get worse

A YOUNG BOY BATTLES AGAINST THE ODDS TO BECOME A TOP FOOTBALLER!

LIMP-ALONG LESLIE

Leslie's through again!

LESLIE THOMSON lived at LOW DYKE FARM with his aunt and uncle, ARNOLD and LUCY SMITH. Leslie's parents were killed in a road accident and Leslie suffered serious leg injuries which left him with a limp. Leslie was determined to equal his father in two ways—by playing football for DARBURY RANGERS and by training a champion sheepdog. Now he was taking part in his first-ever football match, for the village team.

The goalkeeper's coming out at me, and the back's covering him. I'll keep going!

Shoot, Leslie!

Leslie's walking the ball round the goalkeeper!

And now he's walked it into the goal! Leslie's scored again!

Slow but sure, that's you, Leslie! You've never played in a proper game before, yet you've got that terrific ball control. How do you do it?

I've practised every minute I could find for as long I can remember, Joe. On my own, out on the moors. This limp slows me down, so I have to find other ways of getting results.

The game continued—

Leslie's found himself space again. He seems to be thinking two moves ahead all the time.

He's beaten the lot of 'em! Like he'd got the ball glued to his toe!

Leslie's really got 'em worried! Three of them trying to stop him!

BDY. 21.3.81 L1

Above Limp-Along Leslie reappeared in the pages of *Buddy* in 1981 – 30 years after his debut in *Wizard*. He was one of D.C. Thomson's most enduring football characters

MELCHESTER ROVERS v TYNECASTER... 22 OF THE FINEST PLAYERS IN THE FIRST DIVISION. BUT IN A LEAGUE MATCH THAT HAD EVERYTHING, ONE PLAYER IN PARTICULAR STOOD HEAD-AND-SHOULDERS ABOVE THE REST...

RACEY'S ROCKET! IT'S THERRRRE!

ROY of the ROVERS

THAT'S HIS SECOND GOAL OF THE MATCH AND HIS FIFTY-THIRD IN LEAGUE AND CUP GAMES THIS SEASON!

ROY RACE! ROY RACE!

IT WAS A NIGHTMARE OF A GAME FOR THE TYNECASTER 'KEEPER. A FEW MINUTES LATER, ROY SCORED WITH A *HEADER*...

THREE!

AND THEN, FOR GOOD MEASURE, HE PRODUCED A *LOB* OF EXQUISITE TIMING...

FOUR!

TALK ABOUT A 'COMPLETE' PLAYER! ON THIS KIND OF FORM, NO GOALKEEPER IN THE WORLD COULD STOP HIM!

ROY'S PERFORMANCE THAT DAY GAVE THE MEDIA A LOT TO TALK ABOUT...

...MELCHESTER'S NEXT HURDLE IS THE SEMI-FINAL OF THE F.A. CUP! BUT WITH THEIR PLAYER-MANAGER IN SUCH DEVASTATING FORM, THE DRAW CAN-NOT HOLD ANY FEARS FOR THEM!

THEY'RE THE DIRTIEST TEAM IN THE LEAGUE!

THE HUDFIELD HACKERS

That's as far as you go, mate!

OUCH! Foul, referee!

The PENWICK DISTRICT Under-18 League was rough and tough. And the toughest team in the league was HUDFIELD AMATEURS. Their stop-at-nothing style had earned them the title of THE HUDFIELD HACKERS.
Hudfield were leading 1-0 against CARHAM in the second round of the PENWICK CHALLENGE CUP when DANNY HEETON tackled an opponent hard—very hard!

for Tuffy. He is fostered to the Blackley family, but they are thieves and wasters. Mr Blackley deals in stolen goods, while their wastrel son does not work, taking money from Tuffy or simply stealing it. Tuffy gets a break when he is invited to join Westingham Rovers' youth team. His performances gain him a chance to play in the first team, where he plays well, helping them to win the cup by beating Newford Town. With Tuffy's help the Blackley family are arrested, but Tuffy needs to leave Westingham. He signs as an apprentice for Fourth Division Southtown United, where he lives with the Slaymans, the manager's family, but they treat him like a slave and force him to live in the garden shed.

Tuffy plays for the first team, though, and is spotted by First Division Modchester United. The Slayman family try to block the move; however, the switch to Modchester eventually takes place. But Tuffy's problems continue, with accusations of theft and more trouble with authority. It all comes good in the end, with Tuffy playing for the first team on a tour of the US. The story proved so popular that, along with Limp-Along Leslie, it was transferred to *Victor* (6 August 1983), when *Buddy* folded.

Another popular *Buddy* story was "The Hudfield Hackers" – "They're the dirtiest team in the league" (15 August 1981). The Penwick District under-18 league was rough and tough. And the roughest, toughest team was the Hudfield Harriers, their stop-at-nothing style earning them the title of the Hudfield

Above The tough-tackling Hudfield Hackers appeared in *Buddy* from the start (15 August 1981)

Left Roy of the Rovers, England's most decorated footballer, continued to grace the pages of various publications until May 2001

2 Darbury Rangers amateur goalkeeper, scrap dealer Charlie "Iron" Barr, had smuggled two young boys out of East European country, Bulgaria, while the team were there to play Starjevo in the European Cup. At training one day, manager Ted Ingram had some good news for Charlie—

THIS IS OFFICIAL CONFIRMATION, CHARLIE. LAZA AND IVO HAVE BEEN GIVEN PERMISSION TO STAY IN THIS COUNTRY.

TERRIFIC, BOSS!

ONCE ALL THE FORMS HAVE BEEN COMPLETED IVO'LL GO INTO AN ORPHANAGE AND LAZA'LL SIGN FOR DARBURY AS AN APPRENTICE.

MAYBE YOU OUGHT TO PAY ME A SCOUT'S FEE, BOSS.

AMATEURS DON'T GET FEES, CHARLIE . . . NOW GET BACK TO WORK. WE'VE GOT A TOUGH LEAGUE GAME ON SATURDAY AGAINST MANEBRIDGE.

I'M ON MY WAY, BOSS.

Charlie was soon in action—

IRON BARR

WOW! BRILLIANT, CHARLIE. MANEBRIDGE ARE GONNA FIND IT HARD TO GET PAST YOU!

On Saturday, Ted gave the team a warning—

LISTEN, FELLAS . . . THE REFEREES ARE CLAMPING DOWN ON ANSWERING BACK. SO TAKE IT EASY. THE GUY WE'VE GOT TODAY WILL SEND YOU OFF IF YOU SO MUCH AS LOOK AT HIM THE WRONG WAY!

Manebridge attacked from the kick-off—

HECK! THEY'RE FAST!

SP. 19.11.83 IB1

Hackers. Bullied by their manager to take an aggressive approach, the team goes too far in one match, and the league eventually forces the manager to resign. The new boss, Bert Haynes, believes the Harriers are a talented footballing team and encourages them to cut out the rough stuff. The new approach does not please everyone, though, and rifts start within the team. With the new style beginning to get results, some of the teams who have previously suffered at the hands of the Harriers seek revenge. Ultimately, Hudfield beat favourites Thrillby Park to win the league.

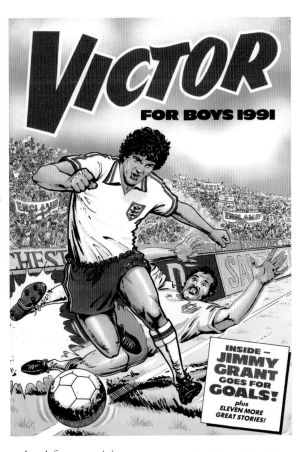

uddy also turned back the clock by introducing a series of one-off, stand-alone stories under the generic title of "School for Soccer". The series kicked off with a full-page front cover story about Cranley College, a boarding school for promising footballers (20 February 1982). The story had echoes of a 1940s story that ran in *Hotspur* called "They're Football Daft at Hotspur Hall". As well as providing a conventional education, the young players get full football training to prepare them for a professional career. The school is run by ex-pro Matt Naylor. What kid would not want to go to a school like this? And it gets better; at the end-of-term assessments league managers are invited to see the pupils perform and to offer them terms. Two friends, Gary Maddox and Bob Hooper, perform well, and Maddox is offered a deal by Eddie Donley of Barford City (a Malcolm Allison-esque character, complete with big hat, big cigar and fur coat). He refuses to sign, preferring to join a club with his friend Hooper; they join Clive Weston's Ragley United, an upcoming club: "'You've made a wise choice, boys, Clive and United are on the way up. They'll pass Eddie on the way down.'"

Buddy continued the emphasis on schoolboy football with "Target Wembley" (21 August 1982), a story about Langthorpe Comprehensive's Under-18 team. They were having a terrible season, losing their first six games in a row. This is due to manager "Screamer" Sorensen, who knows little or nothing about football. Langthorpe are entered into the English Schoolboys U-18 championship, the final to be played at Wembley. Sorensen is given the target of getting the team to the final.

The school caretaker watches the team train and is unimpressed; it transpires he is Jim Kyle, an ex-pro. He agrees to coach them in secret, teaching them football skills rather than the strength training favoured by Sorensen. Jim's

Above Even when the comics ceased publishing, the stars still enjoyed a popular following in the pages of the annuals

Facing page The much-travelled Charlie 'Iron' Barr turns up in the pages of *Spike* (19 November 1983)

secret training starts to pay off and the team progresses through the rounds. But the team is forced to play Daniel Fogerty, the son of Councillor Fogerty, who has done a deal with Sorensen. The scheme is uncovered, and Langthorpe win the final without the ineffectual Daniel; Sorensen is fired and Jim Kyle officially takes over the training of the team.

Buddy was to last just two and a half years. Despite its mix of comic strip stories, star features and use of photography, the comic merged with *Victor* on 6 August 1983.

The merger left D.C. Thomson with just three boys' comics – *Victor*, *Spike* and *Champ*. *Spike* launched on 22 January 1983. One of its leading men was an old favourite – Charlie "Iron" Barr. As well as a regular picture strip the comic also carried an "Iron Barr Sports Round-up" page, which included a quiz, football trivia and readers' letters. Charlie Barr's arrival on the football scene was unusual to say the least. It began just outside the stadium of Danbury Rangers, the club our old pal Limp-Along Leslie plays for. Charlie had arrived to pick up some scrap metal, and while he was there he watched a practice game. Charlie is less than impressed with the Danbury goalie and lets him know as much. The keeper would surely have regretted his response to Charlie: "'You've been yapping on since you got here. If you can do better, loudmouth…'

'Well, I can't do any worse! Okay, I'll have a go. Just a sec while I get my working boots off.'"

Charlie plays barefoot in goal, saving everything the Danbury players throw at him. He is invited to join Danbury, and agrees on the condition that he will remain an amateur. With Charlie on board Danbury complete a League and Cup double, and Charlie is called into the England squad. But after Charlie helps

Below Johnny Tough proves that, regardless of background, there is good in everyone (*Spike*, 5 November 1983)

Above Regarded by many as possibly the best football serial, "We Are United" was an enduring story with a number of players based on personalities of the time. The successful story transferred following the demise of *Champ* to *Victor*, in April 1984

MAGIC MAN

The MARACANA STADIUM, BRAZIL. EIGHTY THOUSAND FANS WITNESSED ANOTHER PULSATING GOAL BY THEIR WING-STRIKER, MEZINO...

MEZINO! MEZINO!

IF THAT IS THE LAST GOAL YOU SCORE IN BRAZIL, IT IS A MEMORABLE ONE!

THE WHOLE COUNTRY WILL MISS YOUR SKILL!

Above "Magic Man" reflected the increasingly international aspects of the English game, and also the personalities who became involved both at management and board level (*Hot Shot*, 13 August 1988)

Right Tony Jordan was "Striker" (*Hot Shot*, 19 November 1988)

Danbury win the European Cup he comes under pressure for his place and decides to move on: "'I've had some great times at Danbury. Deep down they will always be my club.'"

While the Charlie "Iron" Barr stories were timeless tales, "The Taming of Johnny Tough" had a contemporary feel (15 November 1985). It concerns a young tearaway, Johnny, and his struggle to become a top-class professional footballer. Johnny is taken to see a Dr James Barton, a child behavourial specialist. While there, Johnny spots some pictures of Barton playing football; the doctor was once a semi-pro. Johnny's salvation is at hand, for he "would give anything to be a professional footballer". Barton decides to take Johnny under his wing and to toughen him up. He takes him away from his bullying and abusive father to an island where he gets plenty of fresh air and exercise. Johnny becomes part of a group of youngsters with footballing potential but from troubled backgrounds.

Eventually, Barton arranges a trial for Johnny with Fourth Division Penford City. They sign him, the doctor's work is done.

However, the market for boys' comics continued to decline at this time and, like its predecessor **Buddy**, **Spike** had a very short life. After just 15 months and 67 issues it closed (28 April 1984), to be swallowed up by **Champ**. That comic (launched 25 February 1984) represented D.C. Thomson's last throw of the dice in the boys' comic market. Its crowning glory was the soccer strip "We Are United", described by Graham Kibble-White in his tome, *The Ultimate Book of British Comics*, as "one of the best soccer strips ever". "One of the most realistic football stories around, the opening episode was appended with a list of stats and figures about the club's fortunes and a picture of its home ground, the Mill. In this opening instalment, United's board broke the news that the side had run out of money and was going to have to transfer off some of its more lucrative players. A dead cert for the knacker's yard, however, was ageing captain Joe Pearson – 'Your first-team days are numbered, old man!' mused talented-but-lazy Welsh midfielder Terry Evans in a particularly malicious thought-balloon. By the end of the issue, the team had been asset-stripped, but Pearson, rather than being consigned to the scrapheap, was offered the role of manager when the board decided they could no longer afford the present incumbent's expensive boozing and cigar-chomping ways. 'This is what I've always dreamed about,' declared a fist-clenching Joe, 'My life-long ambition.'

With players like burly defender Tug Wilson ('cop that'), punk Alex 'Hedgehog' Jones, going-to-seed journeyman striker Willy Barnes and the callow Benny Grainger in the side, Pearson's inspirational brand of leadership ('Don't stand like a bunch of dummies! We've got to win this match! Move!!') and inevitable last-minute clearances from the goal line re-ignited the side's fortunes. That, and various superstar signings, including Scottish talent Kevin Nicklish (a compound of Kevin Keegan, Charlie Nicholas and Kenny Dalglish) from rival side Southpool, Charlie 'Iron' Barr from *Spike* (inherited when the two titles merged in 1984) and 'Limp-Along' Leslie Thomson, last seen playing in the pages of the now-defunct *Hotspur*. All of this helped give the strip a kind of soap opera feel, and in its time 'We Are United' tackled realistic issues such as merchandising, the stars' private lives and football hooliganism." One of these "stars" was Terry Evans, a George-Best type of character, fond of womanising, drinking and gambling – strong stuff for a kids' comic.

The strip was "interactive" to a degree, with readers invited to contribute to the storylines and characterisations. Also, the stories were divided into two separate chapters, giving the impression of a "game of two halves".

Champ, however, lasted only until 28 April 1984; "We Are United" moved to the *Victor*, D.C. Thomson's last remaining boys' comic. When that comic finally folded, on 21 November 1992, the Scottish publisher's long association with boys' football comics finally came to an end.

Pretty much all that was left was IPC's *Roy of the Rovers*, although the company did test the water once again with the stunningly illustrated comic *Hot Shot*, "fronted" by England international Gary Lineker. It launched on 13 August 1988 and included stories such as "Magic Man" and "Family Fortune". In "Magic Man", Mezino, a striker, plays his last game for Brazil before shocking the football world by signing for lowly First Division northern English club Grimthorpe Rangers. Grimthorpe are owned by Karl King, a pop star and football fanatic. King sacks his manager, and decides to run the club, promising a new all-out attacking strategy. The strategy works and Grimthorpe move up the table.

"Family Fortune" centres on a football-mad family from the rough side of town. Kenny Fortune is an aspiring goalkeeper who gets a chance to play for Second Division Parkside FC in a friendly when the first-choice keeper is taken to hospital. The opposition are First Division Westam Wanderers, for whom his brother Keith is the leading scorer. Despite losing 7-0, Kenny is given another chance and plays well in the youth team.

Also featured was the story "Striker". Its leading man is Tony Jordan of Second Division Cranville Athletic. The club is struggling at the bottom of the division, and at the end of a game which ends in another defeat the players are advised that the club is bankrupt. Jordan asks his father, who owns Jordan Industries, to fund a takeover, which he does, also offering the club £1,000 for every goal his son scores. This is to the disappointment of Kevin Musgrove, Cranville's financial director, who has plans to buy the ground and sell it for housing, making himself a millionaire in the process. The involvement of Jordan

Below *Hot Shot*, with its stylish illustrations, featured the continuing saga that was "Family Fortune" (19 November 1988)

Speech bubbles (part of image):
AND ON THE TOUCHLINE AT STUDLEY...
IAN! I DIDN'T KNOW YOU'D BE HERE TODAY!
I WAS A LAST-MINUTE REPLACEMENT. SO YOU'RE WELCOME TO SERVE UP SOME CLASSIC ACTION FOR ME!

Left "Andy Steele Playmaker" was another hero in *Hot Shot* (29 October 1988); when the comic folded he transferred to the *Roy of the Rovers* comic

Senior is not appreciated by the players, who believe he is favouring his son. Tony is made player-manager, and is also picked to play for England.

One of the leading characters in **Hot Shot** was "Andy Steele Playmaker". The story was sponsored by Quaser Sports, with their logo emblazoned on the team's shirts. Andy had grown up in a succession of children's homes until, at 12 years old, he is fostered by Bill and Margaret Steele. Bill Steele is an ex-England international who encourages Andy to become a playmaker. At 15 (the youngest player ever to play in the English First Division), Andy is selected for Millside City's first team against Brookhampton, whose players decide to "bring him down to size". Not only does Andy show up the thugs using his superior skills, he also provides the passes for all three goals in his first game. Andy's talent is recognised by Italian giants AC Juvenzo, who offer £2 million to Millside for his signature, "…and the answer is no. Andy Steele is not available at any price."

Andy Steel went on to appear in the **Roy of the Rovers** comic, where he ended up playing for big-name Spanish side Real Santania, along with his team mate and fellow prodigy Kevin Radnor. He never, however, signed for Melchester Rovers.

Hot Shot was not to last, though, finally folding in 19 January 1989, with many of the stories coming to an inconclusive end.

That left just Roy Race and his **Roy of the Rovers** comic, which battled on in true style until 23 March 1993. The title was published monthly from September 1993 for 19 issues before that, too, was abandoned. Roy did make a comeback, however, in the launch issue of the BBC's *Match of the Day* magazine (May/June 1997). That title was to last for four years, ceasing publication in May 2001. And so the final chapter ended and they thought it was all over. But as long as we dream and fantasise, the comics and our heroes live on…

THE ULTIMATE FANTASY FOOTBALL COMIC

WE HAVE PUT TOGETHER A COMIC FROM THE ARCHIVES, COVERING THE PERIOD FROM 1910 TO THE 1970s. IT INCLUDES:

GREAT STORY ACTION FEATURING COMIC BOOK FOOTY STARS FROM DOWN THE AGES

THE ULTIMATE FANTASY FOOTBALL COMIC

GREAT COMIC CARDS TO COLLECT — INSIDE!

Can you beat Know-All? He appeared regularly in the pages of *Scorcher*, 1970-1974

Know-All

He's Soccer's Mister Big-Head! See If You Can Catch Him Out.

ANSWERS BELOW

HERE'S A WELL-KNOWN REFEREE, REG MATTHEWSON, WHOM MANY OF YOUR DADS WILL HAVE SEEN PLAYING FOR BOLTON AND SHEFFIELD UNITED IN THE 1950's!

ACTION FROM ST. ANDREWS, AS LIVERPOOL'S PETER CORMACK (LEFT), AND JOHN ROBERTS OF BIRMINGHAM LEAP HIGH FOR A CROSS. BOTH THESE FINE PLAYERS HAVE REPRESENTED WALES DURING THEIR CAREERS!

GOAL! PETER SHILTON OF LEICESTER DIVES, BUT PETER OSGOOD'S SHOT IS ON ITS WAY INTO THE NET FOR CHELSEA. DO YOU KNOW THAT NEITHER OF THESE GREAT SIDES HAVE EVER WON THE CHAMPIONSHIP OF THE FIRST DIVISION?

A RACE FOR THE BALL BETWEEN DUNCAN FORBES OF NORWICH CITY AND LEEDS UNITED'S JOE JORDAN. DUNCAN (LEFT), HAS BEEN A WONDERFUL SERVANT FOR "THE CANARIES", AND HAS NEVER PLAYED FOR ANY OTHER CLUB!

ONE FOOTBALL GROUND I MUST GO TO IS THE CITY GROUND, HOME OF NOTTINGHAM FOREST. HAVE YOU BEEN THERE BEFORE?

FOREST DON'T PLAY THERE, KNOW-ALL!

Answers: 1. Correct. 2. Rubbish! John Roberts plays for Wales, but Peter Cormack is a Scottish international. 3. Wrong, Know-All. 4. Wrong again—Duncan was previously with Colchester. 5. You're right this time, Know-All. Leicester have never been First Division Champions, but Chelsea were in 1955.

The Blue Crusaders were extremely popular before the Great War. This story is from 1910

THE 'BOYS' REALM' FOOTBALL LIBRARY.

EVERY THURSDAY

1/2 D

"DOWN ON THEIR LUCK!"

| JACK NOBLE | THE BLUE CRUSADERS | TEDDY LESTER |

Vol. 3. No. 57.   Week Ending Saturday, October 15th, 1910.

DOWN ON THEIR LUCK

A Stirring Tale of "The Blue Crusaders."

By A. S. HARDY.

THE FIRST CHAPTER.
A Match at Moor Field—The Blue Crusaders in Trouble—Prospects of the Cup-Tie.

IT was the Saturday before the Second Round in the Ties for the English Cup was to be played, and not for many years could such a windy day be remembered.

Hoardings had been blown down, chimney-pots had been hurled into the streets, men and women had been whirled off their feet. Accidents had been numerous, and a long list of casualties were expected when the morning's newspapers came to hand.

The Blue Crusaders, playing at home at Moor Field, had been congratulating themselves that they had not a hard match to play in meeting Birmingham, for the Birmingham team were third from the bottom of the League table, and the Blue Crusaders were second to Newcastle at the top.

The Blue Crusaders started the game in finished style, and, having won the toss, they were able to rush the ball down to the vicinity of the Birmingham goal almost from the kick-off.

They took it leisurely, not because they underrated their opponents, but because there would be plenty of time to score in forty-five minutes.

They rattled the crossbar, they hit the goalposts, they bombarded the Birmingham goalkeeper, but, all the same, there were not many shots that had anything but direction to recommend them. There was no sting behind them.

The Blue Crusaders' powder was damp!

Occasionally the Birmingham forwards, nerved to desperation, broke away, but their attacks were easily staved off, and Fowkes easily repelled the few stinging shots that were sent to him. But the half was drawing to a close. The minutes were flying fast. There was not much time in which to get those winning goals, and Birmingham would have the wind with them in the second half.

Fowkes was the first to realise that the match was by no means won, and ten minutes before half-time, after catching a ball from the Birmingham centre-forward, he punted it down the field, and rushed it nearly to the halfway line.

"Hang it all, lads!" he said. "Get a goal or two! We shall want 'em if we don't look out!"

The Crusaders' forwards were roused at that.

They dashed into the game with a vim and nerve that were irresistible, and, putting on all pace, they swarmed in the vicinity of the Birmingham goal. The crowd roared itself hoarse in an ecstasy of excitement. Then Drew, from the left wing, put in a perfect centre, and his chum Harry Ewing slammed it past the Birmingham goalkeeper.

That was number one.

From the kick-off the ball was carried down, and sent out to Arthur Drew again, and, with twinkling feet, he dribbled it along the touchline, leaving the half-back opposed to him hopelessly in the rear, converging in towards goal as he went.

Then the right full-back came charging down upon him. The opponent was above his weight, and Drew fell full length on the turf, whilst the crowd booed. But the charge was fair enough, though perhaps a little rough.

It was soon plain that Drew was hurt. His comrades clustered round him, and the trainer called out and the doctor was sent for. Then the lad was carried off, his face drawn with agony.

The referee threw down the ball, and Thomson, the Crusaders' inside-left, placed it accurately right in front of the net, where Green, the International, was waiting to receive it; and biff! a twist of the head, and the ball had been sent past the goalkeeper for number two.

There wasn't any time left for more, and the teams returned to the dressing-room with the Crusaders two up.

They came out for the second half with only ten men. Drew was too badly injured to turn out. The lad had twisted his foot as he went over, and both the ankle and the cartilage of the knee were badly wrenched.

As the Crusaders faced that hurricane of icy wind which had prevented Birmingham taking the ball down the field in the first half they shivered with cold, and Harry Ewing, whose face was ghastly pale, and whose nose was red, and whose eyes were watering, shuddered as he spoke to his comrade in the centre.

"Dick," he said, "I don't know what's the matter with me, but I've been cold ever since I got out of my bath this morning. I've never seemed to have got warm. Even the game hasn't warmed me up. I do hope I'm not going to be queer."

"You ill!" answered Dick Green, with a smile, but at the same time looking anxiously at his chum. "Of course you're not! Why, you've never been ill in your life—not really ill! Just you warm yourself up with a brisk run first chance you get, my boy!"

At that moment there came a sneeze from behind him, and turning round, Dick Green saw that David Moran, their crack half-back, was looking seedy also.

"What's the matter, Dave?" he said. "There's

DOWN ON THEIR LUCK.

nothing wrong with you, is there? Though I must say that you seemed to be a bit slack in the first half. I suppose you were saving yourself up for this?"

"Saving myself up for this?" cried David Moran gloomily. "I wish I could say I had been, Dick! No; the fact is I feel rotten. I've caught a downright bad cold. It's in my bones. I've got it in my back, my knees, my shins—everywhere. I wish I could get a hot bath and go home to bed."

"It won't be long now," said Dick cheerfully.

The wind was whistling and shrieking through the stand, and the ground presented a half-deserted appearance now, for so assured had the local supporters become of a victory for the home side that they had gone home to their cosy firesides and their teas, content to rely on the evening football newspaper for the report of the match.

When the ball was set in motion the Birmingham lads kicked it down the field with a huge lunge, and the whole forward line went after it in hot haste, dashing past the Crusaders' halves like a tornado.

They missed the ball, however, and Shepherd, the home right-back, cleared with ease. But he failed to keep the ball low, with the result that the wind caught it and swept it high into the air, and the next moment a roar of astonishment went up as Fowkes was seen to catch the ball right under the bar, and then dance a pirouette with all the Birmingham forwards round him before he could clear.

It was an earnest of what was to come.

Harry Ewing, who had done fairly well in the first half, was now playing listless football. Poor fellow! He was not in a fit state to play the game. He could see two footballs sometimes, through the haze in his eyes. And how his head ached! He made sure then that he was going to be very ill indeed unless he was very careful.

David Moran was now unaccountably missing the ball and letting the Birmingham forwards get away. They rushed past Hammond and Shepherd, and gave Fowkes the time of his life.

The crowd began to stare. Though they realised that the wind was practically playing the game for Birmingham, they also knew their lads were not within fifty per cent. of their true form, and they wondered what was up.

Then a Birmingham forward, with a surprise shot at close range, got the ball past Fowkes, the goalkeeper being unsighted by his own backs, and there was only one goal between them.

Fowkes looked grimly determined. He was frozen to the marrow by that bitter cold wind. He was shivering, too, but he determined that the game should not be won by Birmingham. Then, of a sudden, he found the whole of the Birmingham forward line racing towards him like mad.

Their centre was now in possession of the ball.

They had rushed it through from the halfway line, and had caught the home backs napping, and Fowkes knew that only himself could save the game.

He watched the movements of the forwards like a lynx. He anticipated the passing of the ball, and he was on the man to whom it was given like a flash.

The goalkeeper went down. Somewhere between nineteen and twenty stone struck the earth with a tremendous thud, and he had seized the ball in his hands. But the men in blue shirts were swarming around him. To have attempted to have got rid of

FOOTBALL LIBRARY.—No. 57.

the ball would have been fatal. The only thing to do was to hold on.

They kicked at the ball in their endeavours to get it out of his hands. The boots flashed round him.

Then the referee suddenly blew his whistle. They helped Fowkes up. He looked pale and ill. It took the attention of two trainers five minutes to bring him round.

He went back to his goal and the ball was thrown down. Birmingham got possession, and Fowkes had to save instantly, and no sooner had he punched one shot out than another was sent in with terrific force.

Fowkes caught the line of its flight, and flung himself across the goal with outstretched hands. He just missed the object by an inch. It went past him into the net, and, after hitting the post with his body with terrific force, for the second time during the match Fowkes was laid out. This time he was really hurt, and, after a stoppage, he left the field supported by Shepherd and Hammond.

With Fowkes and Arthur Drew off the field, and Ewing and Moran seedy, Birmingham, with the wind in their favour, danced round the homesters to a merry tune, and Birmingham had won by four goals to two when the final whistle blew.

The doctor was busy in the Crusaders' dressing-room, and no sooner had he patched Fowkes up and sent him home, with the intimation that he would come round and make a further examination of him within half an hour, than he uttered an exclamation of dismay at the sight of David Moran extended, groaning, on his locker.

"What's the matter with you, my lad?" he said, going to him and turning him over. One look at the lad's face, and he uttered an exclamation of concern. "It's the influenza," he said. "You must go home. Go to bed at once, and I'll send you some physic during the evening. Hallo, Ewing! Why, you've got the 'flue, too! Bless my soul! I shall have all of you on the sick-list, I'm afraid, unless you're careful! I strongly suspect that Fowkes has a couple of ribs broken, and Drew won't be able to play for three or four weeks with that wretched ankle and displaced cartilage of his."

The players exchanged meaning glances.

"It's a good job," said Shepherd, the right full-back, grimly, "that we've only got Barsley to play in the Cup-tie next Saturday. We should cut up a bit rough against a crack team with four or five of our best players on the sick-list, I reckon."

And the others gloomily nodded assent.

THE SECOND CHAPTER.
The Second League Match at Barsley — The Last Straw—The Burning of the Stand.

THAT same Saturday afternoon the League match at Barsley had been played to almost empty benches. Gainsborough had opposed the Second League club. They came with a fair record, and, to the unenthusiastic comments of the onlookers, Barsley, whose shooting was appallingly bad, managed to bring off a goalless draw with a little bit of the best of the luck.

The beggarly fifteen hundred spectators wended their way homewards as soon as the final whistle had blown, and many disparaging remarks were heard concerning the team and its management.

The players retired, glad that it was all over. They were a loyal set of lads, youngsters most of them, who had not as yet had years of League

5

THE BOYS' REALM FOOTBALL LIBRARY.

experience. The few veterans in the team were what are termed "has beens" by clubs so situated that they can afford to secure the services of only the very best.

Yet these "has beens" had a steady influence upon the rest of the players, and had there been more enthusiasm in Barsley and more "go" in the management, matters might have considerably improved.

Barsley had scrambled through the First Round of the English Cup, and in the Second Round they were drawn to meet the Blue Crusaders at home. It was a lucky draw in many respects. It was a draw which would have put most clubs on their feet. In Barsley, however, little enthusiasm was shown over the match.

"We don't stand a chance!" one downhearted supporter had said when the draw had been announced in the paper. "The Blue Crusaders will swallow us. I'm hanged if I'm going to come and see my team eaten! If we had a few decent players it might be different, but we haven't got a lad worth looking at."

That was the general opinion.

As Manager Grimshaw stood, hands in pockets, in the deserted stand, and looked gloomily at the crowd, sparse and dejected, whom he could see making their way along the street towards the town, he heaved a deep sigh of regret.

A smartly-dressed, good-looking man of between thirty and forty years of age, who had watched the match from the reserved seats, and who had been eyeing Grimshaw for some time, at this made his way to where the Barsley manager was standing.

"Well, Grimshaw," he said, with a cheery sort of smile, "this doesn't say much for the gate next Saturday, does it?"

Mr. Grimshaw turned with a start, and looked the other up and down.

"No, sir," he said, "it does not. I think I've seen you before somewhere, although I can't rightly recall your name."

"Oh, my name is Wentworth, and I am manager of the Blue Crusaders Football Club!"

In a moment Grimshaw had extended his hand. He was smiling heartily now.

"I'm glad to see you, sir!" he said. "We are pursued by bad luck, Wentworth. Do what we will, we cannot make things pay. The crowd won't come. Their jeering remarks upset the players. The lads either can't or won't try. They are a nice lot of lads, too! Egad! I'd give something to know how I could arouse football enthusiasm in Barsley! The town wasn't happy until it had its first-class football club, and now they've got it, I'm blessed if they'll come and support it!"

Manager Wentworth stroked his chin reflectively.

"You'd a very bad gate this afternoon," he said. "And yet, to my mind, your lads played anything but bad football. They seemed down at heart, that was all. But I must say that your surroundings are very depressing. Are you in debt, Grimshaw?"

The manager set his feet wide apart and looked fearlessly in the Blue Crusaders' manager's eyes.

"Mr. Wentworth," he said, "we owe far more than we can hope to pay, unless things change for the better. The club is nearly £3,000 in debt. Look at this stand! We had promised our supporters a new one this season, and we meant to construct the ground on up-to-date lines. We can't do it. The town grumbles. We can't help that. Unless things

change for the better we shall have to shut down at the end of the season, and it will be good-bye to League football in Barsley!"

"Well, look here," said James Wentworth, "I have a proposal to make, Grimshaw. Mind you, I have no interests of my own to serve. My lads, given their share of the luck, could just as easily beat yours, either at home or away. We have a tremendous following at Browton—in fact, I could guarantee at least a 20,000 gate. How many will you get here?"

"Ten thousand, if we are lucky," said Mr. Grimshaw, with a sombre shake of the head.

"Just so! And your prices are lower than at Moor Field. Well, transfer the tie to Browton. I'll give you an extra £200 for doing so. That will help the club through. You want the money. I don't make the offer because I fear my lads would be beaten here, but because I think it will help you along."

For a moment Manager Grimshaw's eyes gleamed brightly, and his cheeks glowed red with enthusiasm. Then he shook his head dolefully.

"No, Mr. Wentworth," he said. "I can't do it. I'm a strange sort of man. I don't think I was ever cut out to make a commercial success. I can't do it. It's against my principles. We shall have to play at home, and trust to the Barsley folk turning out in their thousands. If we are to go under, nobody shall be in a position to say, when the club is no more, that we haven't acted straight by them all through the piece."

James Wentworth shook Grimshaw by the hand.

"I admire you, Grimshaw," he said. "I'm hanged if I shouldn't have done the same thing. Well, I wish you luck next Saturday, that is all."

While they had been speaking the day had been drawing in fast. They could scarcely see across the ground now, and as the cold wind swept shrieking and whistling through the stand, shaking the crazy structure to its very foundations, James Wentworth drew his coat-collar about his throat.

"Let us get out of this, Grimshaw," he said. "It's neither good for man nor beast. What a wind! There'll be some strange upsets of the League form this afternoon."

James Wentworth was smoking a pipe, which he had refilled during the conversation, and lit by means of a fusee. As he walked along the stand now by Grimshaw's side a sudden gust of wind tore the lighted tobacco out of the bowl of his pipe, and sent it whirling along the stand to a corner where some dust and rubbish to feed on were to be found where the wind had swept it, and the sparks began to revel in mad ecstasy, racing over the dust like imps of fury. In a moment or two there was a glowing heap in the corner, and the dry woodwork began to scorch. The grandstand of the Barsley football enclosure was on fire.

The friendly managers went down to the office, and remained until the teams had departed.

One of the Barsley players—a good-looking, fair-haired lad—smiled a "Good-night!" at Mr. Grimshaw.

"That's Howell, isn't it?" said James Wentworth sharply.

"Yes; our centre-forward, and a good lad, too. He only needs more experience to turn out a tip-top player."

They strolled along together to the gate and passed out, saying "Good-night!" to the groundsman, who

DOWN ON THEIR LUCK.

remained to have a last look round before locking up the enclosure. The two managers walked down the street past the stand, talking together thoughtfully, and they had hardly reached the far end before James Wentworth pulled up, sniffing the air.

"There's a smell of burning!" he cried, holding on to his hat as a fierce gust of wind threatened to blow it away. "It's burning wood! Why, there can't be anything the matter with your stand, can there, Grimshaw?"

"No," said the local manager. Then, as a flash of light suddenly lit up the darkness, he opened his mouth wide with astonishment and horror, as, pointing to the stand, he said: "By Jove, there is, though! The stand's on fire! And all my men have gone home! By the time I ring up the fire-station and have the engines down here the fire will have burnt the place out! Quick, Wentworth, come back with me! Let's try and get the hose out and save the old structure. If the stand goes that will be the last straw. We shall have to close up then!"

The two managers raced back to the wicket door set in the big gate, and, clambering through, faced the astonished groundsman.

"Why, what on earth's the matter, sir?" said the groundsman, his mouth wide open in astonishment.

"The hose—the hose! Quick, Ripley!" gasped the manager. "The stand's on fire!"

With a cry, the man rushed away, and was soon fumbling at the door of the toolshed with a bunch of keys. His very impatience rendered the task of opening the door more difficult. But the hose had been brought out within a minute, and they unrolled it whilst the man screwed one end of it to the cap of the hydrant. Then they rushed the nozzle forward and swung round to face the stand.

It was too late! The wind had fanned the blaze into a fury. The wood was cracking and burning. A portion of the roof was already alight, and masses of charred and blackened timber were falling into the fiery vortex below. The wind was sweeping the flames along the stand. The structure was doomed. The broad jet of water from the hose was sent hissing and spluttering into the flames, but only seemed to feed the fire.

Swept onward by the wind, the flames spread at a tremendous rate, and soon it was impossible to face the furnace. Grimshaw felt his hands blistering and his face scorching, and he drew back, letting the hose drop from his nerveless fingers.

Outside in the street he could hear the crowd yelling. There was much laughter and booing on the part of the spectators.

"It's the best show we've ever seen on the old ground," said one of them ironically; "and it ain't cost us anything. It's a sight more worth seeing than bad football. Look at the old rabbit-hutch burning! Hurrah, hurrah, hurrah!"

The remarks were received with derisive laughter and ironical cheers.

Then the fire-brigade arrived. But from the first they saw that the task was hopeless. Nothing could save the stand with such a wind blowing. Presently the whole roof fell in with a crash, a mass of sparks floated heavenward, and the fierce blaze of light began to fail.

As he saw the charred boards bend and heave, and realised that the ground was rendered practically useless for the purposes of the Cup-tie, Grimshaw looked earnestly at James Wentworth.

"Sir," he said, and his voice was thick and husky,

"does your offer to change the venue of the match hold good now?"

"Now more than ever," remarked the Browtonian; "and this time, Grimshaw, you will have a perfectly valid excuse. The Barsley men can't blame you for playing the match at Moor Field now."

"All right," said the Barsley manager. "Then we'll play the game at Browton."

THE THIRD CHAPTER.
A Big Crowd at Moor Field—Excursionists from Barsley—The Blue Crusaders Lose the Match in a Good Cause.

BARSLEY'S final misfortune—the burning of their stand—instead of ruining the club, as Grimshaw had predicted, had quite the contrary effect. It brought the precarious condition of the club firmly home to the minds of its supporters.

Letters were published in the local papers during the course of the week, and a sigh of relief was felt when the public was assured that the stand had been covered by insurance.

Then James Wentworth, the Blue Crusaders' manager, had written a letter to the "Barsley Argus," in which he plainly stated that he had endeavoured to get Manager Grimshaw to consent to the Cup-tie being played at Browton before the stand was burnt down, but that Manager Grimshaw had refused, having the interests of his club's supporters always first in his mind.

"If the stand had not been burnt down," said James Wentworth, "I could never have got the Barsley team to play at Browton, even had I offered their manager £1,000 to change the venue."

James Wentworth knew his public. In a few days Grimshaw had been lifted from the mire of oblivion in which he had languished for so long, and exalted as a hero. A wave of football enthusiasm swept over the town, and so many and so eager were the inquiries at the railway-station as to the terms for an excursion to Browton for the Cup-tie match that two specials were given to them, and, to his astonishment, the football manager saw that there was a likelihood of the club doing well, after all, if the slightest bit of luck came their way.

The luck came. The team were conveyed to Browton on the Friday afternoon in order that they might escape the unwelcome attentions of the enthusiasts in the excursion trains and avoid travelling on the morning of the match.

They put up at Peter Simple's, at the Half-Way Inn, which is situated exactly opposite the Moor Field Football Ground.

The Barsley players met some of the Browton players in the spacious billiard-room on the Friday night after dinner.

"Come to beat us?" asked Shepherd, the Crusaders' right full-back, as he shook hands with the handsome, fair-haired Howell.

The Barsley centre-forward shook his head.

"I can't say," he remarked. "We haven't won a match of any kind for six weeks. Still, we don't funk. We mean to do our best. We sort of realise that it will be our last chance, and we want to make the most of it."

"Well, youngster," said Shepherd, regarding Howell thoughtfully, and thinking what a fine-built lad the Barsley centre-forward was, "you will have more than an outside chance if your boys have their hearts in the game. Fowkes, our goalkeeper, won't be able to play. He's got two ribs broken, and it'll be a few weeks before he will turn out again. Harry Ewing is down with influenza. David Moran, our crack centre-half, is down with it, too, only in his case there's pneumonia as well. He's in bed, and was so bad in the middle of the week that the doctor thought he mightn't pull through. Then we've got Arthur Drew, our outside-left, crocked; and so you've got more than a chance."

It was encouraging news for Howell. Not that he was the sort of lad that would be put off his game by the reputations of any team, however great they might be.

How the crowd tumbled up the hill from the town the following afternoon! They came in their thousands, most of them wearing the blue-and-white favours of the homeside.

There were quite twenty-five thousand people on the ground when the teams turned out, and they were still coming up from Browton Town.

A steady wind was blowing from the direction of the moor. It was worth the having at the start.

Howell, as captain, tossed for choice of ends. Shepherd, captain for the Blue Crusaders, vice Fowkes, injured, called to the coin and lost.

The Barsley supporters cheered again. Dick Green set the ball in motion for the Crusaders, and, with Barsley setting about their task with diffidence, the blue-and-white forward line, their blue crosses showing up well upon their white shirts, broke clean through.

Dick Green, receiving a perfect centre, slammed in one of the shots for which he, a great International, was famous. It went straight and true to its mark. A roar of "Goal!" went up, and then a yell.

The Barsley goalkeeper had thrown himself across space and got his hands to the ball, clearing in the most marvellous fashion.

While yet the shouts and plaudits of the crowd rang in his ears, and before he could get up, Dick Green was on the ball again, ready to send a swift return into the tenantless goal; but in his eagerness he trod upon the ball, his ankle slipped round, and he stumbled.

As his shoulder hit the ground young Howell dashed up and cleared with a flying kick that lodged the ball into touch at the halfway line.

The referee stopped play so that Green could be attended to. It was some minutes ere he was able to continue, and then he ran down the field with a perceptible limp and his face drawn with agony.

It was apparent that Green would be of little further use; but still, the onlookers thought that the remaining mighty ten of Browton Town would be

too good for the despised eleven of Barsley. They counted without Howell.

Moran's substitute at centre-half found that he had an eel to deal with. Shepherd and Hammond, as time and again they dashed to the rescue of their harassed halves, stared with amazement at the lightning-like and subtle movements of one of the cleverest forwards they had had to deal with that season. And when at length Shepherd slipped up when essaying to stop Howell's progress with the ball, and saw the red-shirted player dash past him for goal, and Hammond unable to come across in time to check him, he fairly gasped.

The goalkeeper thundered out with a terrifying run. With grim, set, and flashing eyes, Howell only saw the goal space, and, shooting just before the goalkeeper crashed into him, he sent the ball flying into the net.

He had scored first goal for his side, and the thunderous roar of applause was like sweet music in his ears.

Barsley had tasted blood in the presence of 25,000 spectators, who applauded that clever goal, like the sportsmen that they were, instead of jeering at them, as the Barsley home supporters had continually done.

They went ahead at such a pace, and played such a sterling forward game, that their rushes were irresistible, and before their line was beaten back they had scored two more goals, and led at half-time by 3 to 0.

In the second half they devoted almost all their energies to defence, tactics for which they could scarcely be blamed, and they succeeded to the extent that the Blue Crusaders could only pierce their defence twice, and the end came with Barsley victorious in the Cup-tie by 3 goals to 2.

Arthur Drew, who had watched the game from the stand, was sad at heart that day.

"We should have won in a canter," he murmured, "if we could have had our full team out."

Manager Wentworth laid his hand on the lad's shoulder.

"Yes, my lad," he said; "but we don't want all the luck to come our way. That win has saved Barsley. Their team won't go to pieces now, and they'll soon have another stand built."

He proved a true prophet—in fact, Barsley, encouraged by their away victory over the most famous team in the land, played like an inspired eleven in the Cup-ties, and were not dismissed until they were defeated at Sheffield by Newcastle in the semi-finals, and by that time they had taken £2,500 out of the Cup. THE END.

("*The New Crusader,*" *a fine, complete football yarn next week.*)

Next Week!

"THE NEW CRUSADER,"

A Magnificent Complete Tale of

JACK NOBLE & "THE BLUE CRUSADERS,"

By A. S. HARDY.

Also an Extra Long Instalment of

"THE BOYS OF SLAPTON SCHOOL."

DANDY FOOTBALL FUN YARN BEGINNING BELOW.

THE CLASSIEST GOALKEEPER IN BRITAIN!

THE LIVING AUNT SALLY.

ONE of the hands at Ticker's Travelling Show and Circus put his head into the tent where Mr Ticker was writing a letter.

"There's a feller after a job, boss," he said.

Mr Ticker stopped writing and looked up eagerly.

"He must be some good, I suppose, or you wouldn't have worried me," he said.

"He certainly looks a likely lad," answered the man.

"Bring him in, then, but don't tell him anything."

The owner of the travelling show rose to his feet and stepped to the other end of the tent, where lay half a dozen footballs.

A moment or two later a rather tall, loosely-built lad entered the tent and looked round. There was a quaint twinkle in his eyes, giving him the appearance of always wearing a smile.

"You're looking for a job, I understand?" said Ticker.

"Yes," was the reply.

"Huh! Can you catch?"

"Catch?" repeated the lad, looking puzzled.

"Yes, catch this."

As he spoke Mr Ticker snatched up two of the balls and flung them at his visitor, who gasped with surprise, but nevertheless caught the balls skilfully.

"Some more," said Ticker. "Drop those you're holding just now."

More balls flew at different angles, but the astonished lad caught them all.

"I say," he asked anxiously, "are you feeling all right?"

"Quite," replied Ticker. "I was just trying you. I've got a job going and you may suit. Come along with me. What's your name?"

"Bentley—Bill Bentley."

"Well, see how this suits you, Bill."

Ticker led the way to a long, oblong-shaped booth. At one end there were several footballs and a number of tennis balls.

"This is my 'Shy-at-Him' show," explained Ticker. "Your job is to stand at the other end while customers shy and kick balls at you."

"Thanks for our little chat," said Bill. "Good morning. I'll find my way out."

"Hold hard! This is a good job, lad. You'll get three quid a week and your board and lodging."

"Which hospital is your last man in?" asked Bill.

"The Royal——" began Ticker, and then coughed. "Um—er——" he stuttered nervously. "He—er—left to get another job."

Bill grinned and looked along the booth.

"Three quid a week and board and lodging is not to be sneered at," he said to himself. Then he added aloud—"I'll have a go at it."

"Got to give you a proper test first," declared Ticker. "This is a very popular part of my show, and I've no use for a dud."

Then he called to some of his men, and told them to let fly at Bill.

A moment later the lad was jumping and dodging like a flash of lightning. His hands and feet kept flying out here and there, now kicking, now catching, and hardly a ball went past him.

"It's a deal," exclaimed Ticker suddenly. "Bill, you're engaged. Come on and I'll fit you out with a costume. You can start work this evening."

"Yes, and I wonder how long it'll be before I'll be carried out," remarked Bill with a grin. "Still, I'll keep going as long as I can, as the man said when he fell off the church steeple."

Presently Bill found himself in possession of a football jersey, a pair of shorts and boots, and red stockings.

He partly undressed to see how his uniform fitted, and Mr Ticker whistled softly as he looked him over.

"My word!" he said. "You've got a chest on you, Bill. And some muscles, too. Let's try them. Why, you're cast-iron, lad!"

"Stop tickling me, boss!" protested Bill. "Let me get into my glad rags."

The brightly-coloured garments fitted him well, and Mr Ticker rubbed his hands as he looked his new hand over.

"I've certainly struck very lucky," he said to himself.

The big show was standing on a common just outside the city of Ironmoor. As he got back into his ordinary clothes Bill glanced towards the buildings, and saw a large board standing up. On it were the words, "Ironmoor United F.C."

"I suppose you'll be open to-morrow afternoon?" asked Bill.

"You bet we will. It's Saturday to-morrow."

"That's dished my idea of watching the United," Bill said.

"Want to see them?" asked Ticker.

"Yes."

"Well, you'll get your chance to-night. They told me to send word as soon as I'd got another man on this job. They spend a lot of money here. They say it helps them in their training."

"Taking shots at me?" asked Bill. Ticker nodded.

"Where's my hat?" said Bill. "I can still find my way out."

"You've taken the job on," said Ticker, "and you don't seem to me to be the sort to let another man down. You aren't a quitter, are you? him-

Dandy FREE Gift

"SURE SHOT SPRING GUN"

To Be Given Away Next Week

Full particulars on page 13.

Why is yesterday like football ?

"No," replied Bill, "only a fool. I'll stay."

TICKER sent word to Ironmoor United that the "Shy-at-Him" booth was open again, and Tommy Mitchell, the skipper, said that some of the boys would be along.

As soon as the show opened Bill was kept hard at work, and the number of people who seemed anxious to hit him in the eye with a tennis ball, or find his wind with a football, was remarkable.

It was easily the most popular booth in the show, and Bill heaved a few sighs as he watched the queue of people lined up, waiting their turn to shy at him.

"I've put up a notice to say that the booth is reserved at seven o'clock," said Ticker, while balls were being collected and flung back to the eager people. "That's the time the United are coming along."

"What do I do now ? Say 'thank you' ?" asked Bill.

"You're getting on all right, aren't you, my lad ?"

"Oh, fine," exclaimed Bill. "Stand clear, the storm's beginning again."

Mr Ticker dashed out of the booth, and then tennis balls and footballs came whizzing through the air at poor Bill.

He could not stop them all, of course, but it was amazing the number he did hold off.

Tommy Mitchell and his chums came along a little before they were expected, and they made their way at once to the booth.

"Got your shooting boots on, Tommy ?" asked Joe Walker, the inside-right.

"Yes, Joe," answered Tommy with a grin. "I shall bore holes through this fellow."

Then they reached the booth and stood and watched. They saw a young crowd flinging all sorts of balls from all angles and at all speeds at Bill.

Out shot his hands, up came his knees, up swung his boots, he leapt to the left, he leapt to the right, he jumped, and he ducked, and he caught ball after ball in an amazing manner.

"My aunt !" exclaimed Tommy Mitchell. "This fellow is made of springs."

"And he looks as if he's made of cast-iron, too," said Joe Walker.

"Just what I said, lad," remarked Mr Ticker, who came along at that moment. "I said that, and that's what I'm going to call him. Cast-Iron Bill is his name, lads."

Then he turned to the waiting queue.

"No more to line up here till half-past seven," he said.

By half-past six Bill was glad of a rest, and he sat down heavily.

"Ready for the United, aren't you ?" asked Mr Ticker anxiously.

"Sure !" answered Bill. "Except for two likely black eyes, a loosened tooth, three lumps on my head, and a swelling on my neck, I'm fine—couldn't be better."

"I thought they'd take to you," said Ticker. "Meet the Ironmoor lads, Bill."

Each of the players was introduced to Bill, and he was very interested in meeting them, for he was a keen follower of football.

It was the United's first season in First Division, and they had made a poor start, having lost all their so far.

"People say we ought to be on a job like this instead of being in the First League," said Tommy Mitchell. "Still, we're triers. Now, then, Cast-Iron Bill, are you ready ?"

"Who's Cast-Iron Bill ?" asked the lad.

"You are," replied Mr Ticker. "I hadn't told you yet. That's the name I shall bill you under."

Bill grinned, and took up his position at the end of the booth. Then three footballs were placed in a row, and three of the United forwards ran and shot with all their might.

Bill lashed out with his right and his left fists, and punched two of the shots away, while his knee came up and dealt successfully with the third.

"He wants a bit of getting past," said Tommy Mitchell.

Four of the United had a go then, but to their amazement Bill actually managed to stop all four balls.

"He certainly is a marvel," said Joe Walker, turning to his skipper. "Why, what's the matter, Tommy ?" he went on. "Aren't you feeling well ?"

Tommy Mitchell was making queer gulping noises, and his eyes were shining queerly.

He grabbed Joe by the arm, and led him away from the booth.

"Hasn't it dawned on you ?" gasped Tommy. "Here's the very man we've been praying for. He's waiting for us to grab."

"Why—what——"

"You ham !" exclaimed Tommy. "Don't you see that Cast-Iron Bill is a born goalie ?"

"Cer-ummy !" gasped Joe.

"He's seen it at last !" sighed Tommy. "Keep the boys here, and don't breathe a word to anyone. I'm going to run like mad and find Mr Pike, our manager."

Away scooted the skipper, and Mr Ticker stared after him.

"What's the matter with the skipper, Joe ?" he asked.

"He's forgotten something that he remembered," answered Joe hastily. "I mean he remembered something that he'd forgotten, and he bunked before he had time to forget what he remembered."

In the town Tommy found a taxi, and he was driven rapidly to the manager's house.

There he found Mr Pike preparing to do nasty things to a large steak and a pile of fried potatoes.

"Don't want me, do you, Tommy ?" Pike said. "I'm likely to be busy."

"Mr Pike, you've got to leave that feed," panted Tommy. "There's a wonder goalie waiting to be picked up at Ticker's show, and if you don't jump in quick he'll be snapped up by someone else."

"Is he good enough for me to leave this ?" asked Mr Pike, casting a longing look at the steak.

"I tell you he's the find of the century," answered Tommy. "If we had started the season with him we'd have been at the top of the league instead of at the bottom. Hurry, Mr Pike, before anyone else gets in."

Tommy had kept his taxi waiting, and soon he and the manager were on the road again.

They drove to the house of the managing director of the United, who happened to be at home. He, too, was getting ready to sit down to a meal, but he gave it up when he heard Tommy's story.

Quarter of an hour later they were standing back from the booth watching the United forwards banging in shots at Bill, who continued to save them in wonderful style.

"You've got to remember that he's been doing this for over two hours," said Tommy. "Isn't he a marvel ?"

"Look out !" another whispered. "Here's Ticker coming."

The party drifted on, but they came back again when the coast was clear, and they watched Cast-Iron Bill's amazing performance again.

"Get him !" said the managing director. "If we have to pay him top wages, get him. Look out ! Here's Brotherton coming along !"

Mr Brotherton was the secretary of Ironmoor City, the United's rivals, and he was supposed to have a wonderful eye for picking out talent.

"Leave him to me," said the managing director, hurrying away.

He intercepted Mr Brotherton just before the latter reached the booth.

"Ah, Brotherton, just the man I was looking for," he said. "I want to have a chat with you about that charity match we are going to play. Come on up to my house, and have a spot of supper with me."

"Thank you," replied the secretary of the City. "I was just going along to see what the crowd was watching here. Is it anything good ?"

"Where ? What crowd ?"

Mr Brotherton pointed towards the booth.

"Oh, it's a side show," said the managing director. "They're slinging balls at a chap. You know, a sort of Aunt Sally business."

He linked his arm in Brotherton's and led him away, not breathing easily until they were clear of the show.

Then he took the City secretary home, and kept him there for the rest of the evening.

By nine o'clock Cast-Iron Bill had finished, and suddenly, to the disappointment of the waiting crowd, he held up his hand.

"The show is over," he said. "Good-night."

Then he ducked under the canvas and met Mr Ticker.

"What's the matter, lad ?" asked the owner of the show.

"I'm going for my hat, and you can have this uniform," replied Bill.

"You're not quitting, are you ?"

"I am," answered Bill. "I may be cast-iron, but even iron has its limits. I've had a happy evening, but I'm off now."

"Bill," exclaimed the owner, "I'll make it four pounds a week."

"You might make it forty," replied Bill, "but I should still travel."

He went into the tent and began to change, while Mr Ticker sat with him almost in tears, and pleaded vainly.

"Well," he said at last, "if you won't, you won't. Here's a ten-shilling note for what you've done to-night. Any time you change your mind come back."

"If you change my uniform and put me in armour I might change my mind," grinned Bill. "But now I'm off, as the man said when he fell off the steeple."

Then he went out of the tent, and instantly came on guard, his fists up, for a little group of men rushed at him eagerly.

"Stand off !" he cried.

"It's all right, Bill," said Tommy Mitchell eagerly. "It's us, the United."

"Gosh, I thought you were a crowd of toughs after the ten bob I've worked so hard for," said Bill with a grin. "Well, what's the big idea ?"

Because it's a pastime.

"Ever played football?" asked Mr Pike.

"Have I ever eaten?" said Bill scornfully.

"Who did you play for?" Tommy Mitchell asked breathlessly.

"The village club at home."

"Pros?"

"Not likely," answered Bill with a grin. "They were farm hands mostly."

"Where did you play?"

"Back," replied Bill.

Mr Pike made a choking noise.

"Then nobody knows," he gulped.

"They knew at home," said Bill with another grin, "but I'll keep it dark if you like."

"You're quitting this job, aren't you?" asked Tommy Mitchell.

"Just as quickly as I can."

"Then there's another one waiting for you," said Mr Pike.

"The same sort?" asked Bill. "Good-night!"

"No, lad, we want you to sign on for the United."

"You'll have a try-out in the morning," said Mr Pike, "but there's no doubt in my mind. That suit you?"

"Yes," answered Bill, still feeling a little dazed.

"Where do you live?" asked the secretary. "I must put your address on the form."

"I've got no home at present," answered Bill. "I must find one."

"We've got a spare room at our place," said Tommy Mitchell eagerly. "You come along with me, Bill."

"Sure," answered Bill, adding in a murmur—"I'll wake up soon."

But presently he was at Tommy's home, where he was made very welcome, and it was arranged that he should lodge there.

Next morning he went to the ground with Tommy, and he was fitted out with some spare togs.

Then he went between the posts, and the United forwards set to work to bombard him with shots.

He had no other defenders to help

★✦✦✦✦✦✦✦✦✦✦✦✦✦✦✦★
THE FIRST MATCH.
★✦✦✦✦✦✦✦✦✦✦✦✦✦✦✦★

BILL still felt as if he were in a dream when he went home to dinner with Tommy Mitchell.

But little by little he grew more accustomed to the idea, and he was able to grin about it.

"This time yesterday I was wandering about with a lot of nothing in my pocket," he said, "and now I'm a blinking millionaire. I say," he went on anxiously, "I hope I won't let you folks down."

"You needn't worry about that," smiled Tommy.

The secret of the new goalie had been well kept, and the crowd that poured into the enclosure that afternoon was surprised to see the new name.

"Who's the goalie?" was the question asked on every side.

"I suppose they feel they've got to do something," remarked one pessi-

BILL THE UNBEATABLE.—The four Ironmoor United players shot together, but to their amazement Cast-Iron Bill stopped all four balls!

Bill stopped grinning and stared. Then his grin came back.

"What's the answer?" he asked. "A lemon?"

"I mean it," exclaimed Mr Pike. "We want you to sign on as our goalie. Surely you know you're a big noise as a goalie?"

"I haven't heard much shouting yet," answered Bill. "Are you serious?"

"So much so that we've got the forms all ready made out, and there is a taxi waiting to take you to them," replied the manager.

"Me sign on for a First League team?" gasped Bill.

"One that's at the bottom of the league," answered Tommy. "We're not getting you under false pretences, Bill. We're the mutts in the league so far this season, but we're looking to you to pull us round."

Cast-Iron Bill whistled softly.

"If you really mean it," he said, "lead me to it."

They hurried to the taxi, and away they drove to the secretary's office at the ground, where the league forms were ready.

him, but by his own efforts he kept out shot after shot until the forwards grew tired of trying him.

On the line he saw Mr Pike performing an eccentric dance close to a little crowd of well-dressed men.

"Is he giving an entertainment?" asked Bill. "When does he go round with the hat?"

"They are the directors," replied Tommy. "Mr Pike is just letting off his spirits, for he's so pleased that you're what he thought you were."

"He's beckoning you over, Bill," said Joe Walker.

Cast-Iron Bill ran across, and was introduced to the directors, each of whom shook hands with him enthusiastically.

"You're playing for us this afternoon against Burnleigh Town," said the managing director.

"Not really, sir?" gasped Bill.

"Yes, really," was the reply. "There was no mention of salary last night, but we've decided to sign you on at nine pounds a week."

Cast-Iron Bill could not speak. He could make only gulping noises

mist. "We're in for our usual hiding this afternoon, I guess."

Burnleigh Town came on the field, feeling that they had an easy thing on.

"Two points for us this afternoon unless we all go to sleep," said their skipper.

Then he and Tommy tossed for ends, and presently the teams lined up.

Tommy was right back, and the other back was Harry Wood.

"I don't want to start flinging my weight about at once," said Bill, "but if they crowd in on me I shall be glad if you chaps would give me plenty of room."

"Right you are, Bill," answered Tommy.

Burnleigh started at a great rate. Their forwards rushed down, and in the first minute Cast-Iron Bill was tested.

It was an easy shot, but it bumped awkwardly, and to the dismay of the crowd and the United, it bounced over Bill's hands.

"Goal!" yelled the Burnleigh crowd. But Cast-Iron Bill seemed to tie himself up in a knot, as his body and arms wriggled back in an amazing manner.

He just reached the ball and patted it down before it could cross the line.

Then like a flash he twisted again, and hurled the ball about thirty yards away as two of the Town forwards leapt at him.

Very neatly Bill dodged them, and they both sprawled in the net amidst the loud laughter of the home supporters.

"Phew!" gasped the Ironmoor managing director. "He gave me a shock then. I thought he had missed that easy one."

Back came the ball, and in trying to clear, an Ironmoor half handled in the penalty area, and the whistle sounded.

"Now we go one up!" said the Burnleigh supporters.

Their centre-forward, a notorious sharpshooter and an international, placed the ball and stood waiting for the whistle, looking very confident.

The whistle sounded, the centre ran, and then he shot like lightning for the corner of the net.

But Bill watched for the turn of the marksman's leg and the glance of the eye at the last second, and he anticipated that shot wonderfully.

He leapt as if he were on springs, and his arm shot out and just knocked the ball up over the bar.

A roar of cheers went up from the home crowd, and the Burnleigh centre gasped.

"That was some save!" he muttered.

The corner kick came in with the wind, and again the Ironmoor goal was in danger.

A crowd of players swarmed round it, but through the midst of them appeared Cast-Iron Bill, and his wonderful arms got to the ball and flung it to one of his own men.

He picked out one who was unmarked, and that gave the home team a chance for a breakaway, and they did not miss it.

Up the field they raced, and Joe Walker put in a peach which the visiting 'keeper could not save.

"Goal!" roared the home crowd.

"On play we ought to be one up," sighed the Burnleigh manager. "But it's Ironmoor that's on the lead, not us."

Nettled by this unexpected reverse, the Burnleigh men went all out to get on level terms, and soon they were round the Ironmoor goal again.

Shot after shot was driven in, but Cast-Iron Bill was always in the way. He dodged from side to side of his goal, anticipating shots in a marvellous manner.

"In the name of goodness, where did you find him?" asked one of the visiting directors, staring at Mr Pike.

The happy Ironmoor manager grinned from ear to ear.

"Some boy, isn't he?" he said.

"Some boy!" repeated the director.

"He's a young army!"

The home team was bucked at the wonderful play of the goalie, and it had a great effect on their own game.

The result was that soon they were penning Burnleigh in their own half, and Bill had a rest.

Half-time came with the home team leading by one goal to nil, and as Bill ran off, the crowd rose to him, cheering him to the echo.

In the dressing-room his fellow-players shook his hand, praising him up to the hilt. But Bill only grinned.

"The match isn't over yet," he said.

"I may let you down in the next half."

"If you do I'll eat the goalposts!" exclaimed Tommy.

As in the first half Burnleigh opened with fireworks, and again Cast-Iron Bill was right in the centre of the picture.

He had shots rained in on him from all directions, but he dealt with them as coolly as possible.

He had no time to kick. All he could do was to fling the ball away, and trust to one of his own side to clear.

Then he stopped a red-hot one, and the visiting centre came rushing in. Instead of throwing the ball away Bill waited a second, and then he dodged like lightning.

The centre went crashing into the upright, and Bill had his chance to kick.

He got in a great punt, sending the ball right out to the wing, where the ouside-left pounced on it and streaked away.

Then the visiting goalie had a taste of what Bill had been through, but he did not deal with it so well. A mighty shout announced the fact that Ironmoor had scored again.

The Burnleigh men set their teeth, and they did all in their power to reduce the home team's lead.

They swarmed down, and they shot and shot, from short range and from long, from straight in front and from the side, but always Cast-Iron Bill was in the way.

They tried to rush him and flummox him, but he dodged them coolly, and he cleared again and again.

At last the whistle sounded for time, and the delighted home crowd cheered to the echo the first victory of the season.

On to the field they swarmed, and Bill was lifted shoulder-high and carried in triumph to the dressing-room.

"We've got a wonder!" said the Ironmoor United managing director. "And we've got to keep him. There are some clubs that will move heaven and earth to try to get Cast-Iron Bill, and we'll have to be prepared for things to happen."

★ ◆ ◆ ◆ ◆ ◆ ◆ ◆ ◆ ◆ ◆ ◆ ◆ ◆ ◆ ◆ ◆ ★

THE FIRST OFFER.

★ ◆ ◆ ◆ ◆ ◆ ◆ ◆ ◆ ◆ ◆ ◆ ◆ ◆ ◆ ◆ ◆ ★

THE Ironmoor United managing director had made no mistake when he had said that other clubs would be eager to get hold of Cast-Iron Bill.

Already a move was being made in that direction.

Ironmoor's great rivals were Ironmoor City, and a certain little band of men who were particularly interested in the City were wondering how to secure possession of Bill.

These men were not acting publicly, nor in the true interests of sport. It was simply that they stood to make money if Ironmoor City were successful.

"There's no doubt about it," said one of them, a man named Smeldon, "this fellow Bill Bentley is a wonder. I've never seen anything like the display he gave in goal. We've got to get him."

"Ought to be easy," said a man named Booker. "There's that job going at the mills, all pay and no work. He gets that as well as his full wages as a pro. if he signs for the City. The fellow will jump at it."

"Let's get him and tell him all about it," declared Smeldon.

Booker stepped up to Bill next afternoon when the goalie was out for a stroll.

"Mr Bentley," he said, "you don't know me, but I want to make your acquaintance."

Booker had a very plausible way with him, and Bill was in the mood to be friendly with anybody who seemed at all likeable.

"How are you?" he said with a cheery grin, shaking hands.

"I saw you play on Saturday," went on Booker, telling himself that things looked like being easy, "and I was amazed."

"So was I," exclaimed Bill. "I haven't got over it yet. I was lucky."

"You're not so lucky as you ought to be," said Booker. "It so happens, though, that I am in a position to improve your luck."

Bill stared at him, and Booker pointed to a cafe along a side street.

"Come in and have a cup of coffee with me, and I'll tell you what I mean," said Booker.

There seemed no reason for him to refuse, so Bill went along with Booker and entered the cafe.

There, in a quiet corner, sat Smeldon and another man, waiting for the bird to come into their net.

"What luck!" exclaimed Booker. "There are two friends of mine who can help us."

Soon Cast-Iron Bill was shaking hands with Smeldon and the other man, whose name was Tiddle.

"I've seen all the best goalies in England, Mr Bentley," said Tiddle. "but there's not one to come up to you."

"And the pity of it is that you've got in with such a second-rate lot as the United," added Smeldon. "You could have chosen any team you liked."

"I didn't know what was coming, as the man said when he stepped in front of the Flying Scotsman," responded Bill.

"Now, look here, Mr Bentley," said Booker. "I've got big interests in Ironmoor City, and there's a peach of a job waiting for you."

"Don't care a heap for peaches," Bill said. "I always bite on the stone."

"You won't bite any stone this time, believe me," exclaimed Booker.

Then he outlined his proposal. Bill was to sign on for the City and get top wages, and in addition a big salary for a no-work job at the mills.

"But I've signed on for the United!" he said.

Booker laughed.

"We'll find a way out of that little difficulty," he said. "They nabbed you before you knew what you were doing. I've heard a bit about that. When they signed you, there was no money clause stated at first, and on the strength of that you can get out of it."

"So you want me to turn the United down and sign for you?" asked Bill.

"That's the idea," exclaimed Smeldon.

"Dirty dogs!" murmured Bill.

"Hold hard!" cried Smeldon. "Just think what this offer means to you. Altogether you'll get nearly twenty pounds a week."

"Do you know what you might get?" asked Bill, and his eyes still twinkled.

"No," they answered.

"A black eye each," said Bill. "Good-day."

He walked away, whistling cheerily, and the three men glared after him.

Then Booker went to a window, and nodded to three tough-looking cus-

Because she beats eggs.

tomers who were lounging in the street, and they winked in reply.

"Well, he's no use to us apparently," sneered Booker, "but he won't be any use to the United either, now."

"Can you rely on those three?" asked Tiddle.

"They'll eat the fool!" snarled Booker viciously. "Serve him right."

Meanwhile Cast-Iron Bill had strolled along the street, and the three toughs went after him.

"He'll be easy," observed one of the rogues, Ginger by name.

"Easy as kiss my hand," responded one of his companions.

They followed Bill until chance took him into a deserted portion of the city as darkness was beginning to fall.

"Now we've got him," said Spike, as the third ruffian was called.

They closed in on Bill near the entrance to a gloomy alley, and all three went for him in a body.

Bill sensed the danger instantly, and his loosely-built body seemed to shoot out like a rubber ball, so that he evaded the first rush, and was able to turn his back to a wall.

One long arm shot out to the right, another to the left, and a long leg came up between them.

Ginger's nose became the colour of his hair. Spike thought he had swallowed most of his teeth, and the third man doubled up as he stopped Bill's boot with his belt.

"Well, if there's nothing more for me to stop for," said Bill, "I'll say good-night."

Dull, droning sounds came from the three toughs, and Cast-Iron Bill strolled home. He said nothing to his pals about what had happened.

THE UNITED v. SHEFTON ROVERS.

ON the following day Bill appeared in the streets with some sticking plaster, as well as a cheery grin decorating his face.

It so happened that he met Booker and Smeldon as they came along the High Street.

"'Morning, gentlemen!" he said. "Taken any flowers or fruit to your friends?"

"I don't know what you are talking about, my man," Booker said, and his face took on a pasty hue.

The twinkle came back to Bill's eyes, and he strolled on, and presently met some of the United, for they were going to the ground for training.

"Great pip!" gasped one as he saw the sticking-plaster. "What happened?"

"I cut myself shaving," replied Bill with a grin.

"Do you generally shave your nose and forehead?" asked Harry Wood.

"I like to do the job thoroughly," replied Bill, "as the gentleman said when he sat down under the steam-hammer."

Saturday's match was on the Ironmoor ground, and the crowd was a very large one, owing to the fact that the Ironmoor City supporters turned up strong.

Some of them came for a very special reason, for they wanted to relieve their jealousy by putting Bill off his game. Booker had gathered this little band of barrackers together.

"Divide up into two lots, and one lot get behind each goal, so you can bother Bentley during each half," he had said. "The idea is to rattle this fellow. If you keep on handing him

back-chat he'll lose his temper, and that'll spoil his game. Get me?"

"Yes!" had come the chorus.

"Leave it to me, boss!" another man known as Weedy had exclaimed.

Orders were obeyed, and the City supporters gathered at the back of each goal.

They kept very quiet, however, until the game began, and then they waited eagerly for Cast-Iron Bill to be tested.

Bill's long, loose figure lounged against one of the posts as he waited, but he did not have long to rest, for the Shefton forwards got on the run

A SHOCK FOR THE CENTRE.—The Burnleigh centre-forward came charging in like a bull, but Bill calmly stepped aside, and the next minute there was a thud as the centre's head hit the upright!

very soon after the whistle sounded.

Their centre-forward, a man named Brown, was a well-known sharpshooter, and he had scored quite a lot of goals this season.

Into position leapt Cast-Iron Bill as the forwards swooped down towards the goal, and to Brown it looked as if the goalie had suddenly become all arms and legs.

But he got into position for shooting, and he drove in a beauty.

"Goal!" came a terrific roar from behind Bill.

The idea was to startle him and cause him to fumble the shot, but he caught the ball very neatly, and then drop-kicked it well up the field.

Then he turned and grinned at the disappointed crowd behind him.

When Shefton began to attack again Weedy took a rattle from his pocket, and waited until a swift shot was flying towards Bill.

Then Weedy sounded his rattle fiercely, but the goalkeeper made no mistake, and once more the ball went up the field.

"What was that gentle sound I heard?" asked Bill when he was able to look back. "Did anybody get rattled?"

Just then the whistle sounded for half-time, with no scoring, and Bill went in with the other players.

When Cast-Iron Bill took up his position at the beginning of the second half he found some more back-chat merchants behind him. He turned and surveyed them, then bowed politely to them.

"Talk away, people!" he said.

Then he turned back, and he took not the slightest notice of the City supporters behind the goal.

They yelled with rage while Cast-Iron Bill dealt calmly with the shots that came in, and at length half a dozen policemen came along by the railings.

"Stop that noise," said a sergeant sternly, "or some of you won't be watching a football match next week."

The City supporters grumbled and growled softly.

Suddenly a mighty roar of cheers went up, for at the other end Joe Walker had found the net.

"Let them make a little noise now, sergeant," said Cast-Iron Bill. "I'm sure they're just aching to cheer."

Then he stood with one hand to his ear.

"Roars of silence!" he said.

Soon, however, there was a crowd in front of the goal, for the Shefton men came along in a fierce effort to get on level terms.

This way and that jumped Bill. Now he bobbed, and now he ducked.

From one side to the other he darted, falling twice as he saved a shot, until at last he was able to clear, and the danger was over for the time being.

Cast-Iron Bill did not have much more to do before the whistle sounded for time, and the United had won their second victory of the season.

Next week Bill plays against the dirtiest team in the League! Every one of that team is determined to score, even supposing it means laying out Cast-Iron!

SOME !!!!! ARE ON THE PITCH!

The weird and wonderful, sourced from the comic archives (#1)

With her overcoat discarded, her tam-o'-shanter well on the back of her head, the Crusaders' giant trainer was striding across the ground, waving a red flannel petticoat in front of her.

CAUGHT in the CUP TIDE!

OUR LATEST LONG COMPLETE TALE of the TIES

THE "BOYS' REALM" SPORTS LIBRARY.

The Popular Thursday Athletic Paper for British Boys.

½d

Ere Long could regain his feet, the bull had given a wild triumphant bellow, and was upon him. (See page 7.)

"THE SLACKERS"

A STIRRING TALE OF TOM MANLEY.

Vol 3. No 123. ONE HALFPENNY. Week End.. g Saturday, January 20th, 1912.

NINETY-MINUTE NAPPER

FIREWORKS FLYNN'S FREEBOOTERS

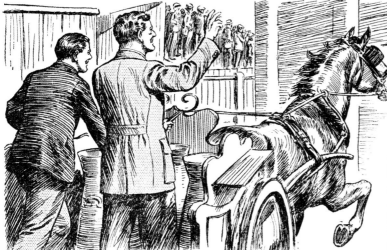

By Donald Dane

THE TELL-TALE PHOTO

"**Y**OU want to see Mr. Flynn, m'sieu? Voila! There he is."

Flicks Deldou, outside-left of the Freebooters F.C., glanced up from the steaming wash-tub and waved a soaking stocking towards the pitch.

The little Fighting Frenchman was up to his eyes in soap-suds and dirty linen, for it was his turn to do the weekly washing at the struggling footer club's ground.

Flicks, however, did not want to miss all the practice. Coming from the pitch outside he could hear shouts and laughter, which showed that his team-mates were having a good time.

But it was hard not to be cheery in the company of Fireworks Flynn, schoolmaster and ex-R.A.F. pilot, who was now directing the fortunes of his old footer team.

The two tall, sombre-dressed men who had arrived at the ground thanked Flicks, then walked out on to the pitch.

"I'll bet that's Fireworks," cried one, pointing to a crowd gathered round the far goal. "Look!"

A ring of players stood peering upwards at a tall, athletic figure standing at one end of the cross-bar above their heads, holding a football in his hands.

Fireworks Flynn beamed down at them.

"I said I would give you a demonstration, chaps," he called cheerfully. "on how to keep your balance. Watch!"

Tilting back his head, and balancing the football against his nose and forehead, the ex-sports master of St. Kit's College commenced a slow walk along the crossbar with his arms outstretched on either side of him.

"My hat! Isn't he a cool hand?" whispered the visitor to his companion. "Don't move or speak till he's finished."

With perfect balance, Fireworks completed his walk along the goal-top as easily as though he were trotting across the pitch.

"There you are, boys," he called. "It's easy when you know how. Try it some day at the swimming-baths. Now then, after it!"

Heading the ball over his admirers below, Fireworks stooped, grabbed the crossbar with his hands, and then, using it as a trapeze, dropped to the ground.

The Freebooters, with a cheer, were off after the ball now, and Fireworks was about to join them when he saw the two visitors. Instantly his face broke into a smile and he stepped over and gripped the first one by the hand.

"Hallo, Wink!" he exclaimed. "What brings you here?"

"Wink," otherwise Wing-Commander Oram, of R.A.F. Intelligence, smiled and looked at his companion.

"I'm afraid this is not just exactly a social visit, Fireworks. Haven't seen you since you were demobbed, have I? Well, well, this is Chief Inspector Hamish. Can you give us a few minutes of your time?"

Fireworks shook hands, then smiled.

"Well, I'm supposed to be doing a bit of coaching just now," he explained. "It's not exactly a cushy job running a football team in one's spare time. But what—er—what can a man so important as Chief Inspector Hamish want to see me for?"

Oram linked arms with Fireworks.

"It's something to do with the team, Flynn. Better excuse yourself to these fellows, and take us where we can talk privately. This is strictly hush-hush, and very important, you see."

Fireworks stared, puzzled and surprised.

"What's up?" he asked, as he showed them into the office and turned on the electric fire. "Why all the secrecy?"

Oram sat down, and nodded to the inspector.

"Better show him, Hamish," he said quietly.

Chief Inspector Hamish opened his pocket-book, took a photograph from it, and handed it to Fireworks. It was postcard size, and showed a football group.

"Hallo," exclaimed Fireworks. "This is a photograph of the Freebooters, one that was taken earlier in the season. There I am, sitting in the middle. It's a full turn-out of all the players we had on our books then. We sold the postcards to raise funds."

He looked up from the card to the two men.

"What's it all mean?" he demanded. "There must be dozens of these photos going about Fulton."

"Possibly," said Oram quietly. "But that doesn't explain how this particular one came to be found in the possession of a dead German in civilian clothes whose body was picked up near a wrecked bomber brought down a few days ago near Ferntickle. He was a German whom we have every reason to believe was one of the Nazis' master-spies, and who was equipped and in every way prepared to land secretly by para-chute, and assume British nationality, even down to a faked identity card."

Fireworks sat up and whistled softly.

"This photograph, found on a spy who was coming here from Germany!" he exclaimed. "You mean the photograph must have been given to him in Germany?"

"I'm afraid so," said Chief Inspector Hamish. "And I don't think it was for sentimental reasons either. Just turn over the back?"

Fireworks did so, to see a few lines in German script which seemed like poetry. Familiar with the language, he translated them rapidly.

"'Once you seek and find my face
  You will know our meeting-
  place!'"

"That's pretty near it," said Wing-Commander Oram. "Now do you get what we're after, Fireworks? This man had an accomplice awaiting him in Britain, probably the same man who sent him that very photograph. And that accomplice has something to to do with the Freebooters. He's one of the persons in that football group.

"You will see that the name of the team has been obliterated, also the names of the players. It was done very cleverly, by an expert, and the paper was reglossed."

Fireworks started, his heart thumping against his ribs.

"B-but it all sounds crazy to me," he gasped out at last.

Hamish shrugged his shoulders.

"I'm afraid you'll have to take this seriously, Mr. Flynn," he said curtly. "Someone connected with the Freebooters is in league with Germany, and we must lay him by the heels, now, at once."

He leaned across the table.

"You're the one person who can help us most," he insisted. "Why, the villain may be out on the field right now. But you must unmask him. This thing has got to be cleared up before he gets wind up, and vanishes to do damage elsewhere. Now, is there anyone of whom you have the slightest suspicion, anyone who could possibly be the man we want?"

WHO IS THE TRAITOR?

Fireworks stared in stupefaction and scorn.

A Nazi agent among the Freebooters. It couldn't be. Why, he knew most of the players well. Yet there were several members of the club whom he really knew very little beyond their activities on the field.

And not all the side were British. There was a Frenchman, Flicks Deldou. There was Stan Stavinsky, the Pole. There was——

Fireworks picked up the photograph again, and glanced at it before replying to the chief's question.

- - - - - - - - - - - - - - - - - -

TWO PLAYERS SHORT—THE GAME SOON TO START THEN BOTH TURN UP ON AN OLD MILK-CART

"No!" he said confidently. "There's no one I have any reason to suspect. It's maybe just a coincidence. That photograph may have been sent to a Fulton man who is a prisoner-of-war, and it then got into the hands of this German you say was a spy."

"Possibly!" said Inspector Hamish. "Nobody will be happier than we if we discover there is nothing to this photo. But in the meantime we must presume it does mean something. We are going to ask you to co-operate with us, Flynn, and keep your eyes and ears open. If anything peculiar catches your notice, then get in touch with us."

He leaned forward, talked earnestly and rapidly for several minutes, Wink Oram joining in. As they finished Fireworks nodded, pocketed the photograph, and shook hands.

"O.K., I'll do as you say," he promised. "But don't expect me to be a Colwyn Dane. The only thing I'm anxious to track down are good players and League points. We're playing Elmwood on Saturday, and—— What the dickens?"

He had led the way to the door and opened it, just as a terrific clamour arose outside.

"Name of a thousand pigs! Gangsters! Unwashed chumps! Help!" shrieked the familiar voice of Flicks Deldou.

Fireworks stared, then he and his companions burst out laughing.

Flicks Deldou, propping up a line of washing, had come to sudden grief as a ball kicked from the field struck his clothes-prop and knocked it out of his grasp.

On top of the unfortunate little Frenchman collapsed the whole of his washing, smothering him completely.

Waving good-bye to his visitors, Fireworks dashed to the rescue.

Flicks was soon extracted, whereupon he looked ruefully at the pile of dirty clothes. Most of them would require rewashing.

"Eet ees not fair!" exclaimed Flicks. "Now I get no practice."

"We'll all stay and help you to finish the washing afterwards," said Fireworks.

Flicks somewhat cheered up, gathered up his washing, dumped it back in the wash-tub, put some more water on the stove underneath the stand, and then joined his pals on the field.

It was a good practice, and after it, having finished the job for Flicks, the Freebooters repaired to the dressing-room to change.

Fireworks looked the lads over quietly. He had already memorised the names of those who appeared on the photograph. Many of them were now present.

Mentally he conned them over: Stavinsky, Beefsteak, Hillier, Waygood, Macrae, Mitchell, Danby, Keillor, Hallam, Twinkler Evans, Flicks Deldou, Peterson, J. Duncan and D. Duncan, Bett, Robinson and Calder, and, of course, himself.

Eighteen players on the photograph, and of these sixteen including himself present in the room. If the Secret Service men were right, then one of the men now with him might be a traitor.

Which one?

"I'll find out somehow," breathed Fireworks. "But while I do it I'm going to see I do as little harm as possible to the Freebooters!"

*   *   *

"HALLO, boys! This is our last practice before we play Elmwood. How's the jolly old morale?"

Entering the dressing-room on Friday, Fireworks Flynn beamed round at the big bunch of lads who had turned up.

It was gone half-past six, and with the lengthening days, the Freebooters could easily get in a good spell of practice before dusk.

"We're all feeling top-of-the-hole, old chunk," said Stan Stavinsky in his quaint English. "We are going to give Elmwood the beans."

"Splendid," grinned Fireworks.

"I'm glad to hear it. D'ye know, the queerest thing happened to-day. Look at this!"

He fished in a pocket and held up a photograph while the players crowded round.

"It's a group of the team," said Twinkler Evans.

"Yes, but where do you think it was found?" smiled Fireworks. "We must have some Fulton Freebooters' fans in Germany. This was taken from the pocket of a dead German whose plane was shot down the other day. It was passed on to me as a souvenir."

"Gosh!" exclaimed Hallam, the schoolboy from St. Kit's.

"Hallo, and there's some German poetry written on the back," cried another. "What does it mean?"

Fireworks shrugged his shoulders.

"I don't think it's of any importance," he said. "I'm going to stick it up in the letter-rack here. Queer, the things that happen in war-time. Ah well, let's get crackin'. Can't waste time."

Placing the card in the rack, Fireworks started to strip, and a few minutes later was leading his men out to the pitch. There they indulged in a hard practice game. As dusk started to fall Fireworks called a stop.

"First class, lads," he cried gaily. "Now I'll pick the team for to-morrow. If you're as snappy then as you've been to-night we'll have Elmwood in the bag."

The team was selected, then the players, one by one, changed and started to take their leave. Fireworks had changed and gone to the office for a minute, and was coming back, just about to enter the dressing-room, when through the half-closed door he saw something that made him catch in his breath with a hiss of surprise.

The dressing-room was empty, but the gurgle of water and a murmur of conversation showed there were still some players in the bath-house, when the figure of Hallam, the St. Kit's schoolboy, appeared.

Hallam was already dressed, and had apparently come back from outside the building. Now, as Fireworks watched, the youngster tiptoed towards the letter-rack, and after a furtive look round, snatched the mystery photograph from the rack, and shoved it into his pocket.

Then he tiptoed out of the room and vanished.

"My hat!" gasped Fireworks. "Hallam! It's impossible!"

Hallam, a pupil from his old school, in league with the Nazis? Surely this clean-limbed, frank youngster was not a traitor. But if not, why had he gone off secretly with the photograph?

Tiptoeing across the dressing-room, Fireworks slipped out into the dusk to take up Hallam's trail. The boy would not be going back to St. Kit's to-night, for he usually spent the Friday night before a match in town at a friend's house.

Fireworks hurried on, and was just in time to hear a key grate in the lock of the players' gate. He saw Hallam's indistinct figure slipping through.

"I'll stick to him," breathed Fireworks.

He gained the gate, passed through it, and continued the trail. Hallam stopped at a bus-halt round the corner of the next street, and waited. The bus was a double-decker, and Hallam clambered up on top.

Fireworks went inside, close to the door, and took a long-distance ticket.

Seven miles outside Fulton, Hallam came down, and got off, along with three others. Fireworks alighted, too, and found himself at a cross-roads in the country. Peering round, he saw that Hallam was vanishing up the road on the right.

In a flash, the Freebooters' skipper was after him, taking to the grass verge, so that his quarry would not hear the echo of his footsteps on the lonely roadway. But Fireworks could hear Hallam's and they served as a guide to him in the darkness.

Where was the schoolboy footballer going? Was he leading Fireworks to some secret headquarters of a Nazi spy organisation?

"If Hallam turns out to be a traitor I'll never trust my judgment again," breathed the footballing schoolmaster. "And if he is I'll have no mercy on him. Ah!"

The footsteps ahead had stopped, and now Fireworks could make out the corn-stacks and outbuildings of a small farm.

He went on, a little quicker than before, determined not to lose his quarry.

But about a hundred yards from the farm, Fireworks received the shock of his life. A figure suddenly leaped from behind the hedge and bore him to the ground.

"I thought someone was following me," snapped Hallam's angry, boyish voice. "Going to waylay me in the dark, were you? Take that, and that!"

Hallam, though a youngster, was well-built, strongly muscled, and in first-class training. Fireworks, flat on the ground, was hard put to it to ward off the furious blows which rained down on him.

Then, just as he was beginning to think that he would have to use sterner measures to turn the tables on his youthful opponent, a shadowy figure appeared behind the schoolboy.

Thud!

A heavy instrument struck Hallam on the back of the head, and he collapsed almost on top of Fireworks Flynn.

"That's settled him," rapped a hoarse voice. "I saw him waylay you. Give me a hand, and we'll carry him over to the yard there. Then you can watch him while I get the police."

Fireworks rose, a little baffled.

"The police!" he panted. "I—er—— Oh, I suppose we can't leave him lying here. I——"

His voice trailed away as he peered at the man who had come to his rescue, and was now asking him if he was all right. Fireworks suddenly realised he could not explain things fully. This had upset his plans to trail Hallam to wherever he was going with the photograph.

He could not tell this stranger the truth.

"Do you live here?" he asked the man beside him, whose face he could not see.

"Yes, down at the village a mile away," came the hoarse reply. "I've got his feet. You take his head. He shouldn't give us any trouble for a few minutes. I hit him hard enough. There's been too much of this hold-up stuff in the black-out around here."

Fireworks bent and took Hallam's head and shoulders. Then, with the stranger leading, they marched towards the farmyard. At last the stranger stopped.

"This'll do, beside that stack," he grunted. "I'll go to the house and phone. You keep an eye on him. He isn't armed, is he? Better search him. I've got a torch."

A light flashed on, and by its aid Fireworks bent down over the unconscious schoolboy and started to feel in his pockets. As he emptied the contents, a pocket-book fell open in his hand, and from it dropped the mystery photograph.

Fireworks reached for it, and was about to pick it up when he heard a slight movement, and turned his head.

But it was too late. Something swished down in the darkness and struck him on top of the head. With a groan he dropped back, senseless.

"That's fixed both of you," snarled a triumphant voice. "Now I'll put you where you won't cause any trouble. I've got what I want."

The speaker whipped up the photograph from the ground, pocketed it safely, and crossed to the brickwork of an old-fashioned well close by.

Removing the heavy wooden cover, he flashed his torch inside, chuckled, and then marched back to where his two victims lay. Taking Hallam first, he carried the schoolboy to the well and tipped him over.

There was a scraping sound, then a dull splash.

The stranger chuckled, went back for Fireworks Flynn, who still lay unconscious, dragged him along, and tipped him in after the schoolboy. Then, battening down the wooden cover, he sped off into the darkness.

THE MAN WITH GREEN HANDS

Fireworks Flynn, groaning, opened his eyes, conscious instantly of being wet through and cold as ice. What had happened to him? He appeared to be sitting in water up to his waist, and as he moved his legs there was the unmistakable feel of another body beside him.

Where was he? What had happened?

Fireworks' brain worked rapidly. At last he remembered. The stranger who had come to his rescue when he had been attacked by Hallam, then the crack on the head.

Fireworks got to his feet, felt for the torch he carried in an inside pocket, and snapped it on.

"My stars!" he panted.

He was standing in a foot and a half of water at the bottom of an old-fashioned well over twenty feet deep, and close by, blood running all over his face that lay half in the water, was young Hallam, the schoolboy he suspected of being a traitor.

"I was tricked," panted Fireworks. "That scoundrel outed me and dropped us both in here. He must have been trailing me while I was trailing Hallam."

Fireworks bent, and raised Hallam up, for the boy, though coming round, was in danger of drowning.

"Hallam! Hallam! Wake up!" rapped Fireworks anxiously, holding the torch in his mouth, and rubbing the schoolboy's face and hands.

Hallam at last opened his eyes and blinked at him.

"Fireworks!" he gasped. "What's happened? Somebody was following me and I laid in wait for him——"

"That was me," said Fireworks. "I followed you because you took that photograph from the dressing-room, Hallam. Why did you take it secretly? What were you going to do with it?"

Hallam blinked.

"I—I just had an idea, sir," he panted. "It was the—the—er—the poetry on the back. Dr. Parkes, down in the village here, where I was going to stay to-night, is a cryptograph expert. I thought it queer that photo being found on a German, and was going to get him to see if there was some coded message in that poetry."

Fireworks gave a gasp of relief. He could not doubt the honesty of Hallam's explanation as he looked into the schoolboy's face.

"You're not the only one who thought there might be some message, Hallam," he said grimly. "I followed you from the dressing-room to-night, but someone else was on the same job—someone who is a traitor—someone who wanted that photograph badly."

"G-gosh!" gasped Hallam. "You mean a—a Nazi agent? Then it must be someone in the team—someone who was there to-night."

"Yes," said Fireworks. "There were sixteen turned up to-night. Take we two out and that leaves fourteen. We've got to find out who followed us, attacked us, then trapped me, and flung us both in here, and we'll have our spy. But first we've got to get out of here. Luckily there was enough water to break our fall, but not enough to drown us."

"We'd better shout, sir," said Hallam.

They shouted themselves hoarse for about an hour, but all to no avail. The farmhouse was too far away, and no one was stirring in this part of the yard.

Again and again they tried it. Then Fireworks had another idea. His torch was going down. He decided to save it, and got to work with a knife on the bricks which formed the wall of the well.

When they had loosened one or two they started throwing them up against the wooden well cover. But when one brick had dropped back and almost brained him, Fireworks had to stop that plan, too.

"There's only one thing we can do. We'll loosen the bricks and make footholes up the wall. Then we'll take turns climbing up and trying to loosen that cover, or banging on it to draw attention."

"O.K.," said Hallam. "It must be late now. Suppose nobody hears us. We might even miss the match to-morrow. And anyhow, we don't know who it was who attacked us."

"No!" rapped Fireworks. "But I've still one trick left. We'll not miss the match, and we'll get the traitor, too."

But it took hours to loosen enough bricks to enable them to climb to the top. Once the footholds were secured, the prisoners took turns to climb up and hammer on the well lid. But their hopes began to fade. It was evident that the well was seldom used, for the water in it was low and stagnant.

They might remain there undiscovered for days.

Fireworks, having climbed up for the umpteenth time, was almost giving it up as a bad job, when he heard a muffled shout, and someone started to lift the cover off.

Fireworks saw daylight at last, gasped, and climbed out to stare at a startled farmer whose dairy cart and horse stood close by. Behind him Hallam came climbing out eagerly.

"Gosh—it's day-time! It's Saturday, sir," he shouted. "What time is it, mister?"

The dairyman, who seemed too amazed to speak, glanced instinctively at his watch.

"It's after two o'clock," he grunted. "But what in blazes are ye doin' in that well?"

Fireworks whooped and turned to Hallam.

"It's after two o'clock!" he yelled. "And the Elmwood match starts at three. Come on, Hallam! This is where we get a milk priority. We've got to be there for the kick-off. All aboard!"

Brushing past the astonished farmer, Fireworks leaped on to the milk cart, seized the reins, and "gee-ed" the horse off. Hallam made a dive after him, and jumped aboard. Then, to the crack of his whip, Fireworks drove out of the yard at top speed.

"Hey, stop!" yelled the startled farmer. "I'll get the police! I'll——"

Running hopelessly, he was soon left behind.

Fireworks was not going to let down his team. He grinned as he looked at Hallam.

"I hope we don't get gaoled for this," he chuckled. "But mebbe if we find out who is the real traitor in the Freebooters we'll get off with a caution."

"Hope o!" laughed Hallam. "But the match matters most now."

The crowd was still pouring into the ground, and it was a few minutes from kick-off time when Fireworks and Hallam arrived in the milk cart amid cheers and shouts of laughter as they dived through the players' gate.

They were just in time to change.

"Thought you weren't going to turn up, Fireworks," said Beefsteak Brown with relief. "We got anxious and phoned, but found neither you nor Hallam were home last night. Something happened?"

"Yes, we had an adventure," replied Fireworks grimly. "But never mind. Let's get the game over first. Everybody else here?"

"Yes," said Beefsteak. "If you hadn't turned up we were going to play Bett at centre, and Peterson at inside-right."

Fireworks had started to change, and was bending over his boots.

"By the way," he said quickly, "someone pinched that photograph I stuck in the rack last night. Hallam was taking it to have it examined by an expert, not knowing that it was a trap, laid by our Secret Service."

He nodded towards the door.

"They've got the pavilion surrounded now. You see it was someone in this room who followed Hallam, knocked him out, then attacked me, and got away with the photograph. But what he didn't know was that after handling that photo, if he didn't wash his fingers in a special solution, they would turn green within twenty-four hours, with a dye that won't come off. It was a trap, and—— Got you!"

Fireworks hurled himself off his locker in a flying Rugby tackle, bringing down with a bang on the floor the one person in the circle of listening players who had whipped up his hands and stared at them.

It was Bett, one of the reserves who would have played in Fireworks' place. As Fireworks bowled him over, and twisted him into a hopeless ju-jutsu lock, the man cursed and raved in a mixture of German and English.

"Tie him up with towels, stick him in the cold spray, and inform the police," rapped Fireworks. "He's given himself away, and I'm proud to think he's not a chap I brought into the Freebooters. Now for Elmwood! Come on! The ref's getting impatient."

The crowd were surprised when a cheering team of players followed Fireworks Flynn out on to the field. The ref, as Fireworks expected, told them to hurry as they were late already.

But even that didn't take the big smile off Fireworks' face.

He'd cleaned up a nasty job, Hallam had proved true-blue, and now he could concentrate on football again. Elmwood were no easy opposition, and they opened smartly, scoring a snap goal in fifteen minutes.

But it was the only goal they were allowed to get.

The Freebooters were out to celebrate, and that early goal jabbed them into action. Fast-moving wings showed the way, and in the front line Hallam at inside-right and Fireworks at centre soon found their shooting boots.

When half-time came, the Freebooters were leading 2—1. In the pavilion Chief Inspector Hamish awaited Fireworks. Bett had already been taken away.

"He confessed everything," explained the C.I.D. man. "He'd been a member of a Fascist group before the war. He'd been tipped off to expect someone from Germany, after he'd sent the photo to an agent in Sweden, and he was too scared to refuse."

Fireworks nodded.

"Then the dead man carried the photo to identify him, I suppose. Well, I'm jolly glad it wasn't one of my young lads, or Flicks, or Stan Stavinsky. Gosh, there's the whistle! Must get out again."

If Fireworks had been full of beans before, he was on top of the world after his half-time chat with Hamish. Elmwood played all they knew, but the Freebooters were unstoppable.

Fireworks scored a hat-trick, Hallam had two goals, and Chic Danby added the sixth. It was an overwhelming victory, and as the team ran in, cheer after cheer rang out. At the pavilion door, however, Fireworks and Hallam turned pale.

There stood the dairy farmer whose cart they had pinched.

"Gosh, hide!" said Fireworks.

But then the farmer turned, saw them, and grinned all over his gruff face.

"I came here to collect my cart," he beamed, pumping their hands, "and also to say I was going to sue for damages. But I saw you play, and now I'll be content with one thing only."

"What's that?" asked Fireworks anxiously.

"A season ticket to the Freebooters' ground," laughed the farmer. "I'm not missing a match after this one, even though I've got to get up earlier than ever to do my milk round!"

Ebenezer, the parrot, does a good turn for the Freebooters in a smashing footer yarn next week.

I CAN'T BELIEVE MY EYES!

The weird and wonderful, sourced from the comic archives (#2)

It was no easy road to the top for Dozy Danny. This is his first adventure in comic strip format, *Hotspur*, August 1961

LOOK! YOUR OLD PAL, DOZY DANNY, IN PICTURES! START READING THIS THRILL-PACKED FOOTBALL STORY NOW!

Every manager wants the footballer with the magic feet!

Dozy finds out why a top-class football team stays at the top **NEXT THURSDAY!**

He made goals, he scored goals, but no one knew anything about this master footballer with the spine-chilling secret! This is the story of the famous Red Lion Library book!

The grim prophecy of the man named Pickford!

But it was several miles before Pickford's caravan could pull off the road and let the car pass.

HOW DID THAT FELLOW KNOW WE WERE GOING TO SIGN ON STRETTON ANYWAY?

SEARCH ME! I THINK HE'S MAD. AND HE'S LOST US VALUABLE TIME!

STEVE, I'VE BEEN TRYING TO REMEMBER. SOMEWHERE, SOMETIME, I'VE SEEN THAT PICKFORD BEFORE.

YOU'VE PROBABLY SEEN HIS PHOTO AS AN ESCAPED LUNATIC. LOOK! THERE'S THE ARSENAL GROUND.

WELCOME TO MANFORD

In the Arsenal boardroom, Mercer and Thornton met John Martin, the Arsenal manager—and got the shock of their lives.

WE'VE COME TO OFFER £55,000 FOR THE TRANSFER OF GEORGE STRETTON TO THE UNITED, JOHN.

YOU'RE TOO LATE, STEVE. WE TRANSFERRED STRETTON TO BARNLEY FIFTEEN MINUTES AGO.

MANFORD ARSENAL F.C.

FIFTEEN MINUTES TOO LATE. IT WAS THAT MADMAN PICKFORD WHO LOST US STRETTON!

YES. HE MADE US LATE. IF I EVER SEE HIM AGAIN I'LL STRANGLE HIM AND BURN HIS CARAVAN.

By coincidence, Redstoke's next game was against Barnley for whom Stretton was brilliant. With five minutes to go, Barnley led 4-0. Pickford was at the game.

BANG IT IN! MAKE IT FIVE!

WHAT A PLAYER STRETTON IS!

WHAT A RUN!

YES, WHAT A LOSS HIS DEATH WILL BE!

WHAT'S HAPPENED?

STRETTON'S COLLAPSED!

Ambulance men and a doctor were quickly on the scene.

GEORGE STRETTON HAS HAD A HEART ATTACK. HE IS DEAD!

STEVE, I SAW THAT GIPSY FELLOW, PICKFORD IN THE CROWD. HE PROPHESIED STRETTON'S DEATH REMEMBER?

I THINK IT WAS JUST A COINCIDENCE—NOT A PROPHECY..

On the Tuesday after the game, the United players reported for training.

MR MERCER THERE'S A MAN OUTSIDE SAYS YOU'RE GOING TO SIGN HIM ON. NAME OF PICKFORD.

PICKFORD! THAT TROUBLE MAKER! SIGN HIM ON! I'LL.. I'LL—

YOU'LL SIGN ME ON. THAT'S WHAT YOU'LL DO! I'M AN INSIDE-RIGHT.

WHAT A HOPE! GET OUT ...NO! WAIT! WE'RE GOING TO HAVE A PRACTICE GAME. YOU CAN PLAY IT!

STEVE, WHAT'S THE IDEA OF GIVING HIM A GAME? WE'VE HAD ENOUGH OF HIM AND HIS CRAZY TALK.

I'M GOING TO GET MY OWN BACK ON HIM. I'LL REFEREE AND TELL OUR PLAYERS TO BE AS TOUGH WITH HIM AS THEY LIKE!

The practice game was the first team attack against the defence. Pickford played inside-right for the attack.

I'VE PASSED THE WORD ROUND AMONG THE PLAYERS. NOW MISTER PICKFORD, YOU'RE IN FOR A VERY ROUGH TIME.

The master mind at inside-right!

Thrills **NEXT WEEK** when Pickford plays his first game for Redstoke United.

GREAT FREE FOOTY CARDS TO COLLECT!

Well, they were if you were a reader of *Scorcher* in 1970

G. Banks *(Stoke)*

M. Chivers *(Spurs)*

G. Gurr *(Southampton)*

C. Lawler *(Liverpool)*

R. Gould *(Arsenal)*

S. Horne *(Fulham)*

T. Wharton *(Bolton)*

D. Wagstaffe *(Wolves)*

Presented free with SCORCHER Feb. 14th 1970

© 1970 IPC Magazines Ltd.

...aools teams and joined Liverpool, where he was born. He was then a centre-half but has since become a great attacking full-back who scores valuable goals. He has gained Youth and Under-23 caps and F.A. Cup and Championship medals.

Presented FREE with
SCORCHER

A very fine goalkeeper. He was born at Wembley and had Youth trials with Arsenal. He played a few games as an amateur with Queen's Park Rangers and then Guildford City, where he was spotted by Southampton and signed in 1964. A six-footer, he flashed into prominence last season.

Presented FREE with
SCORCHER

...N CHIVERS
(Tottenham Hotspur)

Tall, rangy centre-forward who scored 100 goals for Southampton before joining Spurs in January 1968 for £100,000. That season he played several times for England Under-23 teams but last year he suffered a bad leg injury, and was laid up for months. Now he's making a gallant come-back.

Presented FREE with
SCORCHER

9
GORDON BANKS
(Stoke City)

Britain's No. 1 goalkeeper and the first ever to gain 50 England caps. He began with Chesterfield in 1954; spent 12 years with Leicester City and cost Stoke £52,500 in April 1967. In all he has played in more than 400 League games and has been England's goalie since 1963.

Presented FREE with
SCORCHER

MY FAVOURITE SOCCER STARS

16
DAVID WAGSTAFFE
(Wolves)

One of the fastest wingers in the First Division who goes straight for goal. He comes from Manchester and developed with City before making his first team debut in 1960 aged 17. He moved to Wolves in December 1964 for a £30,000 fee and has now made over 150 League appearances for the club.

Presented FREE with
SCORCHER

MY FAVOURITE SOCCER STARS

15
TERRY WHARTON
(Bolton Wanderers)

Dashing, defence-splitting winger with a fierce shot. Born in Bolton, son of a former Manchester City winger, he made his name with Wolves whom he joined in 1959. After more than 200 games he "returned home" to sign for Bolton Wanderers who paid £70,000 for him. The fans love him.

Presented FREE with
SCORCHER

MY FAVOURITE SOCCER STARS

14
STAN HORNE
(Fulham)

Tall, hefty half-back who joined Fulham last February for £18,000 and was appointed club captain. Born at Oxford he had a short spell with Aston Villa before joining Manchester City and gaining experience in their First Division side.

Presented FREE with
SCORCHER

MY FAVOURITE SOCCER STARS

13
BOBBY GOULD
(Arsenal)

Stocky little goalscorer with terrific courage and enthusiasm. Born at Coventry, he joined the City as a youth and became leading goalgetter when they won the Second Division Championship in 1967. A few months later he moved to Arsenal for £90,000. He's very popular at Highbury.

Presented FREE with
SCORCHER

"Billy's Boots" was one of the most popular of all comic football stories. This is from the *Scorcher Annual* 1976

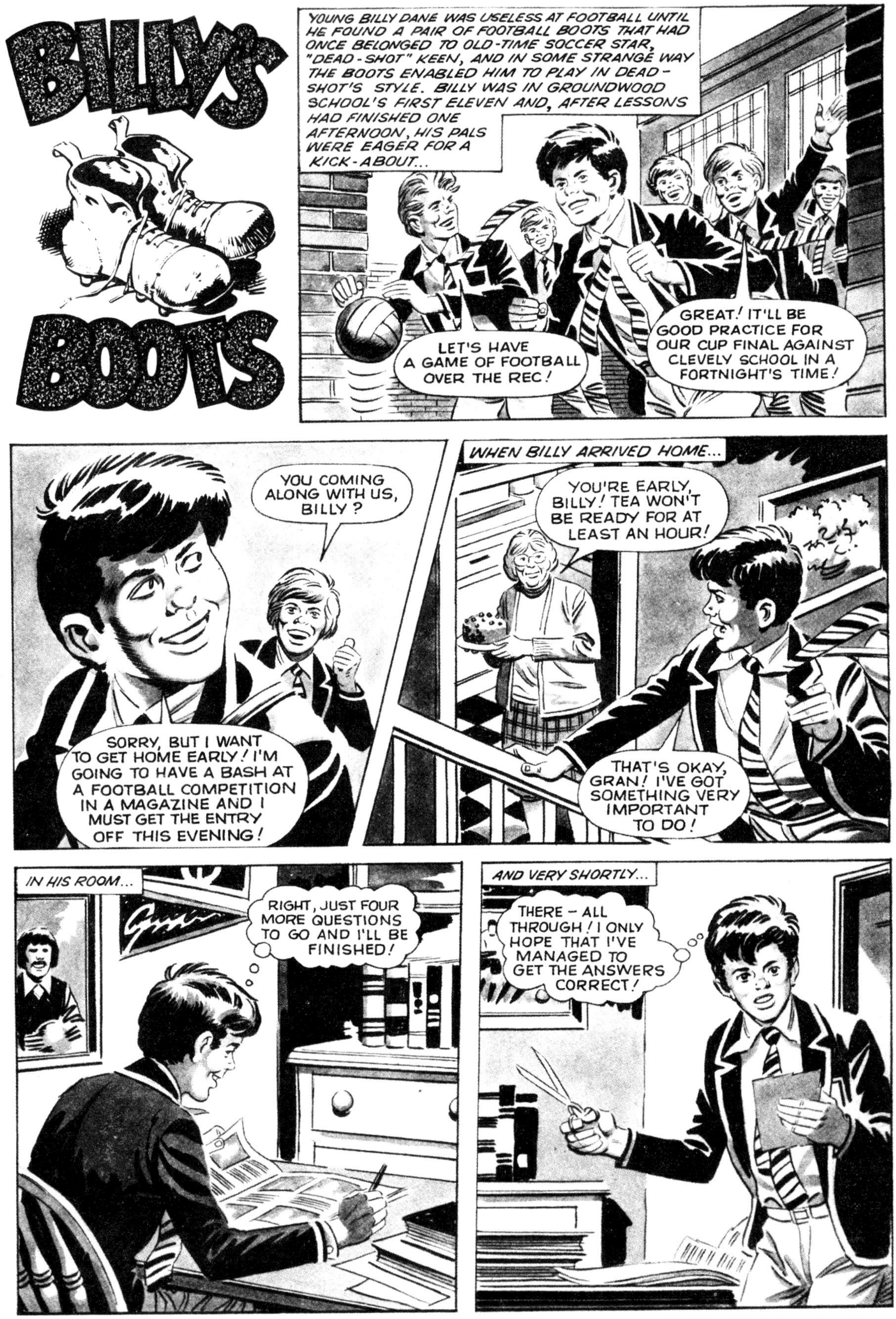
BILLY'S BOOTS
YOUNG BILLY DANE WAS USELESS AT FOOTBALL UNTIL HE FOUND A PAIR OF FOOTBALL BOOTS THAT HAD ONCE BELONGED TO OLD-TIME SOCCER STAR, "DEAD-SHOT" KEEN, AND IN SOME STRANGE WAY THE BOOTS ENABLED HIM TO PLAY IN DEAD-SHOT'S STYLE. BILLY WAS IN GROUNDWOOD SCHOOL'S FIRST ELEVEN AND, AFTER LESSONS HAD FINISHED ONE AFTERNOON, HIS PALS WERE EAGER FOR A KICK-ABOUT...
LET'S HAVE A GAME OF FOOTBALL OVER THE REC!
GREAT! IT'LL BE GOOD PRACTICE FOR OUR CUP FINAL AGAINST CLEVELY SCHOOL IN A FORTNIGHT'S TIME!
YOU COMING ALONG WITH US, BILLY?
SORRY, BUT I WANT TO GET HOME EARLY! I'M GOING TO HAVE A BASH AT A FOOTBALL COMPETITION IN A MAGAZINE AND I MUST GET THE ENTRY OFF THIS EVENING!
WHEN BILLY ARRIVED HOME...
YOU'RE EARLY, BILLY! TEA WON'T BE READY FOR AT LEAST AN HOUR!
THAT'S OKAY, GRAN! I'VE GOT SOMETHING VERY IMPORTANT TO DO!
IN HIS ROOM...
RIGHT, JUST FOUR MORE QUESTIONS TO GO AND I'LL BE FINISHED!
AND VERY SHORTLY...
THERE – ALL THROUGH! I ONLY HOPE THAT I'VE MANAGED TO GET THE ANSWERS CORRECT!

BILLY WENT STRAIGHT OUT AND POSTED HIS ENTRY...

THE FIRST PRIZE IS A VISIT TO THE FOOTBALL CLUB OF THE WINNER'S CHOICE! IT WOULD BE GREAT IF I WON BECAUSE I'D PICK HIGHDOWN ROVERS... THE TEAM DEAD-SHOT KEEN PLAYED FOR WHEN HE WAS A PROFESSIONAL!

A WEEK LATER, BILLY RECEIVED TREMENDOUS NEWS...

HEY, GRAN! YOU KNOW THAT FOOTBALL COMPETITION I ENTERED... I'VE WON FIRST PRIZE!

WELL DONE, BILLY! NOW EAT YOUR BREAKFAST BEFORE IT GETS COLD!

I'VE GOT TO 'PHONE THE MAGAZINE'S EDITOR TO LET HIM KNOW WHICH CLUB I WANT TO VISIT! COR, IT'LL BE GREAT TO GO TO THE ROVERS!

THE VISIT WAS ARRANGED FOR THE FOLLOWING TUESDAY, THE DAY BEFORE BILLY WAS DUE TO PLAY IN HIS SCHOOL'S CUP FINAL TEAM...

IN YOU GET, YOUNG MAN!

'BYE, BILLY! HAVE A NICE DAY!

THANKS, GRAN! I'M SURE I WILL!

VERY SOON, THE CAR WAS ENTERING THE MAIN GATES OF FIRST DIVISION HIGHDOWN ROVERS...

HIGHDOWN ROVERS

IT'S NOT EVERYONE WHO GETS THE CHANCE TO BE TREATED LIKE A V.I.P. — I'M GOING TO REALLY ENJOY MYSELF!

BILLY WAS MET BY THE CLUB'S MANAGER, EX-INTERNATIONAL STAR, BILL REYNOLDS.

HELLO, BILLY! I'M GOING TO SHOW YOU AROUND THE PLACE, SO IF THERE'S ANYTHING YOU WANT TO KNOW, DON'T BE AFRAID TO ASK!

THANK YOU, SIR!

IT WAS A TREMENDOUS DAY FOR BILLY...

THIS IS THE HOME TEAM'S DRESSING-ROOM!

IT'S A BIT BETTER THAN THE ONE WE USE AT MY SCHOOL!

YOU'RE JUST IN TIME TO SEE THE FIRST TEAM IN A FIVE-A-SIDE GAME!

THAT'S ENGLAND STAR MARTIN PAYNE ON THE BALL! HE'S A GREAT PLAYER!

AND BILLY EVEN GOT A KICK OF THE BALL ON HIGHDOWN'S FAMOUS PITCH...

GREAT SHOT, BILLY!

IT WASN'T BAD CONSIDERING I HAVEN'T GOT DEAD-SHOT'S BOOTS ON!

THE VISIT CONCLUDED WITH A LOOK AT THE CLUB'S IMPRESSIVE TROPHY ROOM...

TAKE AS MUCH TIME AS YOU LIKE IN HERE, BILLY!

IT'S FANTASTIC! I NEVER REALISED THAT ROVERS HAD WON SO MUCH DURING THEIR HISTORY!

HEY, THIS IS A PICTURE OF THE HIGHDOWN TEAM AFTER THEY'D WON THE CUP IN THE THIRTIES. BUT MY HERO DEAD-SHOT KEEN IS *MISSING* FROM IT!

I'M SURE HE PLAYED IN THAT FINAL, SO WHY ISN'T HE IN THE PHOTOGRAPH?

I'VE NO IDEA, BILLY! BUT OUR HEAD GROUNDSMAN, TED WILLIAMS, HAS BEEN WITH THE CLUB FOR WELL OVER FORTY YEARS, PERHAPS HE'LL REMEMBER! WHY DON'T YOU HAVE A WORD WITH HIM?

THE VETERAN GROUNDSMAN WAS MARKING OUT THE PITCH...

EXCUSE ME, SIR, BUT DO YOU KNOW IF ANYTHING HAPPENED TO DEAD-SHOT KEEN THE DAY THE CLUB WON THE CUP IN THE THIRTIES?

AYE, I DO, LAD! I REMEMBER IT VERY WELL!

A REAL HERO DEAD-SHOT WAS THAT SUNNY AFTERNOON! HIGHDOWN WERE PLAYING SEADON RANGERS AND THE SCORE WAS TWO GOALS EACH WITH ONLY A FEW MINUTES LEFT TO PLAY!

"...THEN DEAD-SHOT GOT POSSESSION AND SENT A LONG PASS TO A TEAM-MATE..."

"...AND HE WENT HARING INTO THE PENALTY AREA AS THE BALL WAS CHIPPED BEAUTIFULLY INTO HIS PATH..."

"... DEAD-SHOT SCORED A WONDERFUL GOAL! BUT THE SPEED OF HIS RUN WAS SO GREAT HE COULDN'T STOP..."

"... AND HE CRASHED INTO THE POST, INJURING HIMSELF BADLY..."

AYE, HIGHDOWN WON THE CUP THAT DAY, BUT POOR DEAD-SHOT WAS BEING STRETCHERED OFF WHEN THE REST OF THE PLAYERS WENT UP FOR THE TROPHY!

G-GOSH!

ON THE WAY HOME, BILLY WAS WORRIED BY THE GROUNDSMAN'S STORY...

I'M PLAYING IN A CUP FINAL FOR MY SCHOOL TOMORROW... AND WHAT ONCE HAPPENED TO DEAD-SHOT USUALLY HAPPENS TO ME AS WELL WHEN I'M WEARING THE BOOTS! CRIKEY, I DON'T WANT TO BE INJURED!

IN GROUNDWOOD SCHOOL'S DRESSING-ROOM ON THE DAY OF THE FINAL...

I'VE GOT TO TRY AND PUT DEAD-SHOT KEEN OUT OF MY MIND... BUT IT WON'T BE EASY!

GROUNDWOOD KICKED-OFF TO A ROAR FROM THE FANS...

GROUNDWOOD! CLEVELY! GROUNDWOOD! CLEVELY!

AND ALMOST AT ONCE, BILLY FOUND HIMSELF WITH A GREAT CHANCE...

HIT IT FIRST TIME, BILLY!

DANE CAN'T MISS!

BUT...

YAAH! WHAT A ROTTEN SHOT!

MY KID SISTER COULD HAVE SCORED FROM THERE!

I MUST BE STILL WORRIED ABOUT THE DEAD-SHOT KEEN INCIDENT!

BILLY CONTINUED TO PLAY BADLY, BUT BOTH TEAMS WERE FINDING DIFFICULTY IN SCORING. THEN, MIDWAY THROUGH THE SECOND-HALF, WITH THE GAME LOCKED IN A GOALLESS DRAW...

I RECKON WE'RE IN FOR SOME RAIN! THOSE HEAVY BLACK CLOUDS HAVE BEEN BUILDING UP FOR THE PAST HALF AN HOUR!

BILLY WAS THE ONLY ONE PLEASED WHEN THE CLOUD-BURST HIT THE GROUND...

I REMEMBER THE OLD GROUNDSMAN SAYING THAT DEAD-SHOT'S FINAL WAS PLAYED ON A SUNNY DAY! WELL, IT'S CERTAINLY NOT SUNNY HERE, SO NOW I CAN FORGET ABOUT EVERYTHING ELSE AND HELP GROUNDWOOD TO WIN THIS MATCH!

THE RAIN HAD STOPPED WHEN BILLY GOT THE BALL IN THE MIDDLE OF THE PITCH AND SAW THAT HIS WINGER WAS CLEAR...

CRIKEY! THIS IS ALMOST THE SAME SITUATION THAT HAPPENED TO DEAD-SHOT!

THERE CAN ONLY BE SECONDS LEFT TO PLAY, AND I'VE GOT TO GET OUR FORWARD LINE ON THE ATTACK!

GREAT BALL! THE WINGER'S AWAY!

THEN, SUDDENLY...

HEY, THE BOOTS ARE MAKING ME SPRINT UP THE MIDDLE! I-I DON'T WANT TO — BUT I CAN'T STOP MYSELF!

THE WINGER CENTRED THE BALL...

THIS MUST BE GROUNDWOOD'S LAST CHANCE!

LOOK AT DANE — HE'S RUNNING LIKE MAD INTO THE PENALTY AREA!

IT WAS AN IDENTICAL GOAL TO THE ONE DEAD-SHOT KEEN HAD SCORED OVER FORTY YEARS BEFORE...

IT'S THERE!

WHAT A GOAL FROM BILLY!

BUT...

HE CAN'T STOP!

HE'S GOING TO CRASH INTO THE UPRIGHT!

I CAN'T BEAR TO WATCH!

THEN BILLY'S BOOT LANDED IN A PATCH OF SLIPPERY MUD...

AAAARGH!

AND, INCREDIBLY...

HE'S OKAY! HE'S GONE SLIDING PAST THE POST!

WELL DONE, BILLY!

IT WAS THE ONLY GOAL OF THE GAME... AND BILLY WAS ABLE TO COLLECT HIS WINNER'S MEDAL...

THAT WAS A VERY BRAVE GOAL YOU SCORED, YOUNG MAN! YOUR TEAM-MATES MUST BE VERY PROUD OF YOU!

THANK YOU, SIR!

BILLY WAS THE HERO OF THE HOUR...

GROUNDWOOD!

GROUNDWOOD!

BUT FOR THE RAIN I *WOULD* HAVE BEEN INJURED! THIS IS ONE DAY WHEN I'M REALLY GLAD THAT THE BOOTS **SLIPPED** UP FOR ME!

THE END

From the pages of *Score 'n' Roar*, 1970 – Nipper Lawrence was in trouble again!

NIPPER WAS IN TROUBLE AGAIN—FOR CAUSING A CAR CRASH!

"EVERYONE SAYS I'M TOO *TICHY* TO BE A FOOTBALLER!"

LEN DUGGAN – THE INTERNATIONAL MID-FIELD PLAYER! BLACKPORT ROVERS HAVE JUST SIGNED HIM ON FOR THE BIGGEST FEE IN THE CLUB'S HISTORY! THEY RECKON HE'LL BE ON A CONTRACT WORTH OVER A HUNDRED QUID A WEEK!

I'M ON DUTY AT THE STADIUM ON SATURDAY! IF I GET THE CHANCE, I'LL HAVE A WORD WITH DUGGAN, AND TRY AND STRAIGHTEN THINGS OUT! BUT WATCH YOUR STEP IN FUTURE!

OKAY, MR. BRIDGER! THANKS A LOT!

NIPPER SOON FORGOT ABOUT HIS NARROW ESCAPE...

A HUNDRED QUID A WEEK! COR, IF I HAD A JOB LIKE THAT, I'D QUICKLY SAVE UP ENOUGH MONEY TO HIRE THAT LAWYER!

THERE AND THEN, NIPPER LAWRENCE MADE UP HIS MIND...

EVERYONE SAYS I'M TOO *TICHY* TO BE A FOOTBALLER! BUT I'M GOING TO PROVE 'EM ALL *WRONG*... FOR *DAD'S* SAKE! SOMEHOW OR OTHER, I'M GOING TO BECOME THE SMALLEST PLAYER THAT BLACKPORT ROVERS EVER HAD!

THE FOLLOWING MORNING...

IT'S NO USE JUST WALKING INTO BLACKPORT STADIUM AND ASKING FOR A TRIAL! I'LL 'AVE TO MAKE A *NAME* FOR MYSELF FIRST... STARTING WITH OUR SCHOOL TEAM!

ANXIOUS TO GET TO SCHOOL, NIPPER SOON FINISHED HIS PAPER ROUND...

NEWSAGENT'S

SEE YOU IN THE MORNIN', MR. POTTER!

HANG ON A MINUTE, NIPPER! YOU'RE FORGETTING THAT IT'S FRIDAY... *PAY-DAY!*

THERE'S YOUR WAGES... PLUS AN EXTRA TEN BOB FOR DOING JOEY BAKER'S ROUND YESTERDAY! IT REALLY HELPED ME OUT!

GOSH, A WHOLE *QUID!* I KNOW WHAT I'M GOING TO BUY WITH THAT...

MOMENTS LATER, OUTSIDE A SECOND-HAND SHOP...

THEY'RE A BIT EXPENSIVE FOR *SECOND-HAND* BOOTS... BUT IF I'M GOING TO BE A PROFESSIONAL FOOTBALLER, I'D BETTER START COLLECTING SOME DECENT GEAR!

CONTINUED OVERLEAF...

IS NIPPER IN FOR A THUMPING? FIND OUT NEXT MONDAY!

THERE MAY BE TROUBLE AHEAD

It's a hard game… but perhaps, just occasionally, the participants get carried away! It just goes to show that indiscipline is not a new issue

Bronson banged at Dick with both hands; for a few minutes there was pandemonium on the field

THE FREE FIGHT.—" Get off the field, Bentley!" yelled the referee. But Cast-Iron paid no attention—he continued to fight with the opposing forward. What was the reason for Bill's queer behaviour?

FOUL !

Rayne, the deputy goalie, and the opposing centre - forward leapt at the ball together and the young 'keeper lost his head. One fist slammed at the ball, the other caught the centre full on the jaw !

Urged on by Lance Vesey, the players of both sides did their utmost to protect the referee, and no man fought more fiercely than the captain of the Drayton Wanderers.

December 30th, 1922.

Acknowledgements

In creating *Football's Comic Book Heroes* the author and editors needed the dedicated assistance of a number of people without whom the book would not have seen the light of day.

In no particular order we acknowledge assistance received from:

Martin Lindsay, Bill McLoughlin and Roddie Watt at D C Thomson and Co. Limited.
Melanie Leggett, Martin Morgan and Steve MacManus at Egmont UK Limited.
David Abbott at IPC Media Limited.
Bill Campbell and Peter MacKenzie at Mainstream Publishing.
Alan Notton at www.comicsuk.co.uk
Bryan Ceney
Neal Baldwin
Graham Hambly
Richard Heaton
Connor Parker
The staff at the British Library, Colindale.

And, of course, family and friends who have offered support throughout the creative process.

FLEETWAY COLLECTING SCHEME! TOY BARGAINS INSIDE!

VALIANT

6p

EVERY MONDAY

13TH DECEMBER, 1975

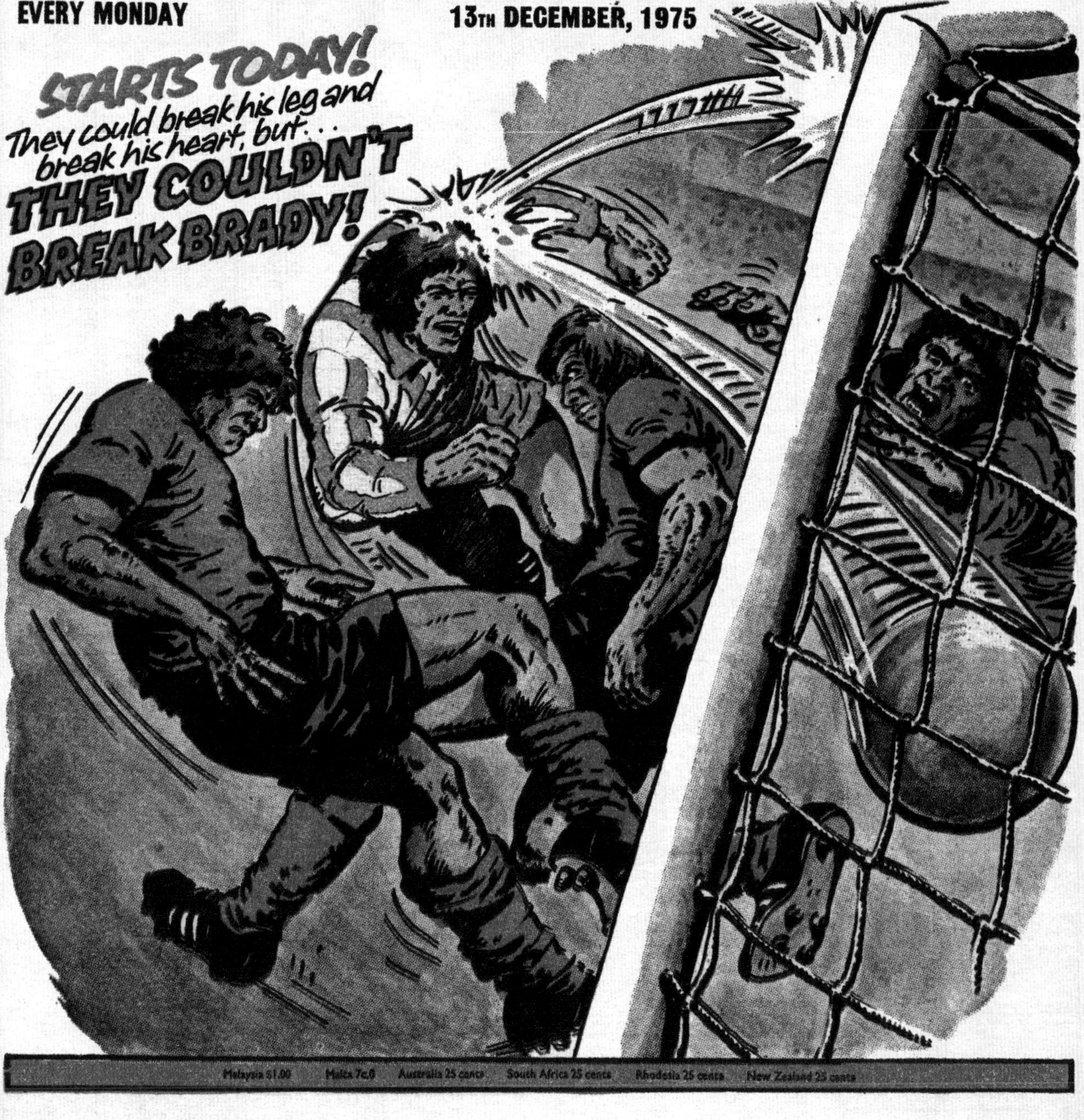

STARTS TODAY!
They could break his leg and break his heart, but...
THEY COULDN'T BREAK BRADY!

Malaysia $1.00 Malta 7c.0 Australia 25 cents South Africa 25 cents Rhodesia 25 cents New Zealand 25 cents